RE-CHARTING AMERICA'S FUTURE

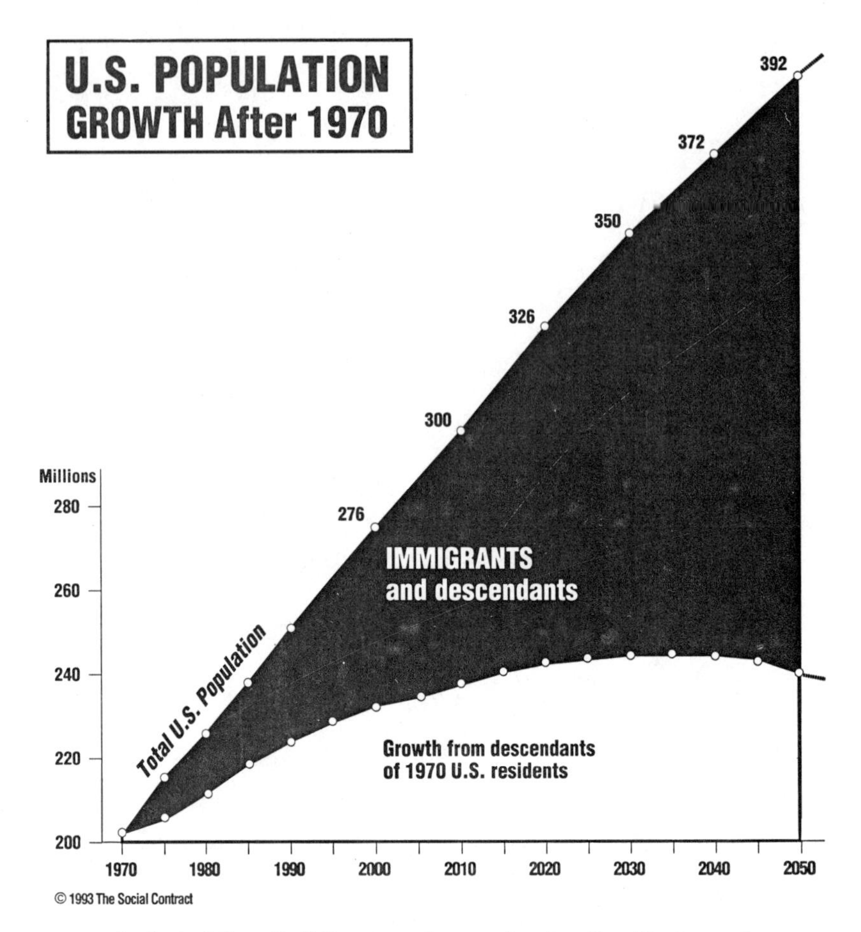

Projected Growth If Congress Leaves Immigration Unchanged

The top line of the chart represents the actual U.S. population from 1970 to 1993, and the Census Bureau's "medium projection" of total population size from 1994 to 2050. It assumes fertility, mortality and immigration levels will remain similar to 1993. In fact, immigration has continued to rise significantly, meaning that population growth actually is on track to be higher than shown here.

The unshaded block at the bottom of the chart (green on the cover) represents *growth* of 1970-stock Americans and their descendants. There were 203 million people living in the U.S. in 1970. Births to that population have exceeded their deaths, resulting in the growth illustrated by the lower block.

The projection of growth in 1970-stock Americans and descendants from 1994 to 2050 is based on recent native-born fertility and mortality rates. The growth would occur despite below-replacement-level fertility rates because of "population momentum." But this segment of Americans is on track to peak at 247 million in 2030 before beginning to drop slowly after 2040. (Source: demographer Leon Bouvier)

The black, upper block of the chart (red on the cover) represents the difference between the number of 1970-stock Americans and the total population. The tens of millions of people represented by this block are the immigrants who have arrived — or are projected to arrive — since 1970, plus their descendants, minus deaths. They are projected to comprise 90% of all U.S. population growth between 1993 and 2050 — if Congress doesn't change the annual immigration level.

RE-CHARTING AMERICA'S FUTURE

Roy Beck

Responses to Arguments
Against Stabilizing
U.S. Population
and Limiting
Immigration

The Social Contract Press • Petoskey, Michigan

Copies are available from:
American Immigration Control Foundation
P.O. Box 525
Monterey, VA 24465

Re-Charting America's Future

The Social Contract Press
316½ E. Mitchell Street
Suite 4
Petoskey, Michigan 49770
Phone: 616/347-1171; Fax: 616/347-1185

Printed in the United States of America.

ISBN: 1-881780-06-6

Table of Contents

INTRODUCTION: The Sabotaged Dream 1

ARGUMENTS Against Population Stabilization

No. 1 **Birth Dearth** **8**
We don't need to worry about U.S. population because WE'RE STABILIZING ALREADY

No. 2 **America the Spacious** **14**
We don't need to stabilize U.S. population because THERE'S PLENTY OF ROOM

No. 3 **America the Wasteful** **32**
We won't have to stabilize population because we can CUT CONSUMPTION TO ALLOW FOR MORE PEOPLE

No. 4 **Cornucopianism** **43**
The U.S. won't need to stabilize population because the FREE MARKET AND TECHNOLOGY WILL SAVE US

No. 5 **Growthism** **55**
We don't want to live without population growth because STABILIZATION EQUALS STAGNATION

No. 6 **Religion** **66**
Population issues are too sensitive to handle because FAITH GROUPS ARE OFFENDED

No. 7 **Globalism** **72**
The focus on U.S. stabilization is misplaced because WHAT MATTERS IS WORLD POPULATION

No. 8 **Irredentism** **79**
We have no right to stabilize population by limiting immigration because U.S. BORDERS ARE ILLEGITIMATE

No. 9 **Fertility Tradeoff** **84**
We can stabilize population without limiting immigration if we CUT U.S. FERTILITY TO MAKE ROOM

No. 10 **Economics** **87**
We can't limit immigration because WE DEPEND ON FOREIGN WORKERS

CONTENTS

No. 11 **Diversity** **103**
We shouldn't limit immigration because
WE NEED FOREIGN CULTURES AND VALUES

No. 12 **Tradition** **113**
Despite pragmatic reasons to do so,
we cannot limit immigration because
WE MUST HONOR OUR IMMIGRANT PAST

No. 13 **Fear of Name-Calling** **125**
It is frightening to agree to limit immigration
because SOME LIMITATIONISTS ARE BIGOTED

No. 14 **Humanitarianism** **136**
No matter what the consequences of U.S. population
growth, we cannot limit immigration because we
have INTERNATIONAL OBLIGATIONS TO THE POOR

No. 15 **Demographic Transition** **160**
Immigration to the U.S. will decline naturally
if we HELP DEVELOP THE THIRD WORLD

No. 16 **Fatalism** **165**
We cannot stabilize population by limiting
immigration because IMMIGRANTS CAN'T BE STOPPED

No. 17 **Freedom** **176**
Limiting immigration and stabilizing population would
require TOO MUCH GOVERNMENT INTERFERENCE

SUMMARY: Our Choices **185**

Sources **194**

Index of Topics **211**

Recommended Reading **214**

Acknowledgements **215**

Introduction

The Sabotaged Dream

For two decades, the federal government has sabotaged the American people's dreams for environmental quality, economic security, and social stability and equity.

The tool: Federal policies that force U.S. population growth.

In 1972, America's Baby Boomers and their older cousins adopted a fertility rate that allows for a stabilized population size. Fertility has remained below that mark. Combined with tough new regulations to lower per capita pollution, the low fertility should have enabled the country to nearly reach the environmental goals set forth in landmark legislation in the late 1960s and 1970s.

But Congress all the while has been flooding the nation with unprecedented waves of foreign workers and their relatives. U.S. population growth has surged. Now, in the 1990s, Americans are faced with a heartbreaking conclusion: Washington has canceled out much of the environmental and social benefits that their choice of small families could have provided. Instead of near-stabilization, U.S. population is on track to grow for centuries.

In effect, Congress has re-charted the future that Americans thought they were creating.

Washington's insistence on population growth further threatens the natural and social order by removing incentives for Americans to continue their environmentally responsible behavior. As Carl Pope of the Sierra Club says, "It's very difficult to say to people, 'You need to have small families because that's going to help your community and your state be environmentally sustainable,' " when Washington doesn't care "how many people may come from other places into your community or state." (Pope, A)

It is time to give close scrutiny to two incompatible blueprints for America in the 21st century:

♦ **The People's Blueprint.** By adopting historically low fertility, Americans have demonstrated a pattern for creating a future with population growing ever-so-slowly until stabilizing around the middle of the next century. (See the green block on the cover.)

♦ **Washington's Blueprint.** By tripling legal immigration levels since 1965 and allowing illegal entries and visa overstays to burgeon, successive Congresses and Administrations have inadvertently set us on a course of perpetual population growth. (See the red block on the cover.)

As any U.S. resident knows, Washington's Blueprint is winning; urban sprawl, worsening congestion and diminishing natural habitats are the rule of American life.

Since 1976, pollsters have found that the majority of Americans object to immigration undermining their decisions to have smaller families. By fall of 1993, 73% of Americans wanted to "strictly" limit immigration. (*Time* magazine poll, Sep. 1993) By a ratio of 7 to 1, Americans believe the country already is suffering from overpopulation. (Roper poll, Apr. 1992) It is no wonder that 60% believe immigration is "bad" for the country. (*Newsweek* magazine poll, Jul. 1993) One-third of Americans are so steamed they want to halt *all* immigration. (CBS/News poll, May 1994)

What Might Have Been

We should pause for a moment to examine what has been lost by Congress moving the nation in a direction contrary to the public's wishes. If the nation's demographic future had rested solely on the fertility choices of American women since 1970 — when the population stood at 203 million — Americans now would be living in this kind of environment:

• U.S. population growth would be winding down by now. Americans would be contending with some 30 million fewer fellow residents than the 260 million we actually have today. Total population would be on target to peak in 2030 at 247 million. From those demographic facts would flow all the following benefits (as will be shown more thoroughly later in the book).

• Traffic volume and congestion never would have gotten as bad as it already is and could be permanently relieved by moderate road-building or mass transit projects.

• Most urban air would meet pollution standards.

• Urban dwellers could delight in the farmland and open spaces at the edge of their cities, confident that population pressures would not require perpetual conversion of agricultural soil and natural habitat into housing tracts, malls, parking lots and streets.

• There would be no further need to drain wetlands and destroy other eco-systems to replace lost farmland and to make room for more residential and commercial sprawl.

- Educational funds could be used to improve existing facilities and programs (especially in core cities) instead of building additional facilities to try to keep up with an ever-expanding student enrollment.

- Americans could enjoy their beaches, parks, waterways and natural spaces, comfortably secure in the expectation that they could return to them year after year without encountering additional congestion or development.

- The Endangered Species Act and other environmental legislation would not have developed so intensely into a never-ending source of conflict between environmentalists and developers.

- We would have more resources per capita, would have to import fewer resources, and would find it much easier to solve the major social and economic problems with a smaller, stabilizing population.

Such would be the United States of the 1990s if Americans had been allowed to benefit from their individual decisions of replacement-level fertility and their costly — sometimes sacrificial — efforts to protect the environment over the last two decades.

Instead, life for the majority of Americans is a daily grind on clogged commuter routes in ever-sprawling metropolitan mazes, breathing unhealthy air and dealing with a deteriorating infrastructure and an increasingly hostile and dangerous social climate — and an economy that widens disparity between affluent and poor.

Why Congress Ignores The Majority

Yet, immigration continues to rise each year. Why? Most Americans appear to have been slow to realize fully what Congress was doing to their future through its forced-population-growth policies. Only in the last couple of years have large numbers of citizens begun to challenge Congress to switch blueprints. Until late 1993, not a single member of Congress had even introduced a bill to cut immigration back toward the traditional levels that had prevailed for decades. Suddenly in 1994, more than 100 of the 535 members of the House and Senate signed onto several new bills that would drastically cut foreign admissions.

But still in place are the powerful forces that have made sure the Washington Blueprint for growth prevailed. Although they represent a tiny fraction of Americans, they have thus far neutralized the majority's wishes in part because they come wrapped in what appear to be strong moral arguments. As Nathan Glazer wrote in *The New Republic*:

> *Few Americans believe our population is too low, our land too lightly settled, our resources unexploited, our industries and commerce short of labor. But our politics, the result of various pressures operating within a framework of decent and generous ideals, end up looking as if we believe all this is true.* (Glazer, A)

In fact, the pressure for population growth also comes from people whose motivation is "ugly and full of self-interest," in the words of former Colorado Governor Richard Lamm. They are employers who want to be able to hire foreign workers in preference to Americans so that they don't have to raise wages or improve working conditions. (American minorities, particularly African-Americans, are especially hurt by these actions.) Others seek growth to reap profits from land speculation or questionable business practices that exploit our country's natural heritage. "Surely the employers' argument cannot be powerful," Lamm said. "It isn't. Its power comes from the fact that it is allied both to the immigration dream and to the politically powerful and seemingly disinterested forces of internationalism, humanitarianism and opposition to racism." (Lamm, Imhoff, A, p.18)

Historian Otis L. Graham, Jr. adds that the moral and mythical veneer often given to immigration policies has distracted Congress from a clear-eyed assessment of its policies. Congress has moved the nation in a direction most of its members don't even realize and in disregard of the national interest. "The result is a disguised population policy called immigration policy, bringing about a demographic future that neither the voters nor Congress consciously selected, and almost certainly would not [select]." (Graham, A, p.22)

How Strong Are The Arguments?

Since Congress is not fully aware of where it is taking the nation or of its reasons for doing so, it is important for the public to help lawmakers examine their actions and rationale. How strong are the arguments against the public's preferred goal of population stabilization? Most policy issues come down to moral questions of what is the right thing to do. Rarely is it merely a question of right *vs* wrong. Rather it is weighing the "right" on each side. Is it parochial, narrow, selfish, foolish, self-destructive or bigoted for the United States to stabilize its population, as the supporters of current high-growth policies variously claim and as even many supporters of stabilization sometimes fret? Or is it possible that in weighing all factors, stabilization is in fact the moral high ground?

Historian Graham sees the country at a cross-roads, facing alternate Americas a century away: "One a population about the size of today, the other nearly twice that size..."

Many commentators have come to accept as inevitable the second, doubled-in-density America and the attendant lifestyle of frenetic adaptations. But there is nothing inevitable or unavoidable about that scenario; it is solely a creation of Congress and its current "Washington Blueprint." Our elected representatives could set us on the road to stabilization tomorrow with the simple passage of a single bill limiting immigration to numbers compatible with the "People's Blueprint."

In the midst of writing this book, I took time for my annual week of leading more than two dozen high school students in building Habitat for Humanity houses on Virginia's Eastern Shore. Although the population of blacks and whites in this area have pre-colonial roots, many experience poverty as great as the newest newcomer from foreign lands. It is easier to see the good results from voluntary action in rural and small-town America. It also is easy to see how federal policies that allow significant immigration into such areas can begin to multiply impoverished conditions faster than other efforts can alleviate them. I dedicate this book to the youth of Mount Olivet United Methodist Church in Arlington, Virginia and to the hundreds of thousands of other teenagers across America who volunteer their efforts in pursuit of environmental and social ideals. My hope is that congressional demographic policies would be set so as not to negate those teenagers' work or the future to which they aspire.

Time is not a friend of today's teenagers. As this book will show, the failure of Congress to act immediately may result in today's American teens living their retirement years in an America with a natural landscape devastated by U.S. population growth. One of the world's oldest conservation organizations, The Izaak Walton League, put it this way: "By its nature, population growth can't be altered overnight — it will require decades to see the results of population stabilization and reduction efforts we may implement today." (Izaak Walton League, c) William Vogt foresaw the coming crunch when he wrote his groundbreaking *Road to Survival* in 1948, connecting human population growth and environmental quality: "The most critical danger is that we shall not realize how short we are of that one non-renewable resource — time. If we wait until next year, or the next decade, to push our search for a solution, then our fate may well be sealed." (Vogt, A)

There were fewer than 150 million Americans in the year Vogt issued his warning and Harry Truman was elected president. Even if Congress were to act in 1994 to halt *all* immigration permanently, that U.S. population of 1948 still would nearly double to around 300 million by 2050, before peaking (if fertility and mortality remained unchanged). If, on the other hand, Congress doesn't act to cut back immigration numbers, we will likely pass 400 million in the middle of the century, not even pausing there on our way to 500 million by the year 2100 — and with no peak in sight. (Census Bureau, E; Bouvier, C)

Opinion polls show that Americans don't want that to happen. Yet, Congress continues to take us in that direction.

The chapters of this book examine the justifications offered for why Washington's population-growth policies should be continued. The academic and scientific evidence offered in each chapter challenges the wisdom of those policies and makes the case for the alternative: allowing *The People's Blueprint* to prevail and our youth to inherit an environmental quality of life that, at least, is no worse than today's.

How To Use This Book

The chapters have several elements:

- Each chapter title states a general claim against population stabilization drawn from those made by groups or individuals who support continued population growth and/or high immigration. Because nobody makes all these arguments for population growth, and because they come from the ideological left and right, many of them are contradictory. The pro-stabilization responses, however, are meant to form a consistent, logical pattern of reasoning.
- The chapter titles and a number of secondary claims are contained in boxes. The reader easily can distinguish between the arguments by supporters of congressional population-growth action (in boxes) and those in favor of population stabilization (outside the boxes).
- After each claim, a short pro-stabilization rebuttal (in large boldface type).
- Following, a paragraph that expands the rebuttal.
- In most cases, further background from various experts that is printed in columns.

The chapters are arranged to be read in sequence. Nonetheless, the format of the book is intended also to allow readers immediately to skip around in the book to arguments that are of the most interest or that are the most troubling. Some may find it helpful to first read the Summary at the end of the book to gain a broad overview of how all the chapters fit together in suggesting public policy options.

Sources, cited in parentheses, can be found alphabetically in the Sources section at the end of the book. There is no ideological uniformity to the sources. They fit in the categories of liberal, conservative, environmentalist, macro-economy analyst, labor union enthusiast, religious, humanist, government official, internationalist, grassroots activist, historian, anthropologist, journalist, Americans and citizens of other countries. I gratefully acknowledge my debt to all of them for their years of study, scholarship, good common sense, and writings that provide the collected wisdom with which I've tried to fill this book.

Weighing Majority Opinion

It is not the contention of this book that the American majority is right because it is the majority. A time-honored truism is that the majority can be, and often is, wrong. In a representative democracy, elected officials do not have to follow the will of the public majority on each issue. We elect representatives to devote time the rest of us cannot muster to the study of public issues. We expect them to protect us from the consequences of quickly evolving popular whims. Indeed, if officials believe the majority is factually, practically or morally in error, they may have an ethical obligation to oppose the majority (always with the knowledge that the public may choose to elect a different representative next time around).

But democratic governance should begin with the assumption that the majority's will deserves priority attention. Barring strong reasons to the contrary, the will of the majority should prevail. The burden of proof rests on those who would create public policy at odds with the majority will. Only 33% of Americans approve of immigration as high as the present level. (CBS/*New York Times* poll, Sept. 13, 1994) Advocates of that majority position must make a convincing case that the majority of Americans have been consistently wrong for two decades to ask to limit immigration and to halt population growth.

For that reason, the format of the book starts with the anti-majoritarian, anti-stabilization arguments and then reveals, we respectfully submit, that they do not stand up under close examination.

Argument No. 1

Birth Dearth

GENERAL CLAIM: We don't need to worry about U.S. population because . . .

WE'RE STABILIZING ALREADY

GENERAL PRO-STABILIZATION RESPONSE:

♦ **When John F. Kennedy was elected president in 1960, we were 179 million Americans; we passed 260 million in 1994, and are on pace to surpass a half-BILLION by the year 2100. Does that sound like stabilization?** (Census Bureau; Bouvier-Grant, A)

♦ **The level of Chinese overpopulation and density that horrified us during our childhood will be the American reality for our great-grandchildren, if current U.S. fertility and immigration levels continue.** (*World Almanac*; Bouvier-Grant, A)

Many Americans are confused by 20 years of headlines that we have a below-replacement fertility rate. We do. But it can take up to 70 years after achieving replacement-level fertility (an average of 2.1 children per woman) before population growth actually stops. "The sudden imposition of any change in fertility will not be fully realized until all have died who were living at the time the change was achieved." (Bartlett-Lytwak, A) The growth from that momentum pales, however, in comparison to the growth we experience from immigration numbers many times higher than traditional levels. (Abernethy, F)

Most demographers project huge population increases far into the future. The facts are easy to come by, and the U.S. numbers are clear: the country is not on a path to stabilize any time over the next several centuries. Anybody who argues otherwise simply is wrong.

Current fertility rates and immigration numbers will push U.S. population past 392 million by 2050 and past 500 million by the year 2100. (Census Bureau, B; Bouvier-Grant, A, pp.76-77) Unfortunately, Congress increased immigration still further in 1990 in the midst of claims by cheap-labor industrialists, immigration lawyers and misinformed commentators that the country faced a coming shortage of people.

Throughout this book, general references to "immigrants" and their numbers include legal and illegal immigrants, refugees and asylees.

CLAIM A: Why worry about U.S. population growth now? The population boom years were in the 1950s and 1960s.

PRO-STABILIZATION RESPONSE:

♦ In fact, the current U.S. population boom is adding people to the country in the same gigantic volume as during the historic Baby Boom years.

It is difficult to visualize fully the magnitude of current growth, but an example or two should help. Immigration and births are on course to add a city the size of Washington, D.C. to the U.S. every three months (Miller, B), and will add the equivalent of the entire population of Japan between now and 2050. (Mehlman, B)

Indeed, the population increase during the 1950s and 1960s of 52 million (most of the famed U.S. Baby Boom) was phenomenal. It dwarfed all other previous two-decade periods. The previous high period (1910s and 1920s) had only a 31-million increase, and that was far ahead of the other periods. (Census Bureau)

Contrary to popular thought, our U.S. growth barely slowed after the Baby Boom, because of increased immigration. The 1970s and 1980s saw 46 million additional Americans.

Census Bureau projections based on current fertility and immigration indicate that growth during the present two-decade period (1990-2010) will equal the record 1950s and 1960s.

CLAIM B: What about the widely publicized claims about a birth dearth?

PRO-STABILIZATION RESPONSE:

♦ The U.S. is a world-class baby factory, producing more than 4 million infants a year and keeping pace with the incredible Baby Boom stork.

The data are clear: we are *not* faced with a birth dearth. Rather, we are in the early stages of a new baby boom caused by the Baby Boom Echo (births to children of Baby Boomers) and by the very high fertility levels of most immigrants. (Bouvier, C)

During the mid-1970s, before annual immigration passed a half-million a year, the media was filled with stories about maternity wards going begging for babies. But, except for a few special situations, that was true for only a short time.

The average Baby Boom year produced 4.03 million babies. The all-time high was 4.3 million in 1957. Annual births fell to 3.137 million in 1973, and slowly have been rising since. Our country has produced more than 4 million babies a year since 1989. (National Center for Health Statistics)

Even though American women today have a far lower fertility rate than the women of 1950, they are having around the same number of total babies, because there were 58 million women of child-bearing age in 1990, compared to 34 million in 1950. (Census Bureau, C,D)

CLAIM C: But isn't the U.S. fertility *rate* continuing to decline, signalling eventual population decline down the line?

PRO-STABILIZATION RESPONSE:

♦ Driven by exceptionally high immigrant fertility, the total U.S. fertility rate has been rising.

Native-born Americans have maintained a birth rate significantly below replacement level since 1972. But the increasingly large foreign-born population tends toward fertility rates high above that level. (Census Bureau)

With a fertility rate of an average of 2.1 children per woman (and zero net immigration, i.e, immigration=emigration), any country's population eventually would stabilize.

Fertility rates fell fairly quickly in the 1960s to below the replacement level by 1972, ending the Baby Boom.

U.S. fertility hit an all-time low of 1.7 in the Bicentennial year of 1976. It hovered just above that for years and has been on an upward path since 1987, threatening to push above 2.1. (National Center for Health Statistics)

In California, the chief destination of immigrants, fertility has soared far above the replacement level to 2.5, twice the rate of Italy, and rivaling some underdeveleped countries. (Oberlink, A)

The fertility of some immigrant groups is more than double that of American natives. Unless immigrants cut their fertility by about a third and natives reduce theirs still further, U.S. population is destined to grow for centuries, if current immigration numbers prevail. (Bouvier, C)

CLAIM D: Maybe we will decide in the next few decades that we've had enough population growth; since Americans are maintaining a zero-population-growth standard with their two-child norm, all we'll have to do is halt immigration at that time and we'll have stabilization when we need it.

PRO-STABILIZATION RESPONSE

♦ **Stabilizing population is like braking a speeding car; one needs to anticipate and act far in advance of the time when one wants to stop the car — or population growth.** (Myrdal, A)

Population "momentum" is a powerful force. The number of births is dependent not only on the number of births to each woman but the number of women of reproductive age. Not until demographic bulges — like the Baby Boomers, the current wave of immigrants, and their own boomlet of children — move through their reproductive years is stabilization possible. Such momentum can drive growth for decades even after replacement-level fertility and zero-net immigration levels are reached. It is not as simple and immediate as turning off a faucet. (Bouvier, C)

Despite below-replacement-level fertility, the 1970-stock U.S. population has grown by more than 25 million because there have been so many Baby Boom mothers having their own babies, albeit at low rates.

The 1970-stock population continues to grow in the 1990s, but not by much. At current low fertility this segment of the population and its descendants will peak at 247 million in the year 2030, well below what immigration pushed total population to by 1994. Beck-Bouvier, A)

In actuality, post-1970 immigrants and their descendants (minus deaths among them) have doubled the population growth between 1970 and 1990, driving the U.S. population past 260 million. (*The Social Contract*, I)

At current fertility, even if Americans decided tomorrow to stop population growth as quickly as possible, and cut off all immigration to do it, U.S. population would continue to grow past the year 2050 and would not peak until it was over 300 million. (Census Bureau, B)

The concept of the "braking distance" of population growth shows the necessity to be far-sighted. "Public policy must stop being reactionary and must begin to be anticipatory if we are to leave any kind of quality of life for our children." (Myrdal, A)

"The effect of this population momentum is that we have to think about the population problem approximately 70 years in advance. Most people, especially political leaders, find it difficult to think about things 70 years in the future." (Bartlett-Lytwak, A)

CLAIM E: If U.S. population growth were a critical problem, our leaders would tell us.

PRO-STABILIZATION RESPONSE:

♦ **The time frame in which the population growth occurs is much greater than election cycles.** (Ryerson, A)

Political leaders are most likely to talk about immediate crises and not address long-range problems, Few things affect a nation more pervasively than demographic change. But it occurs incrementally; it creeps up on us while leaders are looking elsewhere (often at problems that are caused in part, or made worse, by the very demographic change they ignore). It also is easy to put off such sensitive issues to be handled later.

Despite the weaknesses of our democratic system in addressing long-term problems, our nation did have several leaders who recognized the potential for U.S. population problems in the 1950s and 1960s. Presidents Eisenhower, Kennedy, Johnson and Nixon all voiced great concern over U.S. population growth. They gave support to the principle of family planning assistance during that period of high American fertility. (Simcox, A)

Nixon sounded a note of much urgency in 1969 when he said: "One of the most serious challenges to human destiny in the last third of this century will be the growth of the population. Whether man's response to that challenge will be a cause for pride or despair in the year 2000 will depend very much on what we do today." (Simcox, A) He turned his words into action by appointing (jointly with the Democrat-led Congress) the Commission on Population Growth and the American Future, composed of business, labor, environmentalist, minority, academic, feminist and urban leaders to study the population needs of the United States.

After two years of study the commission concluded that there would be no benefits for the country to grow past the 203 million of 1970 and that most economic, social and environmental problems would be easier to solve if U.S. population were to stabilize as soon as possible. Proposed were various kinds of assistance to help Americans maintain a two-child-per-family culture and a cap on immigration so it would not interfere with population stabilization.

Unfortunately, the chance to implement the report was lost in the 1972 election campaign and the subsequent Watergate scandal. Nixon never acted on the report, and no president since has shown much concern about the ever-increasing density in which Americans are forced to live because of federal government policies.

Argument No. 2

America The Spacious

GENERAL CLAIM: We don't need to stabilize U.S. population because . . .

THERE'S PLENTY OF ROOM

GENERAL PRO-STABILIZATION RESPONSE:

♦ **The issue is not space, but carrying capacity. Will U.S. natural resources be able to support future generations at present lifestyles if the population — and thus resource use — increases?** (Miller, B)

♦ **If sustainable living can be defined as enjoying the fruit without harming the tree that produces it, then there is ample evidence that 260 million Americans are already hacking vigorously at the trunk.**

The point of our national life should not be to see how many people can be crowded together at the lowest level of existence. Every increase in U.S. population just adds further to an astounding record of destruction of our natural resources:

- 50% of U.S. wetlands already destroyed; another 300,000 acres lost each year. (World Resources Institute, A; Izaak Walton League, B)
- 90% of northwestern old-growth forests gone; intense pressure to log much of the remainder. (World Resources Institute, A)
- 99% of our tallgrass prairie gone. (World Resources Institute, A)
- 35 states withdraw groundwater faster than it can be replenished. (Izaak Walton League, B)
- 60,000 square miles covered by pavement (Alliance for a Paving Moratorium, A); 1.3 million acres (equal to the state of Delaware) blacktopped each year. (Pimentel, B)
- more than 700 species of native plants and animals threatened with extinction; despite some notable successes

like the bald eagle, the number is growing. (Izaak Walton League, B)

• farmland producing more than half the nation's food supply threatened by suburban growth. (*USA Today*, D)

It is probably impossible to exaggerate the importance of the image of America as a land of limitless bounty in shaping the way we have used and do use the resources of our country. (Shabecoff, A, p.11)

The vast openness of this continental country survives and tempts most of us to question if there possibly can be a population-growth urgency here. But looks are deceiving. The question is not whether there is enough land to divide into suburban plots for 130 million more Americans the next 50 years, but whether our natural resources can sustain the present — let alone additional — population. And can Americans retain any semblance of their culture and lifestyle of personal freedoms amidst such an expansion? (see ARGUMENT No. 17: Freedom)

"Anthropologist Virginia Abernethy argues that the American way of life is uniquely rooted in conservation. A high quality of life in the U.S. goes beyond meeting basic human needs, such as shelter and jobs. It requires 'high-quality recreational opportunities,' and people existing in harmony with 'an abundance and diversity of wild species.' Residents, Abernethy wrote, need 'tolerable work-to-home commuting conditions' and neighborhoods free of crime, plus fundamental education and economic opportunities. When high population prevents people from enjoying any of these things, the quality of life has declined, and the area's carrying capacity has been exceeded." (Izaak Walton League, B)

CLAIM A: You can fly coast to coast in the U.S. and see mostly open spaces, especially in the vast unpopulated West. Surely there is room to grow.

PRO-STABILIZATION RESPONSE

♦ **The vast open spaces through the Midwest are open for good reason — they feed us.**

♦ **Most of the non-coastal West is thinly populated for another good reason: It has little or no economic use and it doesn't have enough water to support agriculture, industry or urban concentration.**
(Brownridge, A)

♦ **The sparsely populated West has little ability to support more people, in part, because its resources already are required to support the mega-cities on California's coast. Los Angeles survives only by importing its water and electricity from Wyoming, Colorado, New Mexico and Arizona.** (Ehrlich, B, p.269)

For each American, it takes many acres of farm, range, forest and other land to feed, clothe, house and provide the materials (and space) for transportation, commerce, residence, recreation and waste disposal. Each additional million Americans multiplies need. We know that someday, if we continue to grow, there will be no excess acreage in this country and that we will be able to add population only by deteriorating Americans' quality of life and the environment. How close are we to that point? Or have we already passed it?

The usual view of the West as unspoiled and boundless is a romantic illusion. "The West has been thoroughly surveyed, mapped, tramped over, prospected and inventoried. All of it has been allocated to some use. The frontier is gone; there is no virgin, idle land waiting to be discovered. Forests, water, rangeland and amenities are being consumed at a rate that cannot be sustained..." (Brownridge, A)

"It takes more than open space to support people. In fact, almost all of that wide open space so often cited is marginal land — land that can't support much life of any kind.... To be habitable, an area must be able to provide water, shelter, food and many other resources for the people who would live there." (Population-Environment Balance, A)

Shifting tectonic plates have rippled much of the West with range upon range of rugged mountains. The flat land between the mountains is high plateau, meaning cold winters and short growing seasons. Most of the West is semiarid, capable of supporting short grass, or it is full-fledged desert. "In short, nine-tenths of the West is too dry, too cold, too steep, or too rocky for crop farming... Mainly because it is useless for farming, half the West was never claimed ... (and) remains in public ownership." Nearly 70 percent of public rangeland has been overgrazed and almost certainly will be able to support fewer livestock in the future than in the past. (Brownridge, A)

Finding more water to enable many more people to engage in agriculture or enlarge the cities of the West is not likely. Virtually every river in the West already has been dammed (throughout their courses, like the Columbia and lower Colorado) or "literally sucked dry (like the Owens in California, the Gila and Santa Cruz in Arizona, and the Arkansas)..." (Brownridge, A) "In the San Joaquin Valley (California) pumping now exceeds natural replenishment by more than half a trillion gallons in a year. By the end of the century, it could rise to a trillion gallons — a mining operation that in sheer volume beggars the exhaustion of oil." (Reisner, A, p.11)

The Colorado River — the very sound of its name conjuring visions of the wild, untamed West carving the indescribable Grand Canyon — has been bled nearly dry by the explosion of population in the West and the voracious appetites of a growing America for more food. Since 1900, farmers east of the Rockies have diverted water from the headwaters of the Colorado on the western slope. Today, more than 20 projects drain its high tributary flows across the Great Divide to provide for constantly growing populations in Denver, Boulder and other east-side cities. They would take more of the water, but federal agreements apportion the rest of the water to California and Arizona. "As I followed the waterway 150 miles below Hoover, I could almost hear the slurping straws of distant cities. On one side of Lake Havasu is the Central Arizona Project (CAP), which carries river water 335 miles eastward to Phoenix and, soon, to Tucson. On the other is the Colorado River Aqueduct, emerging from a pump house able to suck up one billion gallons of water a day for southern California." In dry years, there is not enough to meet current demands of all the users of the Colorado. Even in wet years, the river is drained almost out of existence, with not much more than a trickle of "salt and pesticide-laced runoff from crop irrigation" flowing into Mexico, in violation of our water treaty with that country. (*National Geographic*, A)

CLAIM B: Population growth in the U.S. cannot be a serious problem when Texas alone has space for the entire world's population to live on 1,400 square feet, the size of a house, per person.

PRO-STABILIZATION RESPONSE:

♦ **Overpopulation is not only a matter of overcrowding in the big cities. Even India and China have large areas that are sparsely populated, but virtually everyone agrees they are tragically overpopulated.** (Australians for an Ecologically Sustainable Population, A)

♦ **Why not make the world's people really miserable and just have them stand elbow to elbow in half the**

area of the state of Rhode Island? (Hardin, A, p.121)

Groups like the Cato Institute, that are ideologically wedded to the idea of perpetual growth, do mathematical gymnastics like the Texas example to show how compactly people can live. (CATO, A) But since virtually nobody would choose to live that way, the exercises really have no point. Simple space rarely is the issue in overpopulation problems. If more than 5 billion people lived in Texas and had to live off the resources in Texas, they would all be dead in a week. (Tanton, G)

> CLAIM C: The U.S. should not fear higher population and density, considering how very well — by world standards — the far-more-crowded residents of Hong Kong live.

PRO-STABILIZATION RESPONSE:

♦ **The criterion for determining whether a nation or region is over-populated is NOT land area, but carrying capacity. Does the current number of residents live without damaging the environment beyond its capacity to replenish? For the U.S., the answer is no.** (Population-Environment Balance, A)

♦ **Current population projections suggest a tripling of U.S. traffic congestion by the year 2005.** (Interfaith Coalition on Energy, A) **Is the example of Hong Kong supposed to help Americans feel less threatened by the prospect?**

Hong Kong survives only because it is able to buy excess carrying capacity from other nations. A nation's long-term sustainability is based on its ability to maintain clean air and healthy ecosystems and to have a dependable supply of water, food and energy. (Miller, B) If a nation that fails to meet those standards is overpopulated, the U.S. fits the bill. Each million additional people just make the environmental problems that much worse.

The Hong Kong argument is the same as one long made about the Netherlands. How can one fear overpopulation in a spacious country like America when the Dutch live prosperous lives of high quality and culture? The Dutch have a population density of more than a thousand people per square mile, one of the highest in the world. The simple explanation is that the Dutch can live that way because other parts of the world don't. "In 1984-86, the Netherlands imported almost 4 million tons of cereals, 130,000 tons of food oils and 480,000 tons of pluses (peas, beans, lentils). They took some of these relatively inexpensive imports and used them to boost their production of expensive exports — 330,000 tons of milk and 1.2 million tons of meat... The Netherlands is also a major importer of minerals, bringing in virtually all the iron, antimony, bauxite, copper, tin, etc., that it requires. Most of its fresh water is 'imported' from upstream nations via the Rhine River. The Dutch built their wealth using imported energy.... In short, the people of the Netherlands didn't build their prosperity on the bounty of the Netherlands, and are not living on it now." (Ehrlich, B, pp.39-40,)

Total impact on the environment is a function of per capita environmental impact multiplied by the number of people.

For two decades, the American economy has devoted massive sums of money to reducing the environmental damage done by each person, whether with their cars, garbage, toilets or workplaces. But the government forgot that equally important in the effect on the environment is the number of people driving the cars, flushing the toilets, using fossil fuel and requiring space to live, play, work and bury their garbage.

During the time we were supposed to be putting our environmental house in order, we were filling the house with 60 million more polluters. The result is that we are not meeting our environmental goals.

The federal government's insistence that the population continue growing by nearly 3 million a year reflects a long, shameful side of the American character as noted by many outside observers. Peter Kalm, a Swedish naturalist traveling in America in the mid-1700s, wrote: "The grain fields, the meadows, the forests, the cattle are treated with equal carelessness.... [Americans'] eyes are fixed upon the present gain and they are blind to the future." Alexis de Tocqueville noted in 1832: "In Europe, people talk a great deal of the wilds of America, but the Americans themselves never think about them; they are insensible to the wonders of inanimate nature" and their chief concern is their "march across these wilds, draining swamps, turning the course of rivers, peopling solitudes and subduing nature." (Shabecoff, A, p.14)

A few relatively small countries (Hong Kong has 5.8 million people, the Netherlands has 15.4 million) can depend on the rest of the Earth to expand the carrying capacity they have exceeded on their own lands. But if the U.S. — the third most populous country — persists in outgrowing its ability to feed and supply itself, and its ability to maintain healthy eco-systems, it has neither the moral right to ask, nor a reasonable expectation, that other countries can find the resources to make up the difference.

CLAIM D: Carrying capacity is a vague concept and open to much disagreement. Who can say whether the U.S. has too many people and that the numbers are overstressing the environment?

PRO-STABILIZATION RESPONSE:

♦ **Under current conditions, Americans clearly are exceeding the environmental carrying capacity when 40 percent of them live in areas with air that fails to meet even health standards.** (Associated Press, C)

♦ **Around 1,000 U.S. communities fail to meet clean water standards.** (EPA) **An estimated 15 million Americans now have to drink from unsafe water supplies.** (Zero Population Growth, B)

At current levels of per capita environmental impact, the U.S. has more people than its air and water can sustain. Some day in the future, various changes may make it possible for this many Americans, and maybe more, to live without violating the carrying capacity of the air and water. But prudence would suggest that we add no more people until our air and water meet the quality standards we have established as necessary and desirable.

The author recently drove through Illinois. From the air, Illinois' monotonous, sparsely populated grain fields definitely look like open spaces available for more development. But at a roadside rest stop, a sign reminded me just how totally developed Illinois already is and how environmental resources have been violated to the maximum in order to feed the growing U.S. population:

In 1818, at the time of statehood, Illinois had 8.2 million acres of wetlands, of which only 0.7 million acres remain today, a loss of over 91%. The loss of wetlands continues despite their value for wildlife habitat, flood control, water quality improvement, groundwater discharge and recreation.

> *The small (2-acre) wooded area behind this building is a forested wetland and is protected within the rest area property.*

As I drove eastward and contemplated how wetlands — an essential incubator of biodiversity — had become so rare in Illinois as to qualify as a roadside museum piece, I was puzzled by the sight of a long line of parked cars in the middle of a field up ahead. I was still some 30 miles east of St. Louis. A few seconds later over a slight incline I saw a massive abrasion of the earth. The cars obviously belonged to the workers operating a string of heavy machinery. While wetlands continued to be drained to create more farmland elsewhere, right before my eyes the machines were scraping back top soil from this farmland to plant more urban development for an expanding population in the raw red gash. (Beck)

A map of where most population growth has occurred in the U.S. since 1980 is very similar to a map of where environmental laws are being violated. Population growth has had a direct relationship with dirtier water and air. (Sparks, A)

CLAIM E: If U.S. population growth were a serious threat to the environment, more environmental groups and experts would be warning of the dangers.

PRO-STABILIZATION RESPONSE:

♦ Increasingly environmental groups *are* sounding the population alarm.

Most conservation groups advocate a stable population to protect the environment. Their activism since the mid-1970s, however, has been concentrated on reducing per capita impact on the environment, guarding against the watering down of laws, and fighting specific, immediate threats to various natural resources from development. During the last few years, many organizations have been showing more interest in the population growth that creates the pressure for the development. More than 60 environmental organizations issued a "Priority Statement on Population" in 1991 that stated: "Together, the increase in population and in resource consumption are basic causes of human suffering and environmental degradation and must become major priorities for national and international action." (Zero Population Growth, C)

"It is possible that we have already exceeded our ability to sustain ourselves: Estimates of the population we can support, without damaging resources for the next generation, range from 40 million to 170 million. We are well beyond those limits." (Audubon, B)

In the state with the greatest population growth, "most environmentalists concede that population growth is California's greatest environmental threat.... Thirty-seven animals have become extinct in California since the 1880s. There are 110 endangered or threatened animal species.... Over 200 plants are endangered, threatened or rare... The state flag displays the state animal, the California grizzly, which is extinct in the state. Our state tree, the redwood, is doing somewhat better. Only 90 percent of the original stands have been logged. Ninety-seven percent of the state's wetlands have been lost. Fish populations have dropped precipitously. The Great Valley of California once had 10,000 kilometers of salmon streams. It now has 300." (Oberlink, A)

The nation's most prominent environmental group, the Sierra Club, has called for population stabilization for decades. In 1966, for example, it endorsed creating "federal machinery" to deal with rapid population growth. In 1969, it urged stabilization of the U.S. population no later than 1990. Other policies through the years stated: "All regions of the world must reach a balance between their populations and resources." "Human population growth undermines both natural and man-made communities, and contributes to virtually all global environmental problems." (Sierra Club, D)

"The lesson is clear: conservationists cannot succeed in protecting our natural heritage unless ... population becomes part of the solution... Keep the human population level in balance with the limits of nature's renewable resources, or face the eradication of a way of life." (Izaak Walton League, C)

Among national environmental groups now focusing on U.S. population problems are: the Audubon Society, Carrying Capacity Network, Environmental Defense Fund, Natural Resources Defense Council, National Wildlife Federation, Izaak Walton League, Negative Population Growth, Population-Environment Balance, Sierra Club and Zero Population Growth. (Nowak, A)

Slowly, environmental groups are finding they must address immigration issues if they are serious about the U.S. population size.

"A dedicated environmentalist who carries on about the deterioration of the environment while resolutely refusing to discuss population growth is guilty of over-emphasizing effect and neglecting causes... Once an environmentalist faces the issue of population growth, he finds he cannot avoid the immigration problem." (Hardin, H)

The Sierra Club has urged Congress to conduct a thorough examination of U.S. immigration laws and policies and their impact on the balance between population and environmental resources. (Sierra Club, D)

The Izaak Walton League — begun in 1922 to combat water pollution and other environmental abuses — is one of the oldest and largest of America's conservation organizations. It "recognizes current levels of natural resource consumption and population are not sustainable." It urges government actions that will help stabilize U.S. population. "The League understands international migration must be addressed as part of a comprehensive strategy to manage U.S. population size." (Izaak Walton League, D)

CLAIM F: Compared to residents of many other nations, Americans really don't have much of a crowding problem.

PRO-STABILIZATION RESPONSE:

♦ **Most Americans live at population densities that are among the highest on Earth.** (Fox-Mehlman, A, pp.38-39)

♦ **Americans on the Northeast coast live more densely than residents of El Salvador, the most congested nation in the Western Hemisphere.**

♦ **Coastal crowding is so intense that natural habitat and eco-systems are not surviving, resulting in rapid loss of bio-diversity.**

While much of the interior of the U.S. is used to feed the population and grow timber for its use, about half of all Americans cluster tightly along the narrow band of the Atlantic, Gulf of Mexico, Great Lakes and Pacific coasts. That also is where most immigrants settle and the site of most other U.S. population growth. Unfortunately, the country's most sensitive eco-systems also are concentrated on the coasts.

Most Americans don't live dispersed across the amber waves of grain and purple mountains of America the Beautiful. Even in wide open states like Texas, the vast majority of residents are crowded into metropolitan areas of more than a million people.

Just under 50 percent of Americans live on just 10.5 percent of the continental land mass along the coasts. In 1990, the coastal region of the Northeast had a population density of 767 people per square mile. By comparison, El Salvador, the most densely populated nation overall in the Western Hemisphere, had a density of 671. Haiti — where overpopulation has stripped the land of its environmental inheritance and drives desperate citizens to search for new homelands — has nearly 200 fewer people per square mile than the Northeast U.S. coast. (Fox-Mehlman, A, pp.38-39)

Coastal wetlands are nature's incubator and the ecosystem's natural filters, aiding in the breakdown of natural and man-made contaminants. Many wetlands already have been irrevocably lost under the onslaught of urban development. Louisiana alone loses more than 25 square miles of coastal wetlands every year. Most of the additional 130 million Americans projected over the next 50 years are expected to settle along the coasts. "Ironically, as population grows and encroaches on wetlands, it destroys the ecological basis that supports all population." (Fox-Mehlman, A, pp.38-39)

CLAIM G: We could handle more people if we distributed the population differently.

PRO-STABILIZATION RESPONSE:

♦ **Such redistribution would be ineffective and, at any rate, is theoretical.**

♦ **Most relatively unpopulated areas lack the carrying capacity for large numbers of people. And areas that CAN support more tend to be agricultural.** (Population-Environment Balance, B)

♦ **Redistribution by force of government took place in the old Soviet Union, and in present-day China. Is this a solution Americans will embrace?** (Hardin, G)

The fact is that most of the new population wouldn't want to settle in North Dakota, or anywhere other than the coasts. (*Boston Globe*, A) A growing number of natives are fleeing the coasts for the hinterland. It is tempting to imagine that we can put all the additional population out in those wide open spaces. "The fact that the West is the site of many of the nation's most bitter and protracted environmental controversies should be our clue that population pressures already exist." (Carrying Capacity Network, J)

And there are major moral and practical reasons not to take still more agricultural land permanently out of production in a world increasingly short of food.

One reason to doubt that a major portion of new population will move to relatively sparsely populated areas is the very negative local reaction to the modest shift in population already occurring.

Only a few thousand — in some cases, a few hundred — coastal "refugees" create great social disruption in hinterland communities. And that is from newcomers who are American-born and speak the same language.

"We often hear the 'empty lands' argument from the bi-coastal people who fly back and forth across the country. What these people are really saying is there is lots of room elsewhere — not at their homes on Manhattan Island or in Los Angeles. Now if you go to Montana, Wyoming and Utah, as I have, and ask the people there if they want more neighbors, they emphatically say, 'no.' " (Tanton, G)

The National Trust for Historic Preservation has placed the entire state of Vermont on its list of endangered historic places, because of the number of Americans moving there, fleeing the congestion of the coast. It is evidence that Americans probably do not want to do away with scenic, peaceful places and the charm of small town America just to accommodate another 130 million people. (Carrying Capacity Network, J)

Many moderate-sized cities also resist more growth that endangers the qualities their residents like. An interviewer on an MTV special about Austin asked the mayor for the most important thing he wanted the young TV-viewing audience to know about the Texas capital. "We're full up," Mayor Bruce Todd said. "Come and visit, but don't come here to live." The city ballooned 13% in 1992 alone. "Our attractiveness could be our downfall. We have achieved success — now how do we keep it from destroying us?" (Audubon Society, A)

That's the cry, as well, from small cities and towns across America. Although some very small, depopulated Midwest agricultural towns could use a fresh infusion of newcomers, most Americans living in the hinterland don't want to be the recipients of any major population redistribution — especially on the order of 130 million.

It would be an interesting exercise for the federal government to poll the mayors of every town and city in America and ask how many additional residents they would like or could handle. The total would be helpful information for those setting immigration policies. (*Atlantic Monthly*, A)

"We cannot disperse people to relatively unpopulated areas because the carrying capacity simply is not there." Many such areas require expensive and environmentally questionable schemes just to supply water. (Population-Environment Balance, B)

Dispersal of population may serve to dilute some concentrations of pollution but it vexes mass transit planning. Combined with the rise of flexible job schedules, it makes such energy-saving and pollution-cutting efforts as ride-sharing even more difficult to achieve. (*American Demographics*, A) And a larger but more dispersed population still would require more land for food, recreation, waste disposal, etc.

CLAIM H: America has so much unused agricultural capacity, we should not worry about converting farmland to urban use.

PRO-STABILIZATION RESPONSE:

♦ **Most arable land already is in full production either to feed 260 million Americans, or, in effect, to exchange for resources imported from other countries.** (Pimentel, A)

♦ **Water shortages and the prospect of greatly increased energy prices threaten to make it uneconomical to farm a lot of current agricultural land and may reduce the yields even on our best acreage.** (Fox-Mehlman, A, p.48; Pimentel, A)

The food-producing capacity of America's land — combined with Yankee innovation, massive mechanization and (at least for the moment) cheap oil — is phenomenal. This ability is of major international humanitarian importance. Without that incredible agricultural production, malnourishment around the world surely would be much greater than it sadly already is. But the ability to feed more than 100 grain-importing nations declines as U.S. population grows, converts land out of agriculture, and then eats more of what would otherwise be an exportable surplus. The U.S. annual grain surplus surpassed 100 million tons in the early 1980s. By the early 1990s, it was down to 70 million tons a year. (Brown, A, p.189)

The race to increase agricultural production is resulting in loss of topsoil 20 times faster than replacement. "Even now, in what used to be some of our most productive agricultural regions, soil productivity has been reduced 50 percent, and in some areas, it has been so severely degraded that it has been abandoned." (Pimentel, A)

"It takes decades to replace lost topsoil... Fertilizer is no substitute for the humus and living organisms that make topsoil so nutrient-rich." (Population-Environment Balance, A)

"Despite serious soil erosion, U.S. crop yields have been maintained or increased because of the availability of cheap fossil energy for inputs like fertilizers, pesticides and irrigation." American agriculture has become an energy sink — it consumes more fossil energy than it produces in food calories. About 3 kilocalories of fossil energy are spent to produce every kilocalorie of food. "One cannot help but wonder how long such intensive agriculture can be maintained on U.S. croplands while our nonrenewable fossil energy resources are being rapidly depleted." (Pimentel, A)

Moving away from energy-intensive fertilizers to "green or animal manure will mean reducing present crop yields. Yet, the demand for food will continue to grow as long as population increases." (Population-Environment Balance, A)

A significant increase in energy prices could drive large amounts of land out of production because of the effect on irrigation prices. Consider the Ogalalla aquifer that irrigates much of the midwestern grain belt. In order for that dry region to keep up its grain yields, farmers have been pumping water out of this amazing underground sea — left over from glacial times — faster than rainfall and seepage from above-ground streams can replenish it. In short, they exceed the carrying capacity of the aquifer. They cannot do that indefinitely. The Ogalalla holds two distinctions: it is the largest discrete aquifer in the world and the fastest-disappearing one. The rate of withdrawal over natural replenishment is the equivalent to all the water that flows through the Colorado River. (Reisner, A, p.11)

Further threatening the whole agricultural system, it now takes more energy and more money to pump water from a steadily falling water table. "Millions of acres ... might suddenly go fallow were irrigated farmland to go out of production due to aquifer depletion, rising energy pumping costs and a fall in commodity prices." (Fox-Mehlman, A, p.48)

Indeed, much land not now in production is capable of growing food. But it is arid land. You can't grow food without water, and there isn't excess water to divide up. Agriculture already consumes 85% of all the water used in the U.S. That plus increasing urban water use has resulted in a nationwide groundwater overdraft of use that is 25% greater than the replenishment rate. (Pimentel, A)

The undersupply of water is so great that the cost has risen to the point that many farmers — such as those on the Colorado plains — are finding they can make more money by selling their water rights than by growing food. Thus, even more arable land goes out of production. (Carrying Capacity Network, I)

Not only is our farmland in danger of losing productivity per acre, but population growth is pushing us to destroy an average of 1.5 million acres of arable land per year through urban development and erosion from overuse. When agricultural land disappears under a parking lot, it is gone forever.

(Population-Environment Balance, A) "Asphalt is the land's last crop." (Cutler, A)

Agricultural experts are not in agreement about how high a level of production U.S. farmers can sustain indefinitely. But the double squeeze on arable land is obvious: additional residents require more production to feed them, even as they take farmland out of production through conversion to urban uses, and as they shift water away from agriculture. If U.S. population continues to rise by nearly 3 million a year, the food available for other nations may well continue to fall. (Brown, A, p.189)

The need to feed an unprecedented additional billion people over the next decade is unfortunately coincident with the tapering off of the green revolution. World grain production peaked in 1984 and additional applications of fertilizer are reaching diminishing returns." (Brown, A, p.177, p.184)

The world seemed to be on a never-ending cycle of increased crop yields through 1984. But per capita production of grain products has been declining since then as agriculture fails to keep up with population increase. (Ryerson) During the 1980s, 75 countries experienced a decline in food production per capita. In 1993 alone, 10 million children died from nutrition-related diseases. (National Wildlife Federation, A)

"The easiest ways to expand production have been almost fully exploited. Nearly all of the suitable land and the best irrigation sites are in use.... The natural productivity of the land is falling. Since 1945, 11% of the earth's vegetated surface — an area the size of India and China — has been degraded through soil erosion, salinization from poorly managed irrigation, and overgrazing." (Matthews, A)

While death by starvation or bad water is unlikely to plague the U.S., the situation in the rest of the world raises serious questions about plans for doubling the U.S. population, a move that would decrease greatly the ability of American agriculture to provide food to other countries.

CLAIM I: Since not all experts are certain we've exceeded our agricultural or environmental carrying capacity, we shouldn't rashly act as if we don't have room for more growth.

PRO-STABILIZATION RESPONSE:

♦ The consequences of systematically exceeding the carrying capacity are so serious that the prudent approach for our nation is to stop short of full carrying capacity. There really is no risk in that. Besides, we need a safety margin for years of bad weather and poor harvests.

If the nation wants more people later on and discovers it can handle more without harming the environment or diminishing the quality of life, it always can increase the population then. There will be no shortage of people wanting to come. But decreasing population after discovering its long-term carrying capacity has been exceeded is a much tougher and slower task, and one that may not be possible at all.

"There is no hope of ever making carrying capacity figures as precise as, say, the figures for chemical valence or the value of the gravitational constant." But we can come up with fairly decent estimates. The wise approach is to be very conservative about what the capacity is since the consequence of systematically exceeding it is so serious, with even irreversible results. "The Tigris-Euphrates valley, ruined by mismanagement two thousand years ago, is still ruined." (Hardin, B)

With so much at risk, it makes no sense to insist on absolute proof that excess U.S. carrying capacity is exhausted.

Profit-motivated people may view any policy that doesn't squeeze every ounce of capacity out of our land as a waste of resources. But "even if our concern is mere profit, in the long run the greatest economic gain comes from taking safety factors and carrying capacities seriously. (Hardin, B)

CLAIM J: Perhaps we can make up for any eventual farmland shortage by turning to the bounty of the oceans for food.

PRO-STABILIZATION RESPONSE:

♦ **The oceanic fish catch has peaked. About 60 percent of the fish types tracked by the United Nations are categorized as fully exploited, over-exploited or depleted.** (*Washington Post*, R)

"The oceans, long thought to hold unlimited bounty, are emptying. From Iceland to India, from Namibia to Norway, fish catches are decreasing every year. Worldwide, the global marine catch has been declining in fits and starts since 1989." (*Washington Post*, R)

Besides the threat of overfishing, the seas must contend with increasing pollution from the multiplying billions living on their shores. About 60 percent of the world's population lives within 100 kilometers of an ocean shoreline. "Most of the wastes created on land end up in the sea and remain trapped near the shore, poisoning the marine environment. Coastal waters contain many vital ecosystems and provide about 95 percent of the living harvest of the seas." (United Nations Environment Program, A)

The fishing industry is trying to keep up production, but there simply are fewer fish in the sea. On a per capita basis, the global catch of fish from all sources fell from 42.8 pounds in 1988 to 39.7 pounds in 1992. (*Washington Post*, B)

An ever-larger world population in search of food, and fishing fleets armed with advanced industrial hunting technologies, have removed fish from the oceans in quantities that exceed the seas' capacity to replenish themselves. For now, it looks as though farmland is going to have to replace lost seafood production, not the other way around.

CLAIM K: Europe has a very high standard of living with some 100 million more people than the U.S. on similar-size land. Surely the U.S. can handle another hundred million.

PRO-STABILIZATION RESPONSE:

♦ **It probably can, if Americans will consent to live with European-style regimentation and restrictions.**

♦ **If the U.S. decided it wanted to reach and then stop at Europe's almost stabilized population size by 2050, it needs to take rather drastic immigration-reduction steps right now.** (Census Bureau, B)

Each country has a culture that molds its residents' conscious and unconscious expectations about how life should be lived. Deep in the American psyche appears to be the need for open space and a high degree of personal freedom. Europeans have to live much more regulated lives as a result of coping with those additional hundred million people. There is little room in Europe for true wilderness experiences or for solitary hunting, fishing and other typical American outdoors activities. Because of the huge influx of immigrants into the U.S. the last two decades, population momentum may force Americans in the next three to five decades to deal with European-type lifestyle choices.

Even if Congress immediately slashed total immigration by two-thirds, the U.S. still would add about 100 million people to its present 260 million and reach Europe's population size by the middle of the next century. Unlike under our present policy, however, growth then would not continue on toward one billion. Instead, the population would stabilize later next century. (*The Social Contract*, H)

The earlier sections of this chapter provide strong indications that we won't be able to grow to Europe's density and preserve our remaining environmental heritage without a great change in Americans' lifestyle.

Debbie Benores-Egger, an analytical psychologist who comes from Arkansas but now is a Swiss citizen, believes that change could be psychologically difficult for many Americans. "I'm committed to the premise that what we create on the outside in our society has a relationship to the inner psyche of a population. Americans have a total sense of open boundaries. This is in essence the American culture." The Swiss, as other Europeans, have evolved a culture within their greater population density to preserve their privacy and to limit opportunities for personal conflict. So they consent to and encourage their government to force the protection of personal boundaries. Just a sampling of means would include: You don't change residence without registering with the government; stores must close after 6 p.m. and all day on Sunday; no baths are permitted between 10 p.m. and 6 a.m. To preserve the farms and the beauty of the countryside, land use is strictly controlled by the government, forcing the price of housing so high that most Swiss never will own a home or even rent a single-family dwelling. And Europeans have far less living space than Americans. (Binores-Egger, A)

Would movement to those kinds of restrictions exceed the cultural carrying capacity of Americans? That is the kind of question we would hope Congress would consider now, before its policies leave Americans no choice.

"The cultural carrying capacity of a territory will always be less than its (environmental) carrying capacity.... Cultural capacity is inversely related to the [material] quality of life presumed. Arguments about the proper cultural capacity revolve around our expectations for the quality of life." (Hardin, B)

If the U.S. is to avoid matching Europe's population density, Congress will need to eliminate virtually all immigration until the current fertility level drops. (Census Bureau, B)

Argument No.3

America The Wasteful

GENERAL CLAIM: We won't have to stabilize population because we can . . .

CONSUME LESS TO ALLOW FOR MORE PEOPLE

GENERAL PRO-STABILIZATION RESPONSE

♦ **True, we can cut consumption 10% per capita, and population can increase proportionately. Then what do we do for the next 10%, and the next? Eventually, the tradeoff cannot continue.** (Hardin, G)

♦ **"No pollution control, energy efficiency, or land preservation programs can be ultimately successful if population increases without limit."** (Sierra Club, A)

Unquestionably, Americans use resources inefficiently and often for frivolous purposes that can be characterized in no better way than "wasteful." Future population scenarios have to be based on an understanding of how much can be cut, how much should be cut, and how much likely will be cut. But *present* population policy must be based on how much consumption *is* being cut.

In order to stop environmental degradation even without further population growth, we would need to cut quite a lot — some say as much as 25% — of our per capita consumption and waste. Only after that much cutting would further reductions in consumption responsibly make room for any more people. Yet, current immigration and fertility levels will double our population late next century. That would require yet another 50% in reductions just to stay even environmentally.

Are such massive reductions physically possible, let alone politically practical? Just one example regarding energy conservation proves they are not: (Nowak, A)

The 1990 National Energy Strategy in its "very high" energy conservation projection found that "*if* specific technologically based conservation initiatives are successful, and can be placed into service across every sector of the U.S. end-use energy system," per capita energy consumption could be cut only 43% by 2030. (U.S. Department of Energy, A, p.20)

"The word *if* in the above statement should not be overlooked; the application of aggressive conservation measures is easier said than done. In fact, because of the costs associated with applying such aggressive conservation techniques, the National Energy Strategy efficiency study concludes that 'this study was not able to say definitely that these initiatives would necessarily have positive net benefits.'" (Nowak, A)

Talk of 43% — not to mention 25% plus 50% — reductions in environmental impact of any kind seems ludicrous when one considers the U.S. report to a 1994 U.N. sponsored air pollution conference.

In 1993, President Clinton had signed a treaty pledging that by the year 2000 the U.S. would not increase its overall emissions of gases that trap heat in the atmosphere and would even reduce them slightly to 1990 levels. But in 1994, a U.S. delegate to the UN conference said: "We are clearly not going to get to the levels we have set under the existing plan. We are grappling with ways to get further reductions, but frankly it will not be easy." (*The Washington Post*, T)

For the sake of argument, let us assume that the U.S. was able to achieve the very optimistic goal of cutting per capita energy consumption by 43%. "What then? No more gains would be possible. At that point, the U.S. would have to begin to live within its energy budget by either letting people go without, or by stopping population growth. Of course, energy consumption is just one component of U.S. consumption. Waste production, food consumption and water use would all have to be reduced accordingly. This is the inescapable conclusion we have simply decided not to face by holding on to the fantasy of solving our problems through reduced per capita consumption." (Nowak, A)

Clearly, the country eventually would have to put a stop to growth. Why not do so now while people still can enjoy amenities, instead of waiting until it is a matter of staying a step above poverty?

"Economic sustainability and environmental quality require eventual population stabilization in each nation, region, state, and community." (Sierra Club, A)

CLAIM A: If Americans cut their consumption enough, we can continue to add 3 million people a year without harming the environment.

PRO-STABILIZATION RESPONSE:

♦ **We probably could for awhile. But the "if" doesn't exist. To continue to grow as though consumption**

already has been cut enough — or will be — is to act irresponsibly on the basis of a non-existent condition.

A favorite rhetorical sleight of hand by supporters of high immigration and population growth is to premise their support on "some reasonable-sounding condition which, they argue, will avert the harm their critics are concerned about. This condition, however, always turns out to be non-existent; indeed, everyone already knows it to be non-existent.... One is reminded of Orwell's definition of doublethink as 'the power of holding two contradictory beliefs in one's mind simultaneously, and accepting both of them.'" (Auster, B)

The consumption argument is immensely popular among people who actively pursue environmental protection but who want people to feel unrestrained about having large families or who want high-level immigrant admissions. They advocate waste and consumption reduction as a way to pursue their environmental goals and their natalist or immigration goals. Most, however, have not thought through about how much reduction will be necessary to compensate for the projected doubling of population. What are the laws and societal changes that would create the incentives, disincentives and coercive regulations necessary to achieve those levels of deep cuts? Only when such plans are laid out will we have any way to test them politically.

Those who hope to persuade Americans to voluntarily make the unspecified — but surely very deep — cuts have their work cut out for them. While we have cleaned up many aspects of our lifestyles, often out of enlightened self-interest, there are no major examples of self-sacrifice in order to accommodate the excess population of other countries who want to immigrate here. Even though most Americans are wildly rich by third-world standards, they hardly feel overly affluent these days. "Salaries and wages earned by the 80% of economically active Americans who are nonsupervisory employees have been in decline for over two decades, a decline that will accelerate." (Nelson, A)

With four-fifths of Americans seeing middle-class economic comfort slipping from their grasp (perhaps quickened by labor market changes caused by high immigration), what is the likelihood that they will voluntarily, and out of a sense of national responsibility, lower their consumption further to make room for more foreign workers? What ties Americans together more than anything is their shared belief in the equality of opportunity in the pursuit of economic success. With the majority having increasing reasons to doubt their chances for success, nationwide sacrifice for *any* goal will be difficult to inspire. (Luttwak, A)

As has been said about Australia: "It is perfectly true that if Australians could turn into environmental angels, then this continent could probably sustain a very much larger population with no more environmental damage than is being done at present. Yet, apart from extreme optimists... few would anticipate such a scenario.... One also needs to avoid the error of thinking that improved public attitudes mean that the destruction ceases. As in the case of old-growth forests, we may indeed care more and more about the less and less that remains to preserve; yet the destruction continues." (O'Connor, B)

To say that the U.S. is not overpopulated "because, if people changed their ways, overpopulation might be eliminated is simply wrong — overpopulation is defined by the animals that occupy the turf, behaving as they naturally behave, not by a hypothetical group that might be substituted for them." (Ehrlich, A, p.40)

Pro-environment proponents of a tradeoff of lower consumption for higher immigration have an honorable proposition. But the only honest way to pursue that tradeoff is to (1) propose the consumption cuts and goals necessary to allow population growth without environmental loss, (2) create legislation and educational campaigns to achieve the goals, (3) wait for results, (4) determine that consumption-reduction goals have been met, and then — only then — allow federal policies that increase population growth through immigration.

One minimum way to know whether consumption has been reduced enough is when all U.S. cities meet clean air and clean water laws, all landfills and other solid waste disposal sites are in federal compliance, and no aquifers are consistently being pumped out faster than they can be replenished. Until then, there can be no honorable, pro-environment justification for encouraging population growth of three thousand persons a year — let alone three million.

CLAIM B: Population growth primarily is a problem for third-world countries, while the major problem in industrialized nations is consumption.

PRO-STABILIZATION RESPONSE

♦ **Argued extensively at the Earth Summit at Rio in 1992, the debates over whether the problem was with population growth or resource consumption masked the fact that we have both kinds of problems.** (Ryerson, A)

♦ In many aspects of living, Americans *are* reducing consumption, but population growth wipes out the gains.

"We are cutting more wood than ever before.... Can we blame this on increasingly profligate consumption? Not at all. We use only half as much wood and lumber per person as Americans did in 1900.... (But) in a single lifetime we have added 175 million people, tripling the population since 1900..." (Brownridge, A)

Between 1973 and 1990, in response to the oil embargo and out of a growing understanding of the need to conserve energy, Americans reduced their *per capita* energy consumption by about 1% per year, but *total* energy consumption increased. Nearly all of the increase was the result of U.S. population growth. (John Holdren, A)

Fuel efficiency of U.S. vehicles improved 32% between 1970 and 1988. During that time, however, total fuel consumed by automobiles increased 41%, primarily due to increased driving mileage as the result of population growth. (Statistical Abstract, A; Nowak, A)

CLAIM C: If Americans would recycle more, there would be plenty of resources for all.

PRO-STABILIZATION RESPONSE:

♦ "The three benefits of recycling — reduced consumption of virgin materials, a reduced solid waste stream and reduced energy consumption — represent only a small fraction of each individual's 'environmental impact budget.'" (Nowak, A)

The net results of recycling usually are a conservation of energy, but sometimes not by much because most recycling processes unfortunately are very energy-intensive. (Abernethy, A)

CLAIM D: If Americans would fully embrace car-pooling and mass transit and reduce auto use, we could handle three million more people a year without having a negative impact on air pollution and energy use.

PRO-STABILIZATION RESPONSE:

♦ **Another huge "if."**

♦ **Americans are moving in the opposite direction. Mass transit accounts for only 5.4% of all commuters, down 35% since 1970.** (Statistical Abstract, B)

"There's no express ramp out of this nightmare of congested roads and before-sun-up commutes. Blame it on booming population.... Most people insist on driving alone ... with only about 13% carpooling." Alan Pisarski, a national transportation policy consultant and author of *Commuting in America*, says: "All this wishful thinking about convincing American people to change their behavior, I don't see happening." (*USA Today*, B)

There is no question that the country would be in better shape in terms of energy and air pollution if the number of private automobile miles could be reduced. Among urban planners and environmentalists there remain many optimists who believe they can entice a larger portion of the population away from their one-passenger autos by improving the appeal of transportation options that are more energy-efficient. But faster than Americans can be weaned, immigration and native population momentum add additional drivers to the roads. Many trends will make it difficult to achieve significant shifts away from private driving. Those trends are driven or exacerbated by the massive growth in the adult population since 1970. Few local and regional governments have tried to, or were able to, restrict development to within existing urban perimeters. Such restriction could have increased population density enough to make mass transit more economical and more convenient. Instead, most population growth has pushed the boundaries so far out as to make expensive rail systems impractical for much of the metropolitan areas. The rise of multiple office and work centers throughout the areas makes it even more difficult to provide mass transit that can serve such spiderweb commuter needs. And as the metropolitan areas grow wider, commuter distances lengthen.

Population increase almost always drives property prices, and most other local costs, upward. That price escalation has been one of the factors making two incomes seem like a necessity in urban households. To juggle family and other responsibilities, and to meet other lifestyle considerations, more people adopt staggered work hours and flex time, making car pool arrangements even less likely. (*USA Today*, B)

Geographically, we are so much larger than Japan or countries in Europe, it is doubtful whether our per capita energy use in transportation could ever be as low. The costs are enormous for retrofitting our transportation systems to provide for a much higher level of mass transit use. Given recent governmental financial difficulties, that kind of money is not going to be available soon. (Bouvier, C)

As important as it is to try to shift to mass transit to be better positioned as oil supplies dwindle, it only postpones the day when population growth has to be addressed. (Miller, B)

CLAIM E: The U.S. could handle many more millions of residents without threatening farmland and natural habitats if Americans reduced the square-footage they required for living spaces and lived in higher-density urban developments.

PRO-STABILIZATION RESPONSE:

♦ **Regardless of how tightly-packed people choose to live, any city can survive only by the constant importation of resources and exportation of wastes, requiring vast areas outside any given urban boundary.** (Carrying Capacity Network, G)

♦ **Policy framers have been unsuccessful in persuading Americans to give up any part of their sense of having a birthright to a single-family detached house in a low-density setting near the natural environment; Americans clearly indicate by their behavior how cherished this goal is.** (Burke, A)

To protect agricultural and natural habitats from further degradation caused by human habitation due to doubling population over the next century, higher density living likely would require building housing on most undeveloped land inside current city limits. On many lots, two houses would have to stand where one does now. Many houses would need to be subdivided for two or more households. Some housing would have to be razed to build high-rises. With good planning and enough money, increasing the density of a city can bring about an improved urban lifestyle — better mass transit, more convenient pedestrian shopping, a more lively social setting. In other words, increased population density can be positive, but not if it means an increase in total population. Even when handled with optimum skill, increased population still places greater stress on already stressed resources outside the cities. (Population-Environment Balance, B)

"In assessing several of the more important effects of humans on the environment, the relative density of humans is irrelevant. While the major benefit of living densely is that energy costs are reduced because people commute shorter distances and live in fewer square feet (reducing heating and cooling loads), other critical impacts are not mitigated in any way: the inputs required in the form of both energy and acreage to feed and provide water for each person do not change. High-density living also raises a variety of quality of life issues, including the trade-off between the social benefit of reduced energy consumption and the individual loss of both solitude and silence." (Nowak, A)

At the annual meeting of the American Association for the Advancement of Science, Cornell University professor David Pimentel unveiled the results of a study that concluded that for "Americans to continue to enjoy a high standard of living and for society to be self-sustaining in renewable energy and food and forestry products, given U.S. land, water and biological resources, the optimum U.S. population is about 200 million." Since that is 60 million fewer than we have today, increasing the density of city living is futile because there obviously are not the resources beyond the cities to sustain that higher population. (Carrying Capacity Network, B)

Changing a city to high-density living is not as conserving of resources as it might first appear. A well-maintained wooden house can last for centuries. In a city with a stable population, buildings are left to stand longer because there isn't so much pressure to replace them. But in growing cities with escalating property values, "many buildings are razed long before their time to make room for higher-density structures." A stable population requires virtually no timber for housing, except to upgrade substandard housing for the poorest residents. But more timber constantly is required for new housing in a growing population. (Brownridge, A)

In a democracy, there is an essential question that also must be answered: Do Americans want to live in more density? If they don't, managed growth is not likely to occur. The majority of Americans' clear preference for a yard, a family room, and proximity to open spaces may mean they simply are in touch with their most basic biological selves. Dr. Edward O. Wilson, the distinguished evolutionary biologist holds that "eons of evolution, during which humans constantly interacted with nature, imbued Homo Sapiens with a deep, genetically based emotional need to affiliate with the rest of the living world.... Meeting this need, according to what is called the biophilia hypothesis, may be as important to human well-being as forming close personal relationships." (*New York Times*, A)

Large sprawling cities may be harmful to mental health. Schizophrenia, a form of mental illness, afflicts about 1% of the Western populations. Sociologists long have known that a far higher percentage suffers the malady in the city than in other areas. While it had been thought that schizophrenics drifted to cities as a part of their self-imposed isolation, a new study published in the authoritative *Lancet* medical journal found that men raised in cities were more prone to develop the psychosis. Research suggested "there is an environmental cause common to cities that puts people at risk of becoming schizophrenic," the study's lead author said. (*New York Times*, E)

Increased urban tensions, crowding and crime are key factors that are driving thousands of middle-class Americans, especially between the ages of 35 and 49, to move their families to other countries, polling shows. (*Money Magazine*, A)

CLAIM F: The cause of loss in open spaces is not population growth from immigrants but from middle-class white citizens moving to new suburbs.

PRO-STABILIZATION RESPONSE

♦ Regardless of who is buying the land and houses on the outskirts of cities, it is population growth that creates the pressure.

The main ingredient of U.S. population growth is immigrants, who primarily settle in the core urban areas. The additional social disruption helps persuade established residents to move a little farther out, making room for the immigrants. This sets up a chain reaction that eventually results in new suburban housing tracts. If established Americans did not move, the foreign workers and their families would have to settle around the outskirts of the cities, as rural migrants so often do in third-world countries. In addition, many immigrants do settle at the edge of cities in suburbs such as Orange County outside Los Angeles and Fairfax County outside Washington, D.C.

CLAIM G: Protecting the standard of living of the hyper-consuming countries at the expense of the world's desperate poor having a chance to move here is immoral.

PRO-STABILIZATION RESPONSE

♦ **It's bad enough that we are profligate consumers; what is to be gained by bringing in more people who want to be profligate consumers, too?** (Stein, I)

♦ **When our population density has reached that of India or Bangladesh, are we morally relieved of admitting unlimited numbers of others?** (Grant, E)

Some of our high consumption *does* hurt the rest of the world, especially when it results in the emissions of hydrocarbons into the air or drains a resource so badly that the poor of the world never have a chance to use it for themselves. In such cases, the bulk of the world's poor are only hurt more when we increase by three million each year the number of hyper-consuming Americans. (Simcox, D)

To the extent that U.S. high consumption retards development of a healthier, safer, more fulfilling and stable quality of life for people in impoverished countries, Americans have a high ethical obligation to consider ways to change that. But the change should benefit the masses in those countries. Allowing a tiny fraction of a percent of them to immigrate — even though the U.S. is harmed in the process — is a symbolic gesture that looks more like penance than helpfulness.

"Demanding a reduction to a 'morally defensible' level of consumption in the United States is an unattainable goal. Any level of consumption above subsistence can always be deemed as immoral, because the residents of subsistence-level economies can always make moral claims on the resources of slightly richer nations." (Nowak, A)

"The United States, for all its riches, is a country not without its own poor. While in the aggregate we may possess far greater wealth than the majority of countries, for the homeless, poor and unemployed here (more than 40 million people), increased immigration results in increased job competition and scarcity of resources." (Nowak, A)

Argument No. 4

Cornucopianism

GENERAL CLAIM: The U.S. won't need to stabilize population because the free market and . . .

TECHNOLOGY WILL SAVE US

GENERAL PRO-STABILIZATION RESPONSE:

♦ **We simply do not know how technology will develop, and so should plan conservatively.** (O'Connor, B)

♦ **Humankind will not have suffered if population growth is less than the advance of technology makes possible, but it may suffer very seriously if hopes for technology prove too high and if the number of people outruns the ability of science to support them.** (Grant, A, p.145)

The mythical horn of plenty in 20th-century America is technology. The true believers in this "faith" expect that new technologies will always act as a cornucopia, pouring out new resources or ways to stretch old resources, and providing solutions to problems of pollution. A variation of this "faith" sees the free-market economic system as imbued with cornucopian powers. There is a strong thread of reality in the thinking of the cornucopians: both technology and the market indeed have had a powerful effect in increasing the size of the pie for most of us. During the last three centuries, technological advancements have gone beyond nearly everybody's wildest imagination in solving intractable problems. Cornucopians assume that the phenomenal pace of advance will continue indefinitely. Maybe it will. But it is an act of faith, not science, to make that assumption. (Grant, A, p.145) The "theo-technology" belief that scientists and a free market economy will solve every problem posed by a perpetually growing population is a form of religion for many economists. It is a religious faith not shared by most scientists, however. (Hardin, G)

CLAIM A: Technology always has saved us in past crises.

PRO-STABILIZATION RESPONSE:

♦ History is littered with the corpses of civilizations which technological change failed to rescue from their attempts to continuously live beyond the carrying capacity of their environment.

Throughout South, Central and North America are the ruins of civilizations — some very advanced — that built up past the ability of their technology to sustain them during times of drought and other natural changes. And in Ireland, the technological breakthrough of the introduction of the potato created a false promise that it could provide for an ever-growing population; the result was devastating famine. The technological promise of the green revolution in developing countries, coupled with medical advances that reduced infant mortality, led third-world peoples to believe that — unlike during most of their histories — they suddenly were capable of handling a fast-rising population; technology and political systems have not been able to accommodate the numbers explosion, leading to widespread privation. "The track record of civilizations that have relied on the promise of technology to survive has been poor, indeed." (Nowak, A)

The danger of the federal government using its immigration policies to force the U.S. to live so close to its population limit can be understood by looking at the effort to sustain more than 32 million Californians in a mostly semi-arid region. After massive engineering marvels that have diverted water from most California streams (so that few can fully support their ecosystems) and that have emptied large, picturesque lakes, the current sized urban population has barely sufficient supplies of water — and that only in years of decent rainfall. (Reisner, A)

But even "plenty of almost everything most of the time does not sustain a biological system over the long run. Living populations are limited by whatever essential factor is in shortest supply under the least favorable conditions. Having sufficient fresh, clean water in most years is not enough.... A single bad season does not usually break down human societies, however, because man devises backup systems.... Ultimately, though, limits show up in the substitute systems." (Abernethy, A, p.171)

With no technological breakthrough to make the desalinization of sea water affordable for any but the most affluent communities, California has little choice but to abandon more and more of the nation's fresh-produce agriculture to divert the water to the growing cities. Because California's population size is at the edge of water crisis even during good rainfall years, it has little slack for handling bad times, as demonstrated during the recent 6-year drought.

Unfortunately, drought may be a much more common part of the future than the last few decades have suggested. In the 140 years from 1850 to 1990, there were 37 years in which California's rainfall was less than 13.62 inches, qualifying as drought. From studying tree rings, scientists know of a drought lasting more than 50 years from the 1760s to the 1820s, and of a 20-year drought from 1865 to 1885. (Peart, A) Recent studies have concluded that monster droughts from A.D. 892 to 1112, and from 1209 to 1350, probably were responsible for ending several indigenous civilizations in the American Southwest. "What we've done in California is fail to recognize that there are lean times ahead," says paleoclimatologist Dr. Scott Stine. Carrying capacity is determined by the lean years, not by the fat, wet ones. "We don't need 200 years of drought to bring us down. At some point, in the 9th year, or the 15th year or the 19th year, the damage is done, and it doesn't matter anymore." (*New York Times*, G)

Until and unless technology provides some kind of guarantee that sufficient water can be provided to the existing-size population during such extended droughts in the future, prudence would suggest that the federal government cease its role in helping to force California to grow by another 700,000 to 800,000 urban water users a year.

CLAIM B: Slowing population growth will merely postpone technological advance by delaying the pressure on the market to create the solutions.

PRO-STABILIZATION RESPONSE:

♦ Necessity and deprivation have a long record of not being timely mothers of invention. People living in the 14th century, for example, were in desperate

need of the medicines that were not invented until after World War II. (Ryerson, A)

♦ Population growth, in fact, reduces our chances of a successful transition to sustainable technologies. (Werbos, A)

The energy challenge is an excellent example of the weakness of this "mother of invention" claim. The present mix of fuels and energy technologies is not sustainable in the long term, even if population could be dramatically reduced. With fossil fuels running down, the U.S. and the world eventually must move toward economies based on sustainable solar energy technologies. The transition, however, will take a long time and cost billions upon billions of dollars. A growing population will multiply the energy demand the new technologies must meet. It also will hasten the decline of fossil fuel supplies and siphon money from the development of technology for transition to solar systems. In short, it will undermine the effectiveness of any technological change to rescue us. (Werbos, A)

Economists quote Aesop that "necessity is the mother of invention." But in our time, "necessity is greatest in wretchedly poor countries like Bangladesh and Ethiopia; but is inventiveness at its maximum in such poor countries? Certainly not." (Hardin, G)

Perhaps some environmentalists can be classified as hostile to or irrationally fearful of technology, but the conservation movement has a long history of respect and even enthusiasm for technological advance. Leaders, though, have generally advised prudence. George Jenkins Marsh, for example, author of the seminal *Man and Nature* of 1864, "believed in the power of knowledge and science to redress the balance between humans and nature.... But he also insisted, in words that would be appropriate in today's newspaper, that 'the world cannot afford to wait till the slow and sure progress of exact science has taught it a better economy.'" (Shabecoff, A, p.58)

In other words, a civilization's lifestyle should be based on current scientific knowledge, not predicated on the promise of unproven technology.

"Undoubtedly, technology and manufacturing processes will evolve over the next 50 years, in some cases outstripping our imagination. However, in view of the fact that the versatile, but polluting, combustion engine is still with us, despite waves of technological innovation over the past century and our growing knowledge of how to bring alternatives on line, it would be the height of folly for our nation to sit back and simply hope that the future will be 'greened' by an invisible hand. (National Commission on the Environment, A)

"In a sense, population growth in the face of our inadequate current technology to sustain the people is akin to borrowing money with no prospect of being able to pay it back. It is a risky gamble which puts the burden on future generations who will suffer the consequences. (Ryerson, A)

CLAIM C: Pollution problems related to population growth will be solved by technological advances that are economically feasible.

PRO-STABILIZATION RESPONSE:

♦ **Those technological advances didn't materialize between 1970 and 1995 to offset the added pollution generated by some 60 million additional Americans.**

♦ **"If current predictions of population growth prove accurate and patterns of human activity on the planet remain unchanged, science and technology may not be able to prevent irreversible degradation of the environment or continued poverty for much of the world."** (U.S. National Academy of Sciences and the British Royal Society, A)

Faith in politically and economically feasible technology solutions for future population growth should be viewed with great skepticism in light of recent performance. Since the nation committed itself to restoring its environment around 1970, "advances have been made in reducing all six of the pollutants specifically identified for control in the Clean Air Act of 1970.... But except for lead in the air, which has gone down by 94% because its use in gasoline was banned, progress has not been very impressive. Many of our cities are still choked with smog, and visibility even in remote parts of the countryside is often limited by pollution from distant sources.... With a growing population and economy likely to create new sources of pollution, the act's goal of pure and healthy air still seems to lie beyond a distant horizon." (Shabecoff, A, p.268)

"Even though some technological solutions may be arrived at, they may simply be too expensive for any country to really contemplate." (Parikh, A)

A definition for "too expensive" may be a cost that the political system will not force society to pay. One suspects that the technology exists to restore the health of the Chesapeake Bay, the largest estuary in North America. But governmental entities in the vast 4,400-square-mile watershed won't require the necessary actions, especially the strict limitations on personal use of the automobile. Auto exhaust, which is carried by rainfall into the Chesapeake, is one of the bay's top enemies. (D'Elia, A)

The issue of imposing an absolute limit on population in the watershed "has got to be on the table," according to the president of the Chesapeake Bay Foundation. (*Washington Post,* U)

The governments of the six states and the District of Columbia, whose residents live in the bay's watershed, are reluctant to regulate human activity to minimize damage to this masterpiece of biological diversity because they perceive the cost of doing so — monetarily and in the restriction of lifestyle choices — as too costly.

Already, high population growth — particularly in the Washington DC-Baltimore and Norfolk-Virginia Beach metropolitan areas — has negated much of the expenditures and lifestyle changes reluctantly made to clean up the bay. "These high population growth rates have directly and indirectly caused its infirmity, including declining fisheries, receding wetlands, vanishing seagrasses and a devastated oyster industry." (Grant, A)

The technological and regulatory challenges are immense without any additional population growth. Consider the once-rich coastal waters off Florida:

"Due to the rapid population expansion in Florida from more than a decade of high-level immigration to the area, the Western Florida Bay is rapidly becoming an ecological disaster. About 450 square miles of the bay, termed the 'dead zone' by local fishermen, have turned from clear waters with teeming sealife to pea-green gruel. Experts theorize that development has drastically reduced the flow of fresh water across the Everglades' sawgrass prairie, changing water temperatures, increasing salinity levels and killing off sea animals and plants. The change in the Florida Bay also threatens the delicate coral reefs off the Florida Keys which depend on stable and precise water conditions for their survival." (*Miami Herald,* A)

"Some ground water in the United States is so heavily contaminated that even state-of-the-art technologies cannot clean it to the point where it is drinkable, according to a study released ... by the National Research Council.... Of the estimated 300,000 to 400,000 such contaminated sites across the U.S., some can be made potable; but in many others, complete cleanup is technically not feasible." (*Washington Post,* 3B)

"The goals of fishable and swimmable surface waters established in the Clean Water Act of 1972 ... also remain elusive. The nation expended nearly $150 billion on sewage treatment facilities between 1972 and 1990, and some of the grosser water pollution that killed most of the commercial stocks of fish in the Great Lakes and turned rivers and coastal waters into open sewers has been reduced substantially." But with 60 million more Americans adding pollutants, perhaps half of surface waters "remain useless for fishing and dangerous for swimming..." (Shabecoff, A, p.268)

CLAIM D: Whenever a resource has grown scarce in the past, a technological breakthrough always has found a way to produce more or provide a substitute. That surely will be our future as well.

PRO-STABILIZATION RESPONSE:

♦ **The belief in infinite substitutability is common among academic economists but is not based on any systematic rationale or buttressed by any evidence other than the fact that the industrial world has been doing pretty well, so far.** (Grant, A, pp.141-142)

♦ **There simply is no substitute for some beleaguered resources like national parks, clean air, water and, above all, the planet's genetic wealth. "The loss of the Earth's biological diversity is one of the most pressing environmental and developmental issues today."** (United Nations Environment Program, A)

Economists are correct to note that the rising price of many declining resources spurs the discovery or recovery of more of that particular resource, or the creation of substitutes out of other resources. But the assumption that such substitution can occur forever, or at all for some resources, is not a fact, but merely an unproven theory that helps economists run their computer models. "Biologists and ecologists have been trying, without success, to persuade the economists that the assumption is terribly dangerous in a finite world on which human economic activity is pressing ever more heavily." (Grant, A, pp.141-142)

To show the foolishness of absolute faith in substitution, consider our dependence on exhaustable oil supplies. For this example, we will use the pre-1973 rate of growth in population and per capita oil use. At that rate, even if every ounce of every single material that makes up the entire mass of the earth could be converted to petroleum, the world would use it all up in just 342 years! (Grant, A, p.142)

"The price of a resource says nothing about total reserves, only available supply. Clearly there is less oil in the ground today than the day the first well was sunk, but the price of a barrel of oil, adjusted for inflation, is lower now than it was 20 years ago. Price tells us only what someone is willing to pay for a resource. Science tells us how much of the resource remains... The notion of infinite substitution is sheer fantasy. Some commodities, compounds and resources have substitutes, others do not. Scientists, for example, have discovered processes for creating gold from other materials, but the processes are so expensive and energy-intensive they are not likely to become cost-effective. The creation of other, more essential resources, like water, are less practical yet." (Nowak, A)

Here's another mind-twister that shows the impossibility of perpetual growth, regardless of technology: Assume that on the basis of current U.S. population and its current per capita usage, we had a one-million-year supply of a resource. Now suppose that instead of stabilizing, our population grew at 2% a year (roughly the worldwide growth rate). How soon would the supply of that one-million-year resource be exhausted? The answer: a mere 501 years. (Grant, A, p.142)

"Should we keep desperately seeking ways, which may or may not work, to support our increasing population rather than dealing directly with the cause of the problems?" (Population-Environment Balance, A).

People who believe there can be no real limits on resources in the U.S. fail to understand that there are many countries around the world which prove the reality of severe scarcities.

Beyond resources such as food, energy, iron and copper that we consider essential for our standard of living, are aesthetic resources which we cherish as essential to what makes us human. Many of those have no substitute, nor can increases in efficiency be of much help. "For example, there is only so much Pacific Ocean beach in Oregon. No more is being made." (Lutton-Tanton, A, p.89)

Think what doubling the U.S. population will do to Americans' ability to enjoy their national parks, which England's late ambassador John Bryce called this nation's "crown jewels" and the best idea America ever had. Currently, 270 million visitors a year are loving the parks to death. "The hustle and bustle people try to escape from in their daily lives is following them straight to the parks." Their vacation in the wild is marked by crowds, trash, traffic, noise and air pollution. Yosemite in California has become so congested that looking down at Yosemite valley from Glacier Point has been compared to viewing the Los Angeles basin. (ZPG, A)

Technology and severe restrictions on how individuals may use the parks could bring some improvements, but the main problem in the parks is too many people. The federal government's blueprint for doubling through immigration the number of Americans who might want to use the parks a century from now poses congestion problems that appear to defy technological solution.

John Muir, way back in the late 1860s, captured the psychological importance of having natural retreats: "Thousands of tired, nerveshaken, over-civilized people are beginning to find out that going to the mountains is going home; that wilderness is a necessity; and that mountain parks and reservations are useful not only as fountains of timber and irrigating rivers but as fountains of life." (Shabecoff, A, p.71)

Cornucopians are going to have a difficult time replacing the resource of space. The skies around many metropolitan areas already are too congested with air traffic. Will the skies remain friendly and air travel available to all Americans if there are twice as many seeking to fly?

A much more serious resource problem is the loss of bio-diversity under the march of expanding populations. "The past two decades have witnessed tremendous advances in the sciences of ecology, genetics and conservation biology... Now we know how important living diversity is to us. From this knowledge has emerged a powerful and broad consensus among scientists that we must redouble our commitment to saving species." (Conservation Biology, A)

In fact, the very basis for many future technological and medical discoveries may be lost if we squander our bio-diversity now. (United Nations Environment Program, A)

CLAIM E: Environmental problems result from poor regulations and enforcement, not from overpopulation.

PRO-STABILIZATION RESPONSE:

♦ **"We are not arguing that population growth is *the* cause of all our problems. What we are saying is that it is a significant contributor to and multiplier of them."** (Bouvier, C)

A pragmatist must always work with the present situation If better regulations and enforcement could improve environmental quality, they should be pursued. But until those goals are reached, population growth should be restrained. It is clear that population growth acts in concert with consumption levels and technology and all the other factors that influence these three. Regardless of the relative influence of these other factors, however, "the vast majority of experts believe that any prudent strategy for dealing with the future must include measures to slow projected population growth." (Moffett, A)

The technology exists to clean up the Anacostia River, Potomac River and Rock Creek that flow through our nation's Capital, for example. That does not mean the area can handle higher population, however. The metropolitan area simply does not have the money and/or political will to use the technology to properly treat the wastes of the more than 7 million (and rising) people already flushing toilets. Despite millions of dollars of improvement in sewage treatment plants, an estimated one billion gallons of raw sewage still pours into the Capital's waterways each year. The water is perpetually dangerous for swimming, the fish considered unhealthy for eating in all but small quantities, and the riverbank esthetics marred by odor. (*Washington Post*, V)

With fewer residents, the treatment plants would be able to protect the health of the rivers.

CLAIM F: The greatest resource of all is the human brain. The more of those we have in this country, the more likely we are to come up with solutions to the problems that face humanity.

PRO-STABILIZATION RESPONSE:

♦ Increasing the number of brains does not seem to be working all that well for Bangladesh, Haiti and any number of other rapidly-growing populations.

No single country has a monopoly on intellectual capacity — brains. However, to the extent that creative ideas are developed elsewhere, modern communications makes it possible for the U.S. to have the benefit of them very rapidly, and without any need to import millions of immigrants. Far better to spend our limited resources on improved education for our existing people.

It is always possible that another Albert Einstein could immigrate. "But we can't run an immigration program admitting millions of people in the hopes of getting another Einstein. It is just not practical... Einstein's greatness had nothing to do with the fact that he was a refugee. Had he been allowed to work anywhere, he would have made great contributions wherever he was. Remember, many great inventors produced inventions in other nations that led to great commercial advances here. Ideas can be freely exchanged more easily than people." (Stein, J)

CLAIM G: Many of the concerns about limits on agriculture, water and urban development are tied to the availability and expense of energy. If the U.S. fully exploits renewable energy sources — solar, bio-mass and wind — those limits on population growth can be overcome.

PRO-STABILIZATION RESPONSE:

♦ **Even sunlight is a limited resource. Although solar and wind power are constantly renewable each day, there are limits to how much energy they supply.**

If the U.S. had the money to convert its whole economy to the use of solar energy, present technology could not capture and convert enough solar power to replace the current level of fossil fuel use. "With a self-sustaining solar energy system ... the energy availability would be one-fifth to one-half the current level. Even if the U.S. population remained at its present level ... a significant reduction in our current standard of living would follow." (Pimentel, A)

Solar power systems require gargantuan surface areas for collectors. Placed on roofs of buildings, they can provide some space-heating. But then there is the need for electricity to run air conditioning, appliances, factories, and to charge the batteries needed to power electric automobiles and mass transit, etc. Vast expanses of land — that could be used for little else — would have to be sacrificed for farms of solar panels and wind mills. (Brownridge, A)

Unfortunately, almost three-quarters of the U.S. land area already is committed to agriculture and commercial forestry. Solar farms will be possible only at the expense of natural habitats. (Pimentel, A)

A massive solar energy system to support 260 million people at reduced levels would be an aesthetic blight. Witness what the wind farms in California's San Gorgonio Pass have done to San Jacinto Peak, "one of the most dramatic mountainscapes in the nation." (Brownridge, A)

Another possibility of a renewable resource is bio-mass, organic material like wood and cornstalks that can be burned directly or converted to a more convenient fuel that can be used like oil. "Recent efforts at biomass conversion (methanol from corn) used more energy than they generated. That problem could be addressed by improving the technology and relying on other sources ... but the dilemma does not end there. Biomass production from agriculture competes with existing uses of the land, and ... agriculture already needs more cropland than it has, for food and fiber production. (Bouvier-Grant, A, p.27)

The use of bio-mass has major limitations. The total amount of solar energy captured by vegetation each year in the U.S. is about 13 x 10^{15} kcal. But 7 x 10^{15} kcal. of that amount is captured by agricultural and forest products. We cannot convert that source of food, fiber, pulp and lumber into energy. Of the 6 x 10^{15} kcal. left, much of it provides the necessary habitat for the nation's bio-diversity. (Pimentel, A)

Yet, when oil supplies run down and prices rise — probably during the next century — we will need huge replacements of energy just to continue to grow food. It takes around a gallon of oil to produce food for one day for the average American. Adding three million people a year to the U.S. increases petroleum consumption by about 3 million gallons of oil every day (about a billion gallons a year) just to feed the extra people. (Bartlett-Lytwak) We currently import 58% of our petroleum.

It will be very difficult to replace that much oil with solar energy. The availability of land will be the major constraint to the expanded use of solar energy systems. We need some of those technological miracles to be able to support our present population once fossil fuels are gone. Why would Congress want to double our population during the next century and burden scientists with even greater energy needs to meet?

One last humbling statistic: When all forms of energy are figured in uniform measures, we discover that to support 260 million Americans we use 40 percent more fossil fuel energy than all the solar energy captured by every living plant in the country. If we burned all our food and annual growth of forest, grass and scrub, we still would be short more than a third of the energy we need. (Pimentel, A)

"Our natural resources and the demands of our infrastructure will not permit the population to stay at the present level for very long without dramatic deterioration of the quality of life. The country needs not [population] stabilization but a rollback.... The message is clear: a demographic future compatible with the requirements of the energy transition, the preservation of our farms and forests, clean atmosphere and water supplies, the forestalling of adverse climate change, and the restoration of a decent life for all ... will come about only if we act now. Fertility and immigration must be reduced." (Bouvier-Grant, A, p.123)

Argument No. 5

Growthism

GENERAL CLAIM: We don't want to live without population growth because . . .

STABILIZATION EQUALS STAGNATION

GENERAL PRO-STABILIZATION RESPONSE

♦ **Most of the finest places to live and work have virtual population stabilization.**

♦ **Fear of stabilization reflects an ideological addiction to growth that relies on an outdated historical perspective and defies current reality.**
(Commission on Population Growth and the American Future)

Twenty-five years ago (with 60 million fewer Americans), an ambitious two-year study by a joint presidential-congressional commission examined population questions. Major representatives of corporations, unions, government and of women's, environmental, urban and ethnic groups concluded:

"We have looked for, and have not found, any convincing economic argument for continued population growth. The health of our country does not depend on it, nor does the vitality of business nor the welfare of the average person." (Commission on Population Growth and the American Future)

CLAIM A: Throughout human history, growth has been the norm. Stabilization violates the natural order of humanity.

PRO-STABILIZATION RESPONSE:

♦ **Significant growth that is noticeable year to year**

— even decade to decade — is a modern phenomenon of only the past four centuries.

It took all of human existence until 1650 for world population to reach one-half billion in size. Although people until then often could think back over a lifetime and notice the rather steady march of population growth, numerical increase was so small that it simply was not a major factor in the daily culture of the times.

The combination of early public health measures and the material advance fostered by the Industrial Revolution led to reduced mortality and higher fertility rates in response to the perception of economic opportunity. (Abernethy, F) That quickly created rapid growth that we now take for granted. In the first 100 years alone after 1650, population burgeoned by 50%, adding another quarter-billion people.

Yet another quarter-billion were added between 1750 and 1850.

Then the next century (1850-1950) saw 1.4 billion in growth.

Since 1950, the world population has expanded from two and a half billion (five times the 1650 level) to five and a half billion. (World Almanac)

This type of growth has occurred in a period that is a mere blip on the timeline of history. There is nothing normal or usual about it, nor any good reason to blindly continue such growth.

Throughout most of history, few cultures exceeded an average of much more than two children per family who lived to adulthood. The four-survivor-child family was common in the U.S. during the 1950s and today among many immigrant groups in the U.S., and in the world's underdeveloped nations. But it is a recent phenomenon.

British academic Jack Parsons conducted a fascinating exercise to see what would have happened if the four-child family really had been the norm in the past. The results are so shocking that they look like the professor must have made a mistake.

Parsons began in the year 1 A.D. with the assumption that the only humans on earth were two infants, one male and one female. In this exercise, all individuals couple off at the age of 25, procreating four children. Everybody dies at 75.

If the four-child family had been the norm, the two people on Earth in 1 A.D. would be replaced by 30 in 75 A.D. Even by 200 A.D., there would be only 900 people on the entire planet.

But by the year 750, global population would have reached 3.4 BILLION, the actual global size in 1967.

Continuing the four-child norm, population in the year 1150 would have been 245,000 billion, more than one person for each square yard of the Earth's land surface. (Parsons, A, pp.108,109)

Obviously, such growth was never the norm, nor can it continue.

CLAIM B: Population growth is so ingrained in our American culture that Americans would have a huge psychological adjustment to make if it were to stop.

PRO-STABILIZATION RESPONSE:

♦ **If Americans couldn't handle population stabilization, they wouldn't have lowered their fertility to below replacement level.** (George High, B)

♦ **The U.S. historical norm that is even more important to the American psychology is freedom to leave urban constraints and to retreat, at least periodically, to natural and rural areas — an option increasingly foreclosed by growth.** (Foreman, A, p.6; Abernethy, F)

♦ **For 40 years, studies have found people in large cities wishing they could live in smaller cities.** (Speare-White, A)

What would it mean to honor our "growth norm" and add U.S. population during the next 200 years at the same rate as the last 200 years? Well, imagine if everybody on all of Earth today were moved into the United States. Now imagine tripling the number. That would be America in the year 2200. The growth norm of the past clearly is a nightmare for the future. (Lamm-Imhoff, A)

Although the entire existence of the United States as colony and nation is within the "growth" aberration period of world history, a more important definition of the American norm has been the people's proclivity toward what Leo Marx called the "middle landscape," a compromise between the primeval wilderness and the urbanized, crowded, deforested surface of much of the Old World. Despite the rapid pace of U.S. population growth, Americans always (until recently) have been able to enjoy middle landscape living because the vast continent was so sparsely inhabited when the first European settlers and then immigrants arrived. (Shabecoff, A, p.20)

To Thomas Jefferson and many of his contemporary nation builders, the middle landscape of farms and small towns intermixed with natural habitats was the proper condition for the successful application of their revolutionary new democratic form of governance. "Americans today still feel a deep sense of need for that idealized countryside..." (Shabecoff, A, pp.20-21)

Unfortunately, the "norm" of population growth is closing off even minor interactions with the middle landscape for most Americans who are condemned to live in metropolitan areas of more than a million residents, often an hour or more away on congested freeways from any true non-urban settings. Not long ago during a much-heralded meteorite shower, thousands of Washington D.C. residents suffered more than an hour of bumper-to-bumper traffic after rush hour in an attempt to move out beyond the reflection of city lights. Unfortunately, they discovered an hour wasn't long enough to reach clear skies. Until recent decades, even poor inner city dwellers could take trolleys to the edge of town for non-urban retreat. Suburban sprawl now has moved the non-urban perimeter too far away for such common respite. Even 10 years ago, rural access by city folks was much easier. But local vehicle miles in the Washington D.C. area have increased 50% in the last decade. Planners expect that the mostly rural counties surrounding the urban area will experience explosive population growth of 85%, 95%, 138% and 176% over the next 30 years. (Kosh, A)

Many harried bureaucrats in the Capital area, as soon as they can scrape together enough savings, buy or build retreat houses in the farms, woodlots or small towns of Maryland, Virginia, Delaware, West Virginia and even Pennsylvania and North Carolina. But if the federal government for whom these civil servants work persists in its current immigration policy, their middle landscape retreats inevitably will be surrounded and their weekend retreats spoiled by exurban development.

Former *New York Times* environmental editor Philip Shabecoff describes the dilemma well with the saga of his family's purchase in 1968 of barren, scrub land far from the city, five miles from a town and a mile and a half from a paved road. He tells how the escape from concrete, steel, gritty air and congestion to the "fresh, quiet forest was just what we were looking for.... When we are up there, living seems more direct and vital." But through the years more families have moved in, and lately developers are beginning to clear the forest, cut new roads and lay out lots for tract homes for other urban dwellers seeking their piece of the American norm. "The quiet and solitude we cherish will be broken. The middle landscape will turn into suburbia." (Shabecoff, A, pp.149-151)

There already are so many Americans that only a lucky few can experience the middle landscape part of their national heritage, and most of them will have to keep moving to stay ahead of exurbanization.

"Since the Second World War, we have gone from being a nation of small-town outdoorsmen to a nation of suburbanites who talk about the zen of standing in a trout stream (or who) go after the sluggish walleye with enough technology to bring in a whale.... There is hardly any wilderness or loneliness left in America, only marked trails, parking lots, and campgrounds that look like RV parks.... This is not an exclusively aesthetic or even a moral dilemma. Our political system was developed for an independent populace of farmers and small-town shopkeepers who knew how to mind their own business. Increased population means more government, more police, more regulations. But the no-limits-to-growth Pollyannas have no complaints about this development.... They appear not to know what we are talking about. So long as profits continue to rise and the interdependent world economy is prospering, they do not worry about air and water quality, the abuse of precious resources, the loss of wilderness." (Fleming, A)

Americans of every race are more satisfied living in towns, smaller cities and suburbs — where the middle landscape is nearby — than in large cities, according to the 1985 American Housing Survey. (Speare-White, A)

CLAIM C: There appear to be no limits to growth in the U.S., other than a lack of human imagination. If there is some ultimate limit, it is so far in the future that we need not concern ourselves with it in the 1990s.

PRO-STABILIZATION RESPONSE:

♦ **"Continuous growth is impossible. We must understand that (growth) can only be a temporary phenomenon to be followed by stability or decline. It is not easy to recognize this — our whole lives cry out that it can't be true."** (Woodward, A)

"Many people seem to find it hard to grasp — or at least to accept — what compound growth means in the field of human population." (Parsons, A) For example, when consumption of anything grows at 7% a year, consumption in the next ten years will be approximately equal to total consumption in all previous history. (Bartlett, B) That cannot continue on a finite Earth. One would think that economists, of all people, would understand the power of compound growth, but they tend to believe that capitalism will allow it to continue indefinitely. (Woodward, A)

It is not uncommon to hear of some hotshot entrepreneur setting goals such as the doubling of business size every five years (approximately 14% a year growth). It doesn't seem like such a hard goal, and many are able to do that, and better, the first five years. But who can keep up the pace? Sales for such a business would have to be over a thousand times as large in the 50th year and over a million times as large in the 100th year. (Woodward, A)

Warren E. Buffett, one of America's most successful investors, recognizes this truth: "In a finite world, high growth rates must self-destruct. If the base from which growth is taking place is tiny, this law may not operate for a time. But when the base balloons, the party ends: a high growth rate eventually forges its own anchor." (Buffett, A, p.190)

Economists assure us we have plenty of certain materials. But they do so on the basis of current population and levels of consumption. We're told that if we continue to use aluminum at the present rate, we have enough raw materials for 68,000 years. We might as well wait 66,000 years or so to start worrying, right? Wrong, because the population is growing and so is per capita consumption of aluminum. At a recent rate of expansion (6.4% per year), we will exhaust the supply in only 140 years. That is the power of compound growth. (Woodward, A)

Even though population growth will be forced to end because of pollution or resource shortages long before people would run out of land to live on, we actually are on pace to use up all the land.

"At current growth rates, how long would it take for the world's human population to reach the absurdity of one person on each square meter of ice-free land? Answer: about 600 years." (Grant, A, p.143) No real limits to growth? Any scientific analysis would conclude that the limits are real and not far around the corner.

CLAIM D: That which doesn't grow dies.

PRO-STABILIZATION RESPONSE:

♦ The populations of Japan and Germany barely grew during the 1980s, yet they were anything but models of dying economies.

Growth doesn't always equal life. Population growth can do to a city or country what cancer does to the human body. There are striking parallels between a typical urban community and a malignant neoplasm, a cancerous tumor with cells that won't stop multiplying. (Browne, A)

California was the model of perpetual population growth during the 1980s. By the end of the decade, all that growth had won the state this summary lead in a special issue of *Time* magazine:

"California confronts the crumbling of its cities, the clashing of its citizens, the glaring challenge to its assumption of uniqueness and special promise.... The crimes seem more vicious, the smog more choking, the poor more sorrowful in the light of fluorescent disillusionment. The mad, fit joggers must run at night if they hope to breathe freely.... In Northern California's ancient forests, loggers fell trees that sprouted 10 centuries ago, and elsewhere in the state, some rural neighborhoods are raising their taxes to buy the surrounding hills before they too are buried beneath the tract houses of yet another tacky instant city." (*Time*, A)

Scientists, using photos from space over time, have noticed similarities between the changing shape of Los Angeles and "the changes visible in petridish cultures inoculated with E. coli bacteria, organisms that live in animal guts. Both the bacterial and human colonies expand in intricate fractal patterns, gradually filling the spaces surrounding them." Many growing cities resemble "bacterial colonies that are on the verge of depleting their nutrient media [leading] to extinction." (Browne, A)

University of Colorado anthropologist Warren M. Hern looks at the growth of U.S. cities and proclaims: "The human species is a rapacious, predatory, omniecophagic (devouring its entire environment) species engaged in a global pattern of converting plant, animal, organic and inorganic matter into either human biomass or into adaptive adjuncts of human biomass. [This process is] similar in many ways to highly aggressive metastatic cancer." (Hern, A)

CLAIM E: With population stabilization, a smaller segment of residents would be young and Americans would live in a more and more drab "used" physical environment and a culture losing its vibrancy.

PRO-STABILIZATION RESPONSE:

♦ **Sweden with a very old population is not exactly less vibrant than, say, Kenya with a much younger population.** (Bouvier, C)

♦ **Every year when journalists and academics measure the liveability of cities, the high scoring cities tend to be the smaller ones.** (Grant, A, pp.9-10)

♦ **Population growth is making large U.S. cities more chaotic, not more vibrant.**

Societies can stop growing numerically while continuing to grow in per capita quality of life, in the arts, in ethical principles and moral strength. Population growth is not necessary for vitality. (Hardin, G)

Societies with population growth often have too high a percentage of young people, with attendant problems of crime and other social disintegration.

"Rapid population growth ... dilutes the influence of religious institutions that seek to preserve society's moral fiber. It empowers the unprincipled and the rootless to tear down vastly more civilizing traditions and riches of culture than they will ever create." (Ikle, A)

Thus, what may be a record number of middle-class Americans are fleeing the U.S. out of a "pervasive sense of disillusionment and pessimism" as measured in a *Money* magazine poll showing "three out of five Americans say the quality of life in the U.S. is getting worse." (*Money*, A)

California, the king of population growth, still looks good to people who are moving from third-world countries. But problems associated with its growth are driving Americans out of the state. (Oberlink, A)

Once cities grow to a certain size, their vibrancy is counter-balanced by increasing frustrations. The MC Communications Group, for example, announces it is moving 1,500 engineers and other professionals to get them out of the traffic and housing congestion of Washington DC to an improved quality of life in Colorado Springs, Colorado. (*Elyria Chronicle-Telegram*, A)

Many Americans aren't particularly interested in vibrancy unless it is accompanied by civility and tranquility. Those conditions are far more likely to exist in moderate-size, stable communities. There, children learn high standards of behavior because "interactions are expected to persist, possibly over generations. Mutual reciprocity — sometimes seen as altruism — is an evolutionarily successful behavior only when individuals recognize each other, expect repeated encounters and opportunities to exchange favors, and can detect cheating on the implicit deal. These conditions ... are often absent in large, impersonal cities." (Abernethy, A, pp.230-231)

A 1994 study found that children were reared in the most wholesome family-life settings in states of relatively low population. Child Trends Inc., a Washington-based research organization, compared the 50 states on nine measures affecting family life, including childhood poverty, incidence of rudeness to teachers, repeat births to teenagers, proportion of two-parent households and parental employment, education level and involvement in schooling. Top states were Iowa, Minnesota, Nebraska, New Hampshire, Vermont and Utah. (*Washington Post*, W)

In most of those states it also is easier for Americans to have a stake in the community through such opportunities as owning their own home. Home ownership appears to be a far easier goal to reach in areas of lower population growth than in higher. The average family in the "stabilizing" Midwest had 62% more income than was needed to buy a median-priced home, according to the National Association of Realtors. But the average family in the rapidly growing West was 10.9% short of the necessary income. (Elyria *Chronicle-Telegram*, A)

Pittsburgh, which lost nearly half its population since 1950, has become a far better place to live. In a recent liveability index, it was rated the best in the nation. But most cities are moving the other way. The average "man on the street" has a visceral fear that "by the time his kids are his age, Tucson will look like Phoenix, Phoenix like Los Angeles and Los Angeles like Mexico City ... that life isn't getting any easier, cheaper, or more fun." (Harvey, A)

CLAIM F: Without a growing population, the U.S. economy would stagnate.

PRO-STABILIZATION RESPONSE:

♦ **What counts is per capita — not gross — economic activity. You don't need more people to improve productivity and incomes, or to trade vigorously with the rest of the world.** (Nowak, A)

♦ **Without a growing population, huge amounts of public money could be diverted from expanding infrastructure and services to investment in the modernizing of the nation's existing capital resources.** (O'Connor, B)

♦ **A country the size of the U.S. gains no new economies of scale by growing still more.** (Speare-White, A)

"There is a certain seductive quality to growth, whether in individuals, in cities, in states or in nations... Cities proudly proclaim that they have surpassed a neighboring metropolis in population." Few cities ever turn down the chance for more jobs and more residents even though the growth may actually diminish average per capita income. (Bouvier-Grant, A, pp.138-140) But in nation after nation — i.e. Japan, Korea, Taiwan, The Bahamas, Hong Kong — rapid per capita economic development occurred only after major population growth ended and the country moved toward stabilization. (Ryerson, A)

One reason for the belief in the necessity of growth is that larger cities originally were formed so that industries there could gain advantages in production from proximity to other producers of goods and services. (Spear-White, A)

Technological advances, however, have chipped away at that "agglomeration" advantage. Outside of a few exceptional industries, most firms and cities of moderate size are large enough to take advantage of all economies of size. (Parsons, A, pp.108-109)

In addition, building up large concentrations of industry and population in a city creates "diseconomies" of scale — increased costs, traffic congestion, pollution and, ironically, more transportation costs because of the great distances across large metropolitan areas. (Spear-White, A)

"We found that a 10% increase in metropolitan population was associated with a 0.2% increase in income inequality. This is quite a modest relationship, but it does suggest that the distribution of income is more unequal in larger metropolitan areas..." (Spear-White, A)

CLAIM G: The housing market would wither without population growth.

PRO-STABILIZATION RESPONSE:

♦ The housing market certainly would change, but gradually to a different kind of vitality more like the European construction industry.

The U.S. has millions of poorly housed people and the homeless who still need housing. Retrofitting existing housing with energy-efficient and solar devices could be a giant source of income for the industry. And, as any homeowner knows, there is no end to remodeling possibilities.

CLAIM H: America's national security would be vulnerable without a growing pool of potential soldiers.

PRO-STABILIZATION RESPONSE:

♦ **"The current size of the American population is more than adequate to support worst-case military scenarios."** (Binkin, A)

With new technologies and geo-political realities, few envisage "any situation that would require tens of millions of Americans to serve in the armed forces." (Binkin, A) There is no sign today and was none during World War II that brute numbers led to victory. (Ehrlich, B) The Gulf War with Iraq showed that the number of soldiers was relatively meaningless compared to the quality of military technology. (Bouvier, C)

Argument No. 6

Religion

GENERAL CLAIM: Population issues are too sensitive to handle because . . .

FAITH GROUPS ARE OFFENDED

GENERAL PRO-STABILIZATION RESPONSE:

♦ **Christian denominations (representing the majority of Americans) and other religious groups, overwhelmingly proclaim the moral obligation to take care of God's natural creation; most of them recognize that the task is undermined by population growth.** (*The Social Contract*, F)

♦ **"We declare here and now that steps must be taken toward ... measures to protect continued biological diversity, and (toward) concerted efforts to slow the dramatic and dangerous growth in world population..."** (Joint Appeal by Religion and Science, A)

Let there be no doubt about it: population issues are sensitive in the world of religion, because questions about the value of human life are taken so seriously. But that has not stopped major religious leaders from addressing them. Signatories of the above-quoted statement of the 1991 Summit on Environment included leaders of:

- the U.S. Catholic Conference (the national social issues organization totally controlled by the U.S. Catholic bishops)
- World Vision USA (the giant evangelical, non-denominational global relief organization)
- the Rabbinical Council of America (a major voice of Judaism)
- and of Mainline Protestant, African-American, and Christian Orthodox denominations.

Because of highly public comments by a few religious leaders, many Americans mistakenly have gotten the notion that religion is hostile to environmentalism and to population stabilization. Such a view is a distortion caused mainly by abortion politics. A 1992 consensus document demonstrated that disagreement about abortion does not have to bar agreement on the environment and population. Fifty religious leaders — some part of the "right-to-life" movement, some part of the "pro-choice" movement and others officially neutral — joined hands in making a statement about the need for population stabilization. The Catholic, evangelical, liberal Protestant, Orthodox Christian and Jewish leaders called upon the U.S. government to adopt policies that would ease American burdens on the biosphere and urged global efforts to stabilize population "by humane, responsible and voluntary means consistent with our differing values." (Joint Appeal by Religion and Science, B)

CLAIM A: The Catholic Church opposes family planning and population stabilization.

PRO-STABILIZATION RESPONSE:

♦ **In 1991, U.S. Catholic bishops spoke glowingly of education, good nutrition and health care for women and children that "promise to improve family welfare and contribute to stabilizing population."** (*The Social Contract*, F)

The Catholic Church in reality does not resemble the caricature often painted of it as encouraging the most rapid population growth possible.

"Even though it is possible to feed a growing population, the ecological costs of doing so ought to be taken into account," the U.S. bishops said in their 1991 paper that promulgated a theology of environmental stewardship. "Our mistreatment of the natural world diminishes our own dignity and sacredness, not only because we are destroying resources that future generations of humans need, but because we are engaging in actions that contradict what it means to be human." (*The Social Contract*, F)

Quoting Pope Paul VI, the bishops wrote: "It is true that too frequently an accelerated demographic increase adds its own difficulties to the problems of development: the size of population increases more rapidly than the available resources." The bishops said that environmental responsibility extends to more aesthetic measures such as preserving remaining wilderness and maintaining "landscapes in integrity."

The clarity of such teaching has been clouded, however, by Pope John Paul II's aggressive political maneuvering against certain population initiatives, such as the UN International Conference on Population and Development in 1994. Yet, the Pope showed sympathy for stabilization when he said: "One cannot deny the existence, especially in the Southern Hemisphere, of a demographic problem which creates difficulties for development." (*The Social Contract*, F)

That there is great dynamism on this issue among Catholic leaders was displayed in 1994 in a study by the Papal Academy of Science. It argued that birth control is necessary "to prevent the emergence of insoluble problems.... To deny responsibility towards future generations" would have devastating consequences, especially in the Third World. It suggested that the birth rate must not "notably exceed the level of two children per couple." (Grant, F)

"I constantly encounter people who believe that it is impossible to reduce fertility rates in many countries of Latin America and the Middle East because of religious opposition to family planning. What is not understood is that the Catholic Church and Islam do not oppose family planning in their teachings.... However, the Church opposes the use of certain means — which it considers artificial — to achieve those ends.... The Catholic Church supports and provides broad-based sexuality education and encourages couples to limit the number of their offspring to those they can afford and nurture." (Ryerson, A)

CLAIM B: The underlying theology of Judaism and Christianity is essentially pro-population growth, as stated in the "be fruitful and multiply" command in Genesis.

PRO-STABILIZATION RESPONSE:

♦ **Judaism for thousands of years has been concerned about protecting God's creation, and for three decades has given leadership to promoting the goodness and importance of birth control and family planning to stop the population explosion.** (Religious Action Center, A)

♦ **God's command to multiply and fill the Earth — given when the very survival of the human race depended upon rapid procreation — appears to have**

been fulfilled. The opposite tendency to overpopulate now is the great problem. (Erickson, A)

The account of creation in the book of Genesis is interpreted by only a small portion of U.S. religious leaders as calling for continued population growth in these modern times. Human procreation, like all other human activities, should respect, and be in harmony with, the natural order that God created, according to a common religious view that has been endorsed by conservative and liberal denominations.

The account of creation in the book of Genesis has long been blamed for creating and encouraging a "growth-at-any-cost" ethic. Few biblical scholars, however, see it that way. After describing the creation of all other elements of the Earth, Genesis states that God created humankind, male and female, and blessed them saying, "Be fruitful and increase, fill the Earth and subdue it, rule over the fish in the sea, the birds of heaven, and every living thing that moves upon the Earth." The account clearly offers the view that the Earth was made to assist humanity: "I give you all plants that bear seed everywhere on Earth, and every tree bearing fruit which yields seed: they shall be yours for food." But just as clearly, the account establishes that the non-human world has intrinsic value apart from humans: "All green plants I (God) give for food to the wild animals, to all the birds of heaven, and to all reptiles on Earth, every living creature." And it goes on to say, "So it was; and God saw all that he had made, and it was very good." (Genesis 1: 28-31, NEB)

The Hebrew understanding of humanity's being given dominion over all of nature is soon placed in the context of stewardship. Throughout the Pentateuch (the first five books of the Bible) are limitations on the use of nature: fields are not to be reaped to the border (Lev. 19:9); the grower may only harvest from trees five years old (Lev. 19:25); the land is to lie idle regularly (Lev. 25:1-12); fruit trees may not be used for siege works (Deut. 22:6). "It is evident that the Bible does not teach that God wills for humans to exploit nature for their own ends." (Dockery, A)

That stewardship context is shared by the largest of all U.S. Protestant denominations, the Southern Baptist Convention. It numerically dominates the conservative Protestant population which includes approximately one of every four Americans. Its annual national conventions have endorsed population/environmental concepts such as these:

"[Human population has] de-forested vast stretches of land and soon thereafter experienced droughts, floods and loss of human life. Human beings have wiped out some species and driven others to the point of extinction without ever knowing their full value as sources of food and medicine. God's Earth is in trouble, real trouble for those who will inherit the Earth from this generation." (Southern Baptist Convention, A)

"The Earth is the Lord's.... Human beings are simply sojourners on God's land. We never own the land. We are simply trustees of it.... Genesis 1:28 tells us that we are to have dominion or rule over creation. That does not mean we are to conquer creation, forcing it to meet our greedy appetites. Proper rule seeks justice and well-being for all in the created order.... Genesis 2:15 tells us to serve and to guard the Earth's resources.... Deuteronomy 22:6-7 calls us to preserve species.... The failure to take care of the Earth is tied to human sinfulness and issues forth in catastrophe. Moral corruption results in ecological crises." (Southern Baptist Convention, A)

"Divine ownership of the Earth requires that we recognize who holds the property rights, acknowledge that our mission is Earth-keeping and get busy tending to our habitat." (Christian Life Commission, A)

"It is for the Christian an act of faith and an act of stewardship, as well as an act of enlightened self-interest, to seek the perpetuation and viability of all the created order until we can discern and discover what purpose God has for every living creature and plant." (Land, A)

Mainline (or theologically liberal) Protestant denominations have been even more direct about the importance of not letting population pressures destroy humankind's natural heritage.

The United Methodist Church, the largest of the mainline denominations, began pressing for population stabilization in the 1960s. Its nationally-approved social platform urges the U.S. government to "develop a national population policy that would include the goal of stabilizing the U.S. population..." Its Washington advocacy office continues to distribute booklets that quote church policies calling on churches to "keep before people the moral reasons why we need to be concerned with the population problem" and advocating the need for each nation to be free to develop policies in keeping with their own needs and cultures to deal with population size. (*The Social Contract*, F)

No denomination has been more forthright than the Presbyterians: "The assumption that couples have the freedom to have as many children as they can support should be challenged. We can no longer justify bringing into existence as many children as we desire." The denomination also calls on the U.S. government to "take such actions as will stabilize population size.... We who are motivated by the urgency of over-population rather than the prospect of decimation would preserve the species by responding in faith: Do not multiply — the Earth is filled." (*The Social Contract*, F)

Readers of *The United Methodist Reporter* were given the opportunity to choose which "good option" had priority over the other. Only 18% of the Methodists said "generous immigration" should have priority over "strict limits on immigration in order to stabilize U.S. population growth," which was considered the priority by 78%. (*The Social Contract*, F)

That survey was in line with a 1992 Gallup poll that discovered that more than two-thirds of Christians were opposed to the chief cause of U. S. population growth — high immigration. In fact, Christians were far more likely to want immigration reduced than were those who identified themselves as "non-religious." The attitudes among Catholics and Protestants differed little. (*The Social Contract*, F)

Argument No. 7

Globalism

GENERAL CLAIM: The focus on U.S. stabilization is misplaced because . . .

WHAT MATTERS IS WORLD POPULATION

GENERAL PRO-STABILIZATION RESPONSE:

♦ **"We are not faced with a single global population problem but, rather, with about 180 separate national population problems. All population controls must be applied locally."** (Hardin, F)

The United States has a duty to itself and the rest of the world to quickly stabilize its own population so as to stop adding burdens on those environmental resources that truly are global and so as to serve as a model for other nations.

CLAIM A: The U.S. population problem is insignificant in comparison to that of third-world nations.

PRO-STABILIZATION RESPONSE:

♦ **Of some 180 countries in the world, only seven have been adding population in greater numbers than the U.S.**

The majority of the population growth hurtling the world toward a disastrous environmental future occurs in The Big Eight — seven third world nations and the U.S.! During the 1985-90 period, United Nations estimates show that China (83 million) and India (80 million) continued to be the growth heavyweights. But the U.S. (12 million) was firmly in the second-tier of mega-growth countries, alongside Pakistan (17 million), Indonesia (17 million), Nigeria (17 million), Brazil (13 million) and Bangladesh (13 million). Iran was next with 9 million. (Bouvier, C)

CLAIM B: The growth in the U.S. is not a critical problem for the world because Americans' affluence can handle growth better.

PRO-STABILIZATION RESPONSE:

♦ **"The U.S., because of its size and consumption habits, is the most destabilizing entity within Earth's fragile ecosystem. Population growth here has a far more profound impact on that ecosystem than growth elsewhere."** (Bouvior Grant, B)

In terms of global atmospheric problems, for example, the rest of the world suffers based on the total emissions from the U.S. In this regard, it doesn't matter whether we have a tiny population with astronomical per capita emissions or if we have a huge population with tiny per capita emissions. What matters is total emissions. No matter what level of conservation and technology we achieve, adding to U.S. population growth increases the total emissions. Where is the population problem worst? If the problem is defined as one of "harm to the environment and depletion of natural resources, the worst problems are posed by the richest countries, those with the most industry and the biggest-spending consumers. By that standard, the United States is way out in front. (*Washington Post*, X)

According to the Washington-based World Resources Institute, U.S. citizens consume 43 times as much petroleum per person as do citizens of India. Americans also consume 386 times as much pulpwood per capita ... and release 19 times as much carbon dioxide to the atmosphere. In the aggregate, according to one estimate, the average American creates 30 times the environmental impact of an average person in a developing country." (*Washington Post*, X)

With about 5% of the world's population, the U.S. produces more than 25% of the world's carbon dioxide emissions which contribute toward the greenhouse effect. "Thus, stopping population growth in the U.S. is essential if we are to protect both the U.S. and the world environment." (Population-Environment Balance, B)

CLAIM C: But the only way to halt U.S. growth is to limit immigration. What good does that do from the world's point of view? Either a person moves to the U.S. or stays home. The world would have the same number of people either way.

PRO-STABILIZATION RESPONSE:

♦ Adding one immigrant to the U.S. is the global environmental equivalent of adding two or three dozen people to poor countries.

"It must be kept in mind that from a global environmental perspective, immigration into the U.S. is not neutral. Immigrants from poor nations ... are frequently very successful financially, and even the less well-off quickly acquire American superconsuming habits." Thus immigration does produce a net increment in total environmental impact. (Ehrlich, B)

Some immigration advocates argue that because most immigrants are poor and take low-paying jobs they don't affect the world environment like the average Americans. But "unless one seriously proposes keeping immigrants and their descendants at a permanent level of low consumption and pollution, one cannot make the case that immigration-related growth hurts the environment any less than native fertility-related growth." (Kunofsky, A)

"Arriving here from less developed countries, grain and legume eaters become meat eaters; walkers and bus riders become car drivers; and users of one gallon of water daily consume 50 here." (Simcox, E)

And even while they remain poor, immigrants may contribute substantial pollution. According to UCLA urban planner Leo Estrada, for example, Latinos in California — who are disproportionately foreign-born — own cars that on average are four years older than those of the general population. Half of all car-generated smog is due to the dirtiest 7% of vehicles — usually the oldest. An additional 5% of cars is responsible for another 25%. (McConnell, B)

CLAIM D: Environmental and population problems are global, requiring global solutions. Stabilizing U.S. population is a piecemeal approach.

PRO-STABILIZATION RESPONSE:

♦ **"Population and related environmental problems can usually be solved only by action at the national, regional and local levels; no global institution that can both develop and enforce effective solutions worldwide exists."** (Population-Environment Balance, B)

Very few environmental problems actually are global. The release of chlorofluorocarbons and hydrocarbons into the atmosphere, and the destruction of ocean estuaries, are two exceptions. But most environmental problems are quite local, with local actions causing the problem for a watershed or a natural habitat. The number of people living in that local area is of critical importance in creating such environmental dangers. (Population-Environment Balance, B)

The environmental problems of a city such as Denver, for example, are not primarily global. The city's problems are smoggy air, water scarcity, threats to the aesthetics and eco-systems of the beautiful adjacent mountains, the congestion of traffic and parks, and the handling of solid and toxic wastes. All of those are affected primarily by local population. It makes a lot of environmental difference to Colorado if ten thousand people immigrate to Denver instead of staying home in the Philippines or Philadelphia, India or Indianapolis. It is entirely possible for Denver to stabilize its population and solve nearly all its environmental problems without Ireland or any other nation doing anything.

The only environmental resources the U.S. has total control over are the ones entrusted to it within its own borders. "We must act now to stabilize our own population size, and perhaps even reduce it, if we are to have any hope of saving our environment and diversity of species and maintaining our quality of life in the long term.... By doing so, we can serve as an example for other countries to follow." (Population-Environment Balance, B)

"Never try to deal with an environmental problem as a global problem if it can possibly be dealt with as a local problem.... If all potholes were to be filled by a Global Pothole Authority, what do you think our streets would look like?" (Hardin, F)

CLAIM E: More and more we are becoming one world and realizing that in this increasingly global economy, individual nation-states are inadequate to major modern tasks.

PRO-STABILIZATION RESPONSE:

♦ **The discrediting of the concept of national sovereignty often comes from international financial and corporate entities who see nation-states as one of the final barriers to their ability to pursue profits without restriction.** (Smith, A)

Repeatedly big business has proven ineffectual in protecting biodiversity. Even nation-states may be too large to do the job, although they have the power to require responsible behavior from business. "It is the local people whose livelihoods depend upon protecting their local environment that have the most concern about conservation of their locality. What is the world but a system of localities?" (Smith, A)

The constant appeal to treat problems as "one-world" is an ideological ploy that obscures important differences between truly global problems and the preponderance of difficulties that are best handled nationally or locally. (Abernethy, A, pp.113-116)

"We are not smart enough or conscious enough or alert enough to work responsibly on a gigantic scale.... In making things always bigger and more centralized, we make them both more vulnerable in themselves and more dangerous to everything else." (W. Berry, B)

"The old dogma was that national boundaries are arbitrary and illegitimate, that we should transfer our allegiance upward to world government, that Robert Frost was right: 'Something there is that doesn't love a wall.' But the new understanding is that the nation-state is one of the essential levels of human government. Modern life is impossible without it; most people will transfer their loyalties down to the clan or tribe, not upward to world government. Robert Frost's neighbor had it right: 'Good fences make good neighbors.'" (Tanton, B)

People and organizations who insist on dealing with environmental and population problems only on a global level miss an essential truism about conservation. It only works if you get the incentives right. Operating as if borders don't matter violates that idea. "Why save, why postpone consumption, why conserve, if the benefit goes to strangers?" (Abernethy, A, p.116)

The idea that self-interest motivates people to conserve is as old as Plato. And the concept that operating without strong boundaries discourages conservation is as modern as the tragic story unfolding on Palawan Island. It contains the Philippines' largest remaining expanse of unbroken forest. "Anthropologist James Eder concludes that population growth is the underlying cause of the disaster. The indigenous tribal community is both growing from within and lacking in political power to resist migrants from other overpopulated areas of the Philippines.... Immigration into Palawan Island is pushing tribal Filipinos out of more and more of their land. With a smaller area to use, they are forced to shorten the fallow part of the agricultural cycle, that is, the years in which forest plots are left to regenerate.... Moreover, tribal Filipinos see the forest disappear to commercial logging and know that their use-rights in trees are no more secure than their forest plots. The best remaining strategy is to join in the plunder." (Abernethy, A, pp.156-157)

CLAIM F: It is improper, impractical and immoral for developed countries to try to have population stability within their own countries without working to improve conditions for other nations.

PRO-STABILIZATION RESPONSE:

♦ A commitment to our own U.S. future does not mean ignoring the problems of the rest of the world. Many developing countries are caught in a population explosion, and the U.S. should make family-planning assistance the first priority in foreign aid. (Bouvier-Grant, B)

The U.S. cannot force population stabilization or environmental protection on other sovereign nations. There is no reason to delay taking care of the U.S. environment as soon as possible, not waiting on any other nation. That means immediately cutting immigration back to a level that serves American environmental needs.

Some nations insist that they have the sovereign right to resist the developed nations' suggestions that they stabilize their populations quickly. With rights always come responsibilities. "A state's right to increase its population must be wedded to the responsibility of taking care of its own people. No exporting of surplus people to other nations. The UN asserts a right of emigration (out of a country) but no right of immigration (into a country), for the right of immigration would amount to a right to invasion, which is intolerable in a world seeking peace." (Hardin, G)

"While the problems of Haitian boat people and other would-be immigrants are heart-rending and real, they cannot be solved by sacrificing our own future. The U.S. has an obligation to its own people and descendants, one that cannot be served by allowing the population to swell to half a billion." (Bouvier-Grant, B)

Argument No. 8

Irredentism

GENERAL CLAIM: We have no right to stabilize U.S. population by limiting immigration because . . .

U.S. BORDERS ARE ILLEGITIMATE

GENERAL PRO-STABILIZATION RESPONSE:

♦ **Nearly all borders are arbitrary, and most land around the world was taken by occupation or conquest from some other people at some time in the past. The whole human social structure would collapse if everybody asserted a right to reclaim ancestral lands either by changing the borders or by open immigration.**

♦ **"Control over entry by non-citizens is generally considered one of the two or three universal attributes of national sovereignty; no government has ever explicitly abrogated this sovereign right..."** (Teitelbaum, A)

Without maintaining sovereignty and strictly enforcing movement across their borders, nations have little way to protect their natural resources. Most moral philosophers "have defended forms of private ownership within nations, and national sovereignty on the international level, as a way of checking abuse" of scarce resources. "That understanding can be found in the Stoic philosophers of Greece and Rome; it can be found in the Church fathers and among the great Scholastic theologians.... The common possession of scarce resources invites abuse." (Green, A)

The natural world provides good lessons about the importance of territories and respect for boundaries. "Animals that are territorial in their behavior live more peaceful lives. The boundaries of any territory are artificial, the result of the accidents of community development. But the genetic predisposition of a species to respect artificial boundaries makes for peace." (Hardin, G)

"The classic irredentist situation involves an area of one nation-state, adjacent or in proximity to another nation-state, which was formerly owned by the latter and has a majority of its inhabitants sharing the same ethnic identity as the latter." Parts of the American Southwest come close to fitting the classic situation. Since the Chicano National Liberation Youth Conference in Denver in 1969, there has been a small but vocal movement to increase the Mexican population of California, Arizona, New Mexico and Texas in order to achieve majority status and further their irredentist aims. The former Mexican territory of the Southwest is referred to as "Aztlan." Chicano nationalists are not united about whether they favor independence for Aztlan itself or seek its annexation by Mexico. (Nelson, B)

Mario Barrera, in his *Beyond Atzlan: Ethnic Autonomy in Comparative Perspective*, indicates that the idea of pulling southern California, northern New Mexico and southern Texas out of federal U.S. control has gained renewed strength in the 1990s, what with the rise of multi-culturalism as a mainstream philosophy and as Latin Americans approach majority status in those areas. Barrera advocates a regional autonomy for the Spanish-culture Southwest that would relate to the rest of the U.S. in ways similar to French-speaking Quebec to the rest of Canada. (Barrera, A, p. 15)

Although outright irredentism is heard publicly in California from time to time, it is more common to hear a modified irredentism that holds that Mexicans should have freedom to come and go as they please in the American Southwest since they once "owned the area." This argument occasionally is mentioned by pro-immigration advocates in more mainstream religious and rights organizations. Another variation of this ideology regards all national borders as illegitimate man-made barriers to human potential and rights. This globalist argument is superficially appealing to many persons who want to stress the universal connections of humankind or the religious brotherhood and sisterhood of all people that transcends any borders. But when actually examining such a concept, virtually no person or group concludes that world anarchy could be prevented without national borders. Even the big umbrella organization of U.S. groups promoting high immigration and population growth acknowledges that "the U.S. has a right and duty to regulate who enters our country." (National Immigration, Refugee and Citizenship Forum, A)

The United Nations affirms that the nation-state — which requires strict borders for its existence — remains an essential unit of human governance. Its Universal Declaration of Human Rights recognizes that sovereignty is the guarantee of a nation's and its citizens' right to regulate entry into one's territory. (Tanton, D)

In the animal kingdom, refusal to honor boundaries greatly weakens the entire species through endless conflicts, "resulting in the disrespectful species being replaced by others. Private property or national property is the human equivalent of animal territory. Without it there is no peace. We must grant the sanctity of national boundaries and the universal right to defend them." (Hardin, G)

CLAIM A: The U.S. stole most of its territory from the Indians, bought much land from other nations under questionable terms and unfairly took the Southwest from Mexico. Our borders are illegitimate and we have no right to be all that picky about who else crosses them.

PRO-STABILIZATION RESPONSE:

♦ **At some point it becomes too late to challenge settled matters — at least some kinds of matters. Borders are probably one of these. It's getting very late in the history of the world to be redrawing national borders, at least without the consent of the inhabitants.** (Tanton, D)

"We have invented the rhetorical gimmick [and legal practice] of the 'statute of limitations.' Without it, the present inhabitants of every country in the world — except possibly the Indians of the Americas, and some unknown tribe in central Africa — would have to pull up stakes and try to set up home elsewhere, only to discover that the present inhabitants of 'elsewhere' are disinclined to slit their own throats in order that 'justice' may be done." (Hardin, G)

Without question, immigration virtually annihilated the cultures and political control of the indigenous peoples of North America — as mass migration has all through human history, with one group conquering the territory of another. By the 1880s only about 200,000 North American "Indians" were left in the United States, the vast majority confined to desolate reservations in the West. (Briggs, A, pp.32-35)

Did the Indians have a moral right to resist the immigration invasion of their lands? Yes. Was the colonization of North America by the European immigrants an unjust act? Perhaps so. Does that mean present non-Indian inhabitants have a moral obligation to get out and move back to the European, Asian, African and Latin American homes of their ancestors? Of course not.

Since all non-Indian residents of the U.S. benefit from an invasion long ago, does that mean they have no right to have borders and enforce the movement across them? Again, of course not. Most people around the world live where they do because their ancestors invaded in some form. And more immigration in the future can only further any injustice to America's indigenous peoples.

Perhaps no group fights harder for immigrants, legal and illegal, than the American Friends Service Committee. When it formed a special committee to study questions about borders, it acknowledged that many Friends consider borders to be so inimical to Quaker values that they should be abolished. But after considerable study and discussion, the committee issued a report stating that "within borders people are better able to establish their own forms of social organization, maintain their unique identities and culture, and pursue their own path to development." It also noted the importance of borders to protect from harmful forces and to provide for "rational and ecologically sound administration.... Administration requires manageable units. It is impossible to manage the whole world." (American Friends Service Committee, A)

CLAIM B: The citizens of Mexico have a right to enter the U.S. Southwest freely, since it was once their land.

PRO-STABILIZATION RESPONSE:

♦ **At the time that Mexico ceded the Southwest to the U.S., there were only around 75,000 Spanish-descent inhabitants in the entire Southwest region. The treaty provided that those who wanted to stay could do so. Most did. Their descendants are not in Mexico, primarily. Most have been here all along, deeply rooted Americans.** (Briggs, A, pp.35-36)

Current citizens of Mexico — few of whom can claim ancestors who lived in what is now the *Southwestern* U.S. in 1848 — have no more claim on free migration to the U.S. than do citizens of Great Britain who can point out that their country once owned what is now the *Eastern* U.S. but lost it in a violent takeover by the Americans.

Few of the people living in the Southwest and California when those areas were incorporated into the U.S. in 1848 had any deep ties to Mexico, which had experienced a very shaky sovereignty for a very short time. Many, of course, were indigenous tribes who had been forcefully incorporated into Mexico. Of the estimated 75,000 Spanish-descent residents, nearly all were products of procreation between conquistadors from Spain and the women of the four branches of the sedentary Pueblo Indian tribes. About two-thirds of them were concentrated in the Taos-Sante Fe area. (Briggs, A, pp.35-36)

The irredentist claims of some Mexicans that the Southwest belongs to them comes down to the argument that "we stole it first from the Indians, fair and square." (Tanton, G)

One of the most vocal leaders of Mexican-Americans, U.S. Rep. Xavier Becerra of Los Angeles, acknowledges that "as a sovereign nation, the U.S. has a right and duty to effectively regulate its borders." (Becerra, 9B)

Jorge A. Bustamante, a Mexican sociologist and noted defender of Mexicans in the U.S., also has stated: "Nobody should deny the sovereign right of a country to determine who will enter and who should be excluded." (Bustamante, A)

Argument No. 9

Fertility Tradeoff

GENERAL CLAIM: We can stabilize population without limiting immigration if we . . .

HAVE FEWER BABIES TO MAKE ROOM

GENERAL PRO-STABILIZATION RESPONSE:

♦ **Another "if" proposition based on a non-existent condition. When fertility drops low enough — if it ever does — then we can consider having high immigration. Lately, U.S. fertility has been *rising*.**

♦ **To make room for the present level of immigration — without raising the population in 2050 above today's size — Americans would essentially need to adopt a one-child-per-family average.** (Bouvier, C)

Many environmentalists are uneasy about taking on the immigration issue. But they must face up to the reality that "for every immigrant admitted, one birth must be foregone. How the mix of births and immigrants is achieved is not a scientific issue, but one to be decided by democratic choice..." (Ehrlich, C)

Let's put in context what a regimen would look like that produced a U.S. population in 2050 the same size as in 1994, while continuing the present level of immigration.

To eventually stabilize a population size and maintain it, women must average 2.1 children each — if in-migration equals out-migration. Americans went below that level in 1972 and hit an all-time national low level in 1976 at 1.7. The rate has climbed recently almost to the magic 2.1 mark. In the meantime, women in densely populated and congested Europe have had the disincentives of cramped housing and high costs of living to help drive their fertility down to a phenomenal 1.6 average. (Bouvier-Grant, A, p.102)

Now for the bottom line. To make room for the present level of immigration and still be able to stabilize the population, American women would have to lower their family size not to their historic low of 1.7, or Europe's basement-level 1.6, but to below 1.2! (Bouvier, C)

That means the average American family would have to be limited to just slightly above one child. Today's young adult and teen women and little girls would have to decide to have only half as many children as their older sisters and mothers. That slash in the U.S. fertility rate by nearly 50% would need to happen by the year 2000, and then be maintained to 2050.

China, with one of the world's most authoritarian governments and regimented societies, can't come close to forcing its citizens to adopt a 1.2-child average, even with the threat of massive food shortages around the corner. It would be interesting to see the literature and educational programs needed to persuade American women to adopt this norm.

To turn Paul Ehrlich's formula around, for every birth American women have above the 1.2-child average, an immigrant admission must be foregone.

Let's assume that Congress passed the most restrictive bill now before it and cut annual legal immigration from 1 million a year to 200,000, and that illegal immigration was cut to as low as annual out-migration. How large could the average family be without generating a larger population in 2050 than now?

The answer is stunning: only 1.5 children! (Bouvier, C)

There are reasons to question whether such a drastic reduction in pregnancies could happen without a massive and coercive campaign to encourage it. And is the country prepared to put pressure on the people with the highest fertility rates — immigrants and poor Americans of all ethnicities — to lower their fertility? What would be the ethical basis for asking American women to have fewer babies when the average native-born fertility already is well below replacement level at around 1.8 — especially when the lowering is to make room for immigrants who tend to have nearly double the 1.5 target fertility rate?

Such a plan certainly would face strong opposition.

"If fertility dropped low enough to accommodate immigration and still let the population stabilize, the U.S. would be embarked on a policy to replace its present population and character with newcomers. Such a policy has never in history been voluntarily adopted by any nation." (Abernethy, F)

"Those communities that are so foolish as to substitute natural children with immigrants will soon disappear from the face of the Earth. The problem of this stupidity solves itself. But is that an argument for being stupid?" (Hardin, G)

All of that will make for interesting debate. For the time being, though, environmental responsiveness would require dealing with the actual fertility of about 2.05. Immigration could and should be tied to the latest official fertility rate and a population-size goal deemed proper to handle U.S. environmental problems. Then when the fertility rate goes down, immigration could rise; when fertility goes up, immigration would have to be cut. Such a system does not place a value on whether it is better to cut fertility or immigration, but it does recognize that while Congress can cut immigration almost immediately with the passage of a single piece of legislation, it cannot — and would not — cut fertility to meet a goal. Thus, population policy always would have to start with the fertility rate Americans choose, followed by immigration levels based on that fertility rate.

Argument No. 10

Economics

GENERAL CLAIM: We can't limit immigration because . . .

WE DEPEND ON FOREIGN WORKERS

GENERAL PRO-STABILIZATION RESPONSE:

♦ **Is immigration necessary for the operation of the U.S. economy? "I've never said it's necessary," said economist Julian Simon, the nation's foremost advocate of high immigration for economic reasons.** (Brimelow, A)

"You don't need more workers to increase productivity anymore, because of technology. You need skills and capital." (Grant, E) The flood of foreign workers in the last two decades has helped transform the American workplace into one with fewer benefits and less job security, and one with a growing income disparity between the skilled and less-skilled. (*Washington Post*, Y,Z)

The examples of countries like Japan should put to rest any notion that advanced economies depend on a constant supply of low-wage immigrants to survive or thrive. Japan's essentially zero-net immigration policy clearly has not prevented "the most remarkable economic performance of the post-WWII era." Even with a relatively stable population size, Japan's gross national product since 1955 increased three times as fast as that of the U.S. (Brimelow, A)

Far from depending on foreign workers, the U.S. economy appears to be polarizing because of them. A 1993 report to President Clinton concluded: "Immigration has increased the relative supply of less educated labor and appears to have contributed to the increasing inequality of income...." (Council of Economic Advisors, A)

U.S. Labor Department statistics reveal the widening gap between the "have" and "have not" workers. For example, the difference in income between a white male college graduate and a white man with only a high school diploma 15 years ago was 49%. The gap has grown to 82% and is widening, "forcing many at the bottom out of the middle class." (*Washington Post*, Y)

Labor Secretary Robert B. Reich explains how immigration makes the society less egalitarian: An employer has two choices. The first option is to invest in workers by upgrading their skills, which enables them to become more productive, which improves their wages so they no longer are low-wage workers. The second option — when immigration policies provide largescale availability of low-skill foreign workers — is to simply hire more low-wage workers. Reich worries that government efforts to encourage workplace training to improve the status of the low-wage work force may be thwarted by the steady supply of foreign workers. (*Washington Post*, Y)

Low-wage workers saw their plight steadily get worse during the massive immigration of the 1980s. The Commission on the Skills of the American Labor Force — co-chaired by former Labor secretaries under Presidents Carter and Reagan — concluded that the heralded U.S. economic expansion during the 1980s was due largely to growing numbers of workers and consumers. But per capita expansion did not look as good. Real wages for 70% of the U.S. workforce had actually declined considerably. (Briggs, A, pp.217-218)

Advocates of high immigration are fond of pointing out that foreign workers raise the *total* output and wealth of the country. But the cost is too high if it comes at the expense of the standard of living for middle-class Americans, says Labor Secretary Reich: "If we have economic growth and most Americans don't enjoy it, we're not succeeding as an economy." (*Washington Post*, Z)

"One of the most important changes in the quality of jobs stems from the private sector's increased reliance on temporary or part-time employees, day laborers and employment services — trends that are encouraged by the ready supply of immigrant workers." More and more jobs are being stripped of their benefits and security under this labor market transformation. (*Washington Post*, Y)

CLAIM A: We need immigrants to pay the Social Security of the Baby Boomers when they begin to retire.

PRO-STABILIZATION RESPONSE:

♦ **If the Baby Boomers really need foreign workers to take care of them in their old age, the time to import immigrants is after the year 2010.**

♦ **Unless all of today's immigrants are Peter Pan, they too will grow old and further add to the**

number of people who must be supported by Social Security. (Mehlman, B)

The idea that immigration will help resolve Social Security fund problems is especially ludicrous in light of a study that reveals foreign-born Americans are taking more out of Social Security than they are paying into it. The study divided Americans into the native-born and the foreign-born. It examined 1992 tax payments and Social Security pay-outs of old age, survivor and disability benefits. In 1992, the native-born paid $19 billion more into the Social Security fund than they took out. But the foreign-born ran a deficit, taking out $2.7 million more than they paid in. "The addition of large numbers of foreign workers to the workforce now ... in the hope of insuring the solvency of the Social Security system would in fact have the opposite effect." Many immigrants simply make too low an income to pay much into the Social Security fund. (Huddle-Simcox, A)

Concerns about Social Security are too narrow. What matters to a country is the ratio of all dependents to the number of people working. Children are dependents, too. There are about twice as many of them as of old people. The retired are dependents who, in effect, rely on current workers to pay their Social Security benefits but also live off their own savings. Children are much more dependent, and costly. Not only do today's working immigrants add to the number of retirement-age dependents in the future, but their high fertility rates add disproportionately to today's number of young dependents. (Grant, A, pp.147-154)

If immigrants are supposed to be helping take care of older Americans, it is odd that they are not doing a very good job of caring for their own parents in many cases. Under current law, immigrants can bring their parents into the country; they promise to care for their parents who are too old to be in the workforce the day they arrive. Large numbers of immigrants, however, soon turn their parents over to the state for support. The 1990 welfare rate among senior Mexican immigrants in California was 21% (compared to 9% for native-born seniors). That's nothing compared to older immigrants from China with a welfare rate of 55%. (Matloff, A)

Many are concerned about something called the "dependency ratio." Demographers use it to measure the proportion of total population consisting of the old (above 64) and the young (below 15), who presumably are outside the labor market and dependent on those who are in it. Concerned observers should be reassured that not much has changed the last several decades in terms of the overall dependency ratio: (Grant, A, pp.147-154)

- The old and the young constituted 39% of U.S. population in 1960.
- Those total dependents dropped slightly to 38% in 1970.
- Total dependency has been around the 35% level since 1980.
- It is true that the proportion of older people will grow. But if the government slows down its importation of high-fertility foreign workers, the proportion of children could go down. Under such circumstances, the young-old proportion of population still would inch upward, but only a few percentile, before leveling off by the mid-21st century.
- Once a nation's population has totally stabilized, the dependency ratio will stay at 39%, where it was when John Kennedy was elected president.

To the extent that the rising number of retirees creates a financial problem, most experts today believe it can be solved largely through policies that slightly advance the age of retirement and delay the age at which Social Security payments begin. (Kirschten, A)

But that may not be necessary. Thus far, we've talked only about dependency in terms of the retired and children. In fact, lots of people between 15 and 64 also are dependents. Although about 66% of the population are age 15-64, only 45% of the population actually works. Thus each worker effectively supports 1.2 non-workers. "If indeed we need more workers, there are ways of improving the ratio. Bring unemployment down.... Find ways of enlisting discouraged workers.... Employ the elderly through programs such as shared jobs." (Grant, A, pp.147-154)

"At some point every society is going to have to go through a period during which its population stabilizes. Eventually, we are going to have to devise a way of dealing with an aging cohort. It cannot be avoided. The longer we postpone, the more difficult it will be." (Mehlman, B)

"To propose more children or more immigration... is — on a gigantic scale — akin to proposing a little drink to cure a hangover. We are presently working off the Baby Boom.... Do we want to 'solve' an anticipated problem that may not materialize when the Baby Boomers grow old by generating more rapid population growth, and, eventually, more old people later on?" (Grant, A, pp.147-154)

"The age structure of a population is unlikely to be decisive in the forms of social organization which emerge. And as we have seen, there are many advantages of population stabilization which seem clearly to outweigh any fears of an older population." (Simcox, A)

Since crime is disproportionately a young male problem, a stable population with a lower percentage in the lower ages tends to be a safer society. (Tanton, G)

CLAIM B: Immigrants start their own businesses and create new jobs; they were the salvation of many urban cores during the 1980s.

PRO-STABILIZATION RESPONSE:

♦ **Immigrant businesses are notorious for hiring other immigrants of their nationality group. American workers seldom benefit.** (Martin, A)

Because so many core cities have been filled with new immigrant businesses as the native population was emptying out, many people have assumed those cities would have collapsed without the foreign influx. In reality, however, the influx may be a major reason why the natives fled. (Tyson, A)

Frank Morris, former executive director of the Congressional Black Caucus Foundation, complains that unemployed, lower-skilled blacks are especially hurt when the businesses in their neighborhood become owned by immigrants. Studies show the predominance of "ethnic networking" in which owners reserve jobs primarily for people of their ethnic, and often language, group. Jobs aren't advertised but offered by word-of-mouth through the immigrant communities, sometimes enticing people in their home countries to come illegally to fill the positions. Immigrant networking has "locked many blacks out of occupations where they once predominated." (Morris, A)

Today's immigrant business owners simply are continuing a form of discrimination against American workers that past waves of immigrants practiced. But the Civil Rights Act of 1964 was intended to make it illegal to hire job applicants on the basis of their national origin. Immigrant businesses, nonetheless, practice such discrimination on a massive scale. "The casualties often are the native-born citizens who also reside in these cities (a disproportionate number of whom are minorities, youth, and women) who are denied the opportunity to compete for such jobs on an equal access basis." (Briggs, A, p.241; Foreman-Peck, A)

Elizabeth Bogan writes in her book, *Immigration In New York*, that thanks to "ethnic hiring networks and the proliferation of immigrant-owned small businesses in the city [that] have cut off open market competition for jobs ... there are tens of thousands of jobs in New York City for which the native-born are not candidates." (Bogan, A, p.91)

It is no wonder that the 25

metropolitan areas with the highest immigration also ranked the highest on the Misery Index created by Rice University economist Donald Huddle. The index measures negative changes in the wage rate, the ratio of labor force participation to population and the fraction of the past year worked. "Declines in these measures mean less work and lower earnings and hence more misery for the unskilled native work force." (Lutton-Tanton, A, pp.38-39)

Various population researchers have discovered that these negative economic forces set in motion by immigrants have pushed large numbers of native-born Americans out of the geographic areas of highest immigration. (Tyson, A)

Even with so many natives moving out of New York City, for example, congestion problems have increased with immigration. A look at Public School 5 in Washington Heights finds twice as many children under 12 as 20 years ago. "There are schools so crowded that teaching is done in shifts.... There are only two school playgrounds for 25,000 children because all the rest have been swallowed up by portable classrooms and makeshift additions. There are thousands of children trapped inside crowded apartments with nowhere to play because of the drug trade and the violence on the streets outside.... High school dropout rates exceed 50% and the homicide rate is among the city's highest.... Many criminologists predict another crime wave in the early part of next century" as this bulge of immigrant children reaches the prime crime age. (*Washington Post*, A)

CLAIM C: There have been reports since the late 1980s that we are facing a labor shortage.

PRO-STABILIZATION RESPONSE:

♦ **"No technologically advanced industrial nation that has 27 million illiterate adults and another 20-40 million adults who are marginally literate need have any fear about a shortage of unskilled workers..."** (Briggs, D)

♦ **Of black teenagers who have graduated from high school or dropped out, only 33% have full or part-time jobs.** (*Washington Post*, B)

With those kinds of statistics readily available, one wonders what people mean when they say the U.S. lacks workers and must import massive numbers of low-skilled laborers from abroad. Sadly, what they often mean is that they don't want to fill their labor needs with African-Americans. (Ray, A)

While the U.S. intentionally imports more than a million permanent and temporary foreign workers a year, the official national unemployment rate in early 1994 was just under 7%. When counting workers who want to work but have stopped looking, the overall rate of unemployment probably exceeds 15%. (Lutton-Tanton, A, p.33)

In 1990 when Congress abruptly increased immigration by another 35% to 40%, a chief justification was a privately prepared report called "Workforce 2000." Former Labor Department official Demetrios G. Papademetriou says the report may have been badly done in part and was "horribly misunderstood." The principal finding was not that the country faced a labor shortage but that it was in danger of not having enough workers trained with skills to meet the challenges of a fast-changing global economy. (Kirschten, A)

Although a cause for concern, such an impending skills shortage should have been a great opportunity for Americans currently shut out of the mainstream economy. In fact, virtually any kind of labor shortage is good news for workers. Without immigration, the nation's governments, schools and businesses would be forced to improve the education, motivation and training of its large underclass. Every potential worker in America would be valued and nurtured, with nobody allowed to languish forgotten in the surplus labor pool of today. But the federal government dashed another dream through its perpetuation of high immigration. (Briggs, B)

The cruelty of Congress' immigration policy may best be seen in the jobless figures for Americans aged 16-24 who are not either in school, the military or in prisons. "People who cannot find a job by the time they are 24 are probably going to wind up defeated, resentful, alienated, and perhaps violent." Many young Americans simply can't grab hold of the first rung of the mainstream job ladder. Joblessness in the 16-24 group is around 35% for white and Hispanic males. It is even worse for others of that age. The unemployment rate is about 50% for white females, nearly 60% for black males and more than 65% for black and Hispanic females. "Granted, some small proportion, particularly of the women, may be home makers or voluntarily living with their parents and not working, but by and large, these people have been excluded by the system... They are getting by on crime and whatever scraps they can earn in the 'informal economy'... The problem is not just bad; it is rapidly getting worse. Don't just think of the social costs. Think of the wrecked lives." (Grant, B)

The Labor Department indirectly acknowledges that the federal immigration program is pouring foreign workers into cities that have too many workers, not too few. Thirty-four of those metropolitan areas where immigrants settle in large numbers are designated by the Labor Department as "labor surplus" areas, meaning they have had two or more years of unemployment at 20% above the national average. That qualifies them for federal procurement preferences. (Center for Immigration Studies, B)

"Our immigration flows now make us poorer ... in that they prevent the labor shortages needed to drive the industrial structure in progressive directions... In a major comparative study covering ten countries, Harvard's Michael Porter has found that such shortages are a beneficial deficit forcing management toward innovation... Employers do not like labor shortages, and workers do not like declining industries. But adjustment is the systems' goal, with rising productivity and national strength the result." (Graham, A)

CLAIM D: Without the immigrants, who would pick our produce? Would we be willing to pay the higher prices for the food?

PRO-STABILIZATION RESPONSE:

♦ **We have a surplus of agricultural workers. We don't need to import additional ones.** (Associated Press, A)

"In a society with an elaborate social safety net, there really is no such thing as cheap labor. It's really subsidized labor, with the costs transferred from the employer to the taxpayers." (Mehlman, B)

Even if the halting of immigration forced a doubling of the price of farm labor — moving workers out of their present poverty — a $1 head of lettuce would go up only to about $1.11. That's hardly a price increase that would send large numbers of Americans to charity soup kitchens. Typically, for every dollar paid for a head of lettuce, the farmer gets about 33 cents. From that, the farmer pays farmworkers 11 cents. Thus, raising the labor cost 100 percent would raise the retail cost only 11 percent. (Martin, B)

The image of immigrants as agricultural workers is a terribly outdated one. More than 80% of immigrant workers compete with Americans in non-agricultural jobs, primarily in major cities. (Population-Environment Balance, B)

Nonetheless, the small portion who do seek farm work are enough to overwhelm the agricultural labor market. The federal Commission on Agricultural Workers found that our fruit and vegetables probably would get picked without bringing anybody else into the country. Thanks to heavy lobbying by some agricultural businesses, Congress has flooded the country with so many foreign farm workers the people who still are able to get work are experiencing a "decline in real wages, a decrease in annual earnings, a decrease in non-mandated benefits and a deterioration in working conditions." (*Fresno Bee*, A)

Such low labor costs may benefit consumers through slightly cheaper produce, but that is more than made up by extra government costs. Poorly paid foreign workers and their families place great new demands on all services. Their children add to the pressure to have to build new schools, for example. The California state government discovered that it needs to build an entire new school every day, seven days a week, for years into the future, just to keep up with the additional student enrollments swelled in large part by immigrants. (California Department of Education, A)

Each new school costs an average of $15,000 per pupil. These are not costs that can be recovered from the foreign farm worker. Looked at this way, that head of lettuce can be mighty expensive. (Bartlett, A)

What would really happen if Congress stopped flooding the labor market with foreign farmworkers? Economist Phil Martin says one cannot be certain but that the best test of what the free-market system will do when forced to rely on native labor may have been when a massive temporary guest farm-worker program was stopped in 1964. Without the availability of cheap foreign labor, tomato harvesting was mechanized. The price of tomatoes became so cheap that it opened the way for the proliferation of chains of tomato-based fastfood pizza restaurants. Currently, there are so many surplus farmworkers, it might be some time after the ending of immigration before labor became short enough to force significant increases in wages to spur technological innovations. (Martin, C)

CLAIM E: Immigrants do jobs Americans won't do. Who would make the beds and wash the dishes?

PRO-STABILIZATION RESPONSE:

♦ **Americans will do any job, if the pay and working conditions are right. The majority of workers in every industry in the country are American citizens. None depends on immigrants for the majority of workers.** (Lamm-Imhoff, A, p.147)

♦ **If you go to Iowa, Wyoming, Kentucky or any number of other places in hinterland America, you**

will find the hotels and restaurants operating just fine on American labor. It is on the coasts that many industries have become addicted to cheap foreign labor.

The mistake commonly made is to look at foreign workers doing a job and assuming that Americans could not be found for it. In many cases there are plenty of unemployed Americans who would take the job if offered. That is demonstrated when federal officials raid worksites and take away illegal aliens. Programs designed to match Americans to those vacated jobs seldom have trouble doing so. In other cases, there may not be a sufficient number of Americans who would take certain jobs being done by foreign workers because the pay and working conditions are so deplorable. The presence of immigrants keeps those wages and conditions from improving to the point that Americans would take the jobs. (Immigration 2000, A) Former Labor Secretary Ray Marshall observes: "Elementary economics suggests that at a time of high unemployment, increased labor supplies depress wages and reduce employment opportunities for legal residents unless you completely segregate labor markets." (Briggs, A, pp.229-230)

The author pulled off the highway amidst a dazzling summer rain and lightning storm, seeking shelter at an all-night gas station in Lexington, Kentucky. The other customers looked as seedy at 3 a.m. as my son and I. After paying the middle-aged woman at the cashier island in the middle of the store, we went to a concession booth at the back and had a young man make subs for us, spreading the mustard freely over freshly baked bread. "Well, Dad," my teenaged son said as we sat down at a little table, "I guess there are two Americans who will get up at 4 in the morning to butter the bagels."

I was puzzled for a second. Then I realized he was referring to an exchange I had a few months earlier on a network TV program. A New York City advocate of high immigration had insisted that without foreign workers the residents of that city would not have anybody to get up at 4 a.m. and butter the bagels. My immediate retort was that Americans are perfectly capable and willing to get up at 4 a.m. But many businesses on the coasts have become so addicted to cheap, compliant foreign labor, they may be convinced American workers aren't available.

Living on the East Coast, both of my sons have become accustomed to certain types of jobs being filled only by immigrants. Every time we venture inland — a hundred miles from the coast is far enough — they always marvel that every one of those types of jobs is filled by English-speaking Americans. (Beck)

Well-to-do professionals often argue that only immigrants can provide their childcare, gardening and housecleaning needs. In fact, many Americans do those jobs now. And there is an ample supply of unemployed, lower-skilled Americans who could be trained to take the rest of those jobs under decent conditions. But one wonders if the affluent Americans seeking such workers aren't really looking for a compliant servant class. (Bouvier, C)

In some cities like Los Angeles, racial attitudes seem to be involved. The city's native-born black population suffers a high unemployment rate, and many more are so discouraged and unskilled they aren't even in the labor force. Yet, lower-skilled jobs are given primarily to Latin Americans. "If the Latinos were not around to do that work, nonblack employers would be forced to hire blacks — but they'd rather not. They trust Latinos. They fear or disdain blacks." (Miles, A)

Think what it means for the well-to-do to insist on foreign workers so they can pay less to care for their children, clean their houses and maintain their yards. It allows them to keep more of their wealth, while Americans who are unemployed and poor remain that way. But if the well-to-do were hiring currently unemployed Americans and paying more because of it, the rich would be a bit less rich and the poor might be significantly less poor. In other words, there would be less glaring disparity in the economic lot of our citizens.

And we should never forget that middle-class taxpayers subsidize the more affluent private employers when they fail to provide sufficient pay and benefits and their employees make up the difference with governmental social services.

Throughout American history, mass immigration has been the great *unequalizer*. Economic studies long have found that economic inequality has increased during periods of high immigration, while the citizenry became more middle-class during low immigration flows. (Williamson, A)

CLAIM F: It is racist and demeaning to suggest that blacks should have those lower jobs that immigrants take.

PRO-STABILIZATION RESPONSE:

♦ Lower-skilled unemployed Americans of any race should have a chance at those jobs; blacks happen to be disproportionately represented in that number.

♦ Many of the immigrants' jobs — in custodial work, construction and nursing, for example — are far above minimum wage and even require high skills.

An impressively large segment of African-Americans has moved solidly into the middle class. (Harrison, A, p.201) But others appear hopelessly trapped in a cycle of jobless poverty along with proportionately smaller segments of other racial groups.

Some low-level jobs of immigrants were much more attractive when Americans were filling them. For example, blacks had most of the good-paying, unionized custodial jobs in downtown Los Angeles office buildings. But nearly all of them have been replaced by non-unionized, lower paid immigrants. (General Accounting Office, A, p.39)

Apparently, some Yuppies sneer at certain kinds of jobs as being beneath the dignity of any American and prefer to see a sub-class of foreigners doing them. But for Americans with few skills and who are unemployed, bottom-rung-of-the-ladder jobs are not demeaning but a wonderful chance for improvement, especially for the under-24 population. (see CLAIM 10-C)

CLAIM G: Many of our industries might be forced to move to other countries if they had to pay the minimum wages and offer the minimum conditions necessary to attract American workers.

PRO-STABILIZATION RESPONSE:

♦ If the only way a company will stay in the U.S. is to employ low-paid foreign workers, it isn't doing anything for American workers anyway.

Arguments that some industries can't survive without immigrant labor are very similar to those 150 years ago and 100 years ago that other industries could not survive without slavery or child labor. (Koed, A)

Why should the most advanced economy in the world try to hold onto industries whose method of operation is to compete with low-wage, underdeveloped countries? (Glazer, A)

Conditions in some countries are so deplorable that it's impossible for the U.S. to compete. "And we shouldn't." When companies threaten to leave to take advantage of those deplorable conditions, let them go. "If a company cannot afford to run a healthful and safe plant, we shouldn't allow them to run an unsafe one. We should let them close. We'll be better off without them. Letting go of dying companies and industries may cause some economic dislocations in the short term. But in the long run it will contribute to the health of our economy. (Lamm-Imhoff, A, p.147)

"I recall an Australian economist confidently pronouncing the end of the Japanese miracle in a talk in Tokyo in 1962. Why? Because Japan could not or would not, for reasons of culture or xenophobia, import labor, as Europe was then doing, and labor shortages would call a halt to Japanese economic growth. Clearly, he had it wrong. The Japanese did not import labor, but did manage to maintain phenomenal economic growth." (Glazer, A)

Nearly all the leaders of the pro-slavery crusade justified the shameful institution on the basis that southern agriculture could not survive without cheap foreign workers — slaves from Africa. Historic economic analysis, however, shows that the South's long reliance on slave labor "slowed the progress of technology and the development of skills that would be needed to compete" in the ensuing industrial revolution. (Koed, A)

Similarly, the textile industry fought vigorously against labor laws. The industry claimed it simply could not survive without youngsters working for minuscule wages. After laws forced an end to the practice, however, the voice of the industry, "The Textile World Journal", expressed gratitude for the laws: "It can be stated without fear of effective contradiction that ... the labor of children under 14 years of age is not only inefficient in itself, but tends to lower the efficiency of all departments in which they are employed..." Perhaps today's businesses that are dependent on foreign workers would make a similar conclusion as the textile owners when they discovered that "economic survival, and indeed prosperity, did not depend upon the exploitation of children." (Koed, A)

CLAIM H: We may have plenty of unskilled workers, but our economy desperately needs to import skilled workers and professionals.

PRO-STABILIZATION RESPONSE:

♦ Immigration can be useful in supplementing the domestic labor market with well-targeted, short-term infusions of specialized labor, but it must not undermine the workings of the domestic labor

market to eventually train Americans for those jobs. (Graham, A, p.27)

The number of immigrants annually admitted "should be far fewer than the number actually needed. Immigration should never be allowed to dampen two types of market pressures: those needed to encourage citizen workers to invest in preparing for vocations that are expanding; and those needed to ensure that government bodies provide the requisite human resource development to prepare citizens for the new types of jobs that are emerging." (Briggs, A, p.246)

A study by immigration experts David Simcox and Leon Bouvier for the Center for Immigration Studies found patterns suggesting that foreign-born professionals are being imported to the detriment of American minorities. There are, for example, 30% more foreign-born Indians who are doctors than African-Americans. Furthermore, foreign-born physicians are paid significantly more than native-born black doctors. People from India and China, not Americans, are getting the best U.S. jobs in physics and computer science. "We have benefitted as a nation from the contributions of foreign-born professionals.... But there is another side to this issue. Why is it that we, the most powerful nation in the world and the one possessing the greatest system of higher education, use a continuous stream of highly educated foreign-born professionals to fill our needs? Could we not instead train our own people, particularly minorities, to meet these needs?... Many graduate programs in the sciences, engineering and social sciences search out foreign students to the disadvantage of the native-born. Our graduate and professional schools must become more aware of their social responsibilities toward our own people.... The admission of so many highly educated migrants discourages our own minorities, distorts the labor market and hurts developing countries through the brain drain that it brings about. It is time to begin producing a new generation of native-born professionals." (Bouvier, D)

Numerous legislative acts and court interpretations of them, including the Supreme Court in 1991, long have held that the primary purpose of immigration laws is to protect American workers, not to help businesses. (Immigration 2000, A)

Manuel P. Berriozabal of the University of Texas sees industry's importation of high-tech workers from foreign countries as a decision to deny the opportunity especially to minority Americans, many of whom have been turned away from science and engineering programs because of lack of funds. (Berriozabal, A)

"Because it takes time for would-be workers to acquire skills and education, immigration policy can be used on a short-run basis to target experienced immigrant workers for temporary settlement who already possess these abilities." But such high-skill labor shortages should not be viewed as a problem to be solved by immigration. Rather, such shortages should "be viewed as an opportunity to educate youth; to retrain adults; to eliminate discriminatory barriers; and to introduce voluntary relocation programs to assist would-be workers to move from labor surplus to labor shortage areas." (Briggs, A, pp.246, 251)

CLAIM I: **A global economy requires free trade, free movement of capital and information, and free movement of people.**

PRO-STABILIZATION RESPONSE:

♦ Immigration counteracts the benefits of free trade.

According to Henry Simons, a pioneer advocate of free-market economics at the University of Chicago: "Free trade may and should raise living standards everywhere.... Free immigration would level standards, perhaps without raising them anywhere." (Reder, B)

The European Union — forming so its member nations can be on the cutting age of global competition in a global economy — has essentially banned its member nations from allowing free movement of non-EU workers across borders. Permission for a foreign worker to take a job in the European Union countries can now only be given on a temporary basis for no more than a year. (Reuters, A)

Noted free-market economist Melvin Reder warned of the dangers of loosening borders back in 1963, just before Congress did just that. Free immigration would cause per capita incomes between nations to equalize, mainly by leveling the incomes of workers in industrialized countries down toward the low wages in the third world. Substantial increases in immigration would especially injure labor competitors of immigrants, notably blacks, recent immigrants already here, and "secondary earner" workers such as married women, youth and aged persons. (Reder, B)

Cuban immigrant George J. Borjas was a firm believer in free trade and open borders when he began his career as an economist in 1980. But now he believes strongly that the U.S. is allowing in too many immigrants with little education at a time when the economy demands ever-higher levels of skills and training. (*Business Week*, A)

"Broad trends that have converged and accelerated since the middle 1970s have split the old middle class into three new groups," Labor Secretary Robert B. Reich said in 1994. "Well-educated and skilled workers are prospering, those whose skills are out of date or out of sync with industrial change anxiously contemplate their prospects, those without education or skills drift further and further away from the economic mainstream." (*Washington Post*, S)

Those assessments bear out Reder's warning in 1963 that increased immigration would slow or end the movement toward economic equality that Americans had enjoyed during 50 years of low immigration. (Reder, B)

Argument No. 11

Diversity

GENERAL CLAIM: We shouldn't limit immigration because . . .

WE NEED FOREIGN CULTURES AND VALUES

GENERAL PRO-STABILIZATION RESPONSE:

♦ **Whatever the arguments for and against diversity, "it is not clear that the U.S. today needs more of it.... Ours is already a remarkably diverse society."** (Graham, A, pp.15-16)

It is clear that the majority of Americans don't crave more diversity or believe that mass immigration is a net cultural benefit to the country. In 1992, well before public opposition to immigration heated up as a national hot-button issue, a poll found that 59% of Americans said immigration makes race relations in our cities worse. (Business Week/Harris Poll, June 1992) And 55% said the diversity of cultures brought in by immigrants "mostly threaten" American culture. (Gallup Poll, July 1993)

To say that the imposition of a foreign culture into an American community is disruptive is not necessarily to say there is anything negative about the foreign culture itself. The point is that differing cultures often tend to clash. And no matter how admirable the traits of a foreign culture, it can produce less than admirable results when introduced too rapidly and in too large of a dose into the middle of a community. (*Atlantic Monthly*, A)

In addition, it must not be overlooked that some practices and attitudes brought in by immigrants are abhorrent to most Americans. (McCarthy, B)

Immigrants' cultural attitudes about the status of women, for example, often clash with American culture. The practice of female circumcision (removal of the clitoris) is a jarring example. So are attitudes about a husband's rights to discipline his wife and children. A Somali woman brought to trial in DeKalb County, Georgia on charges of performing a circumcision operation on her two-year-old niece defended herself by saying it was customary back home. A Chinese immigrant in New York City hammered his wife to death because he suspected her of cheating on him. He received five years' probation after the judge relied on an anthropologist's testimony about the seriousness of infidelity in Chinese culture. (*Time*, B)

"The uninhibited migration over the next few decades of millions of potential political and economic refugees poses a serious threat to all existing cultures and to civilization at large." (Wagenbichler, A)

"Respecting other cultures, even borrowing from them, does not mean we ought to change the underlying principles of our own culture. It is, after all, our culture that makes people want to move here." (Mehlman, B)

The U.S. has a better chance of taking the best from other cultures without the problematic parts if it does so by its citizens visiting and studying other lands, rather than bringing millions of their people to live here. "Closing the doors to immigrants does not mean closing the doors to ideas. Visits can be encouraged both ways." (Hardin, B)

CLAIM A: It is imperative to continue current levels of immigration in order to maintain our diversity and the multi-cultural richness of our lives through ethnic restaurants, festivals, stores, etc.

RESPONSE:

♦ Even if the U.S. took no immigrants for the next 30 years, it still would remain one of the most ethnically and racially diverse nations on the globe. (Martin, Jack, A)

If the point of our immigration policy were to increase diversity, it would spread the admissions more equally around the globe. Instead, immigration policies reserve most slots for migrants from just a handful of the 180-plus countries: Mexico, the Philippines, Korea, Vietnam, Dominican Republic, Haiti, El Salvador, India and China. (Stein, H)

People whose goal is to make certain that European-descent Americans become a minority in the U.S. have nothing to fear from cutting back from immigration. "It is clear that a change in immigration policy would not halt the growing diversity of our country," immigration researcher Jack Martin concludes. Because non-Euro-American residents have much higher fertility rates than the present Euro-American majority, the country would continue to become less "white" and more Latino, Asian and African-American even if nearly all immigration were halted immediately. The U.S. Census Bureau projections for what is likely to happen if the country has "zero net-immigration" show that by 2050 the non-Euro population will be approaching 40%. Latinos will nearly double as a portion of total population from 9.9% today to 17.5%. Other major ethnic groups also would become larger parts of the population: blacks from 12.6% to 17.2%; Asians from 3.4% to 4.2%. (Census Bureau, E; Martin, Jack, A)

Even though mass immigration was stopped in 1925 and not renewed until 1965, the U.S. still had substantial ethnic diversity in 1964. If immigration again were cut back to an environmentally sustainable level, there is no reason why ethnic restaurants would disappear. Cooking secrets will doubtless be passed down to the children of immigrants. Other Americans might even be capable of learning. If citizens felt their choice of good ethnic restaurants was declining, they could seek help from Congress. Providing a sufficient number of ethnic-cuisine chefs would require at most a few hundred — not a million — admissions a year.

Concerning ethnic festivals, is it likely that the huge Mexican-American population, for example, will cease its Cinco de Mayo celebrations just because fewer Mexicans are entering the country? Mass German immigration ended 80 years ago, but many of the old German-American communities still have Oktoberfests. If we crave exposure to other cultures, why not sponsor American tours of the real thing — artisans who have chosen to continue to live in those foreign cultures?

CLAIM B: In all of life, the more diversity there is the better; nature proves it.

PRO-STABILIZATION RESPONSE:

♦ **We have been taught by recent events in Lebanon, Quebec, Israel, the Soviet Union and elsewhere, as well as by daily experience at home, that too much diversity in a nation can be costly.** (Graham, A, p.16)

♦ **California is the main U.S. laboratory for diversity. "The state is dividing and subdividing now along a thousand new fault lines of language and identity.... Los Angeles, for example, is one of the most**

segregated cities in the world — a horizontal patchwork of ethnic and racial enclaves, all almost self-sufficient, inward turning and immiscible." (*Time*, A)

Even in ecosystems, all species do not have full freedom to move to a neighboring ecosystem to increase its diversity. "It is clear that without boundaries, we would not have variety — everything would be one indistinguishable mush." What makes for variety around the world is that every ecosystem does not contain all diversity. (Boulding, A)

Biologists are partly responsible for the prestige of diversity. When a mutant fungus almost wiped out the entire U.S. corn crop in 1970, scientists who had introduced the hybrid monoculture cornstocks quickly backpedaled and convinced us of the importance of genetic diversity in agriculture. Biologists also praise the diversity of species in a habitat. Since that type of diversity is good, does the same judgment apply to human communities? Not necessarily. For the plant, insect or animal in a rain forest, living amidst such diversity means a constant struggle for survival. When humans settle permanently in a rainforest, they realize they have to create a small island in defense against all manner of fleas, lice, rodents, army ants, etc. They have to reduce the diversity of organisms with which they must interact daily. For humans, in other words, organic diversity is a wonderful thing to visit as a spectator sport, but they wouldn't want to live there. (Hardin, G)

Can there be too much diversity in a nation? Yugoslavia had all manner of ethnic, religious and cultural diversity. Why didn't its multiculturalism work? "Where in today's world can we find a truly multicultural society? On close scrutiny, the answer is: nowhere. The necessary prerequisites for such a society do not exist." (Wagenbichler, A)

Columnist Georgie Anne Geyer sees no reason the U.S. should expect to be significantly different from all other nations of the world. After observing nations such as Kuwait, India, Lebanon and the Soviet Union for two decades, she fears something very similar is starting to happen in the U.S. "I felt I was walking through massive delusion ... the breakdown into ethnic groups.... The value systems that held multi-ethnic, multi-religious systems together aren't holding anymore. We're becoming a country not of individual citizens, but of groups." (*The Social Contract*, B)

L.F. Thomay, a Hungarian who migrated to Canada after World War II, has studied numerous countries in Africa, Europe and the Americas. He concludes that massive immigration of different nationalities into other countries inevitably leads to tension and conflict. Immigration can only occur safely when the immigrants are closely related to the host population and enter in small numbers. (Thomay, A)

"There emerges an increasingly bifurcated economy, in which low-skilled immigrant laborers have relatively few opportunities to work their way up into higher paying, skilled jobs and middle-class status. The loss of a middle class, combined with ethnic fragmentation, should be the first real flare in the sky. People have to want to live together, interact and assimilate to get along. At some point this must happen. But can it ever happen if there is no letup in immigration?" (Stein, J)

British academic Jack Parsons wonders if democracy can continue indefinitely when the will of the majority is so resoundingly ignored: "How much homogeneity must you have to hold society together? How much heterogeneity can you stand before it flies apart?" Former Sen. Eugene McCarthy, a co-sponsor of the 1965 act that inadvertently opened the door to mass immigration, says he regrets that the legislation has been one of the reasons the U.S. has lost control of its borders and increasingly is becoming "a colony to the world." (*The Social Contract*, B, McCarthy, A)

CLAIM C: Our strength is in our diversity; the diversity of immigrants made America great.

PRO-STABILIZATION RESPONSE:

♦ **America's strength in the past was not that it was diverse but that it could find some unity in the midst of its diversity. There never was a movement to import more diversity.**

The nation's early leaders were faced with a population of rather modest diversity. John Jay wrote: "Providence has been pleased to give this one connected country, to one united people, a people descended from the same ancestors, speaking the same language, professing the same religion, attached to the same principles of government, very similar in their manners and customs, and who, by their joint counsels, arms and efforts, fighting side by side throughout a long and bloody war, have nobly established their general Liberty and Independence." (*Federalist Papers*, A) The early leaders' task was to unify the population, not to add diversity, notes Arthur Schlesinger in his *The Disuniting of America.* What allowed the country to be great was that the people could be brought under a common culture — "the language of the nation, its laws, its institutions, its political ideas, its customs, its precepts, its prayers, derived principally from Britain." Although different heritages and movements of people have modified that British heritage, "it has nonetheless remained the central tradition of American civilization — until today." (O'Sullivan, A)

All histories of immigration note the clashes among citizens and the various nationality groups during times of high admissions. That the U.S. was able to later bring about harmony and even unity during periods of reduced immigration is no argument for recreating the conditions that produced disunity. (Mehlman, B)

The Ford Foundation funded a major study of cities that experienced high immigration during the last decade, *Changing Relations: Newcomers and Established Residents in U.S. Commmunities* (April, 1993). The prevalent relations among natives and newcomers were found to be competition, tension and opposition. The reason there has not been more overt conflict in communities with large immigrant population growth is that "newcomers and established residents coexist primarily by maintaining their distance from each other ... separation, not integration, characterizes the divided world." (*The Social Contract*, C)

The unity in diversity that made the country great is sadly lacking while Congress allows four times the traditional average of immigrants to pour into the country each year.

"Contrary to expectations, demographers now see evidence from changing regional profiles that the influx of immigrants is provoking sharper racial divisions and white flight instead of greater racial and cultural mixing. 'Rather than leading toward a new national diversity, the new migration dynamics are contributing to a demographic Balkanization across broad regions and areas of the country,' concludes Dr. William Frey, a demographer with the University of Michigan's Population Studies Center. If the pattern continues, new political schisms are likely to emerge between parts of the country..." (Tyson, A)

"Diversity, like other human traits, has its pluses and minuses — more variety, but more conflict. The Japanese say, 'Our strength is in our homogeneity.' They don't need to fight over language, religion, race, ethnicity, nationality, etc. — they can put those energies and resources into building cars and widgets, and accumulating a $50-billion trade surplus with the U.S. We hire lawyers to resolve our disputes — rather than engineers." (Tanton, G)

CLAIM D: Increasing diversity through immigration is necessary to be true to our civil rights principles.

PRO-STABILIZATION RESPONSE:

♦ **The Civil Rights Movement fought to rectify three centuries of slavery and discrimination against blacks. Now, immigrants who just arrived are benefitting from that struggle at the expense of native-born blacks.** (Briggs, D)

♦ **"Immigration is undoing affirmative action's underlying mission to undo history by helping America's black people." Employers are hiring immigrants to satisfy affirmative action goals without hiring blacks.** (Newhouse News Service, A)

The measure of being true to civil rights principles is how an action affects African-Americans, who, according to George La Noue of the University of Maryland, have an "unassailable" moral claim in this country. Immigrants, regardless of their race, have no such claim in regards to affirmative action because they just got here and have no history of past discrimination in this country, says historian Lawrence H. Fuchs of Brandeis University. Immigration/diversity advocates have turned civil rights principles on their head. They lobby for more foreign workers on the basis that they increase "diversity," but the workers are then often used by employers to avoid hiring blacks. (Newhouse News Service, A)

In a landmark series of articles in late 1993, Jonathan Tilove of Newhouse News Service showed how employers are able to use immigrants to subvert the purpose of President Lyndon Johnson's executive order on affirmative action in 1965. The further "diversity" of mass immigration "greases the displacement of blacks by immigrants in jobs from hotels to construction," Tilove reported.

"In the nearly 30 years since affirmative action was born, massive immigration of Hispanics and Asians has transformed America from a nation in which nearly three-quarters of the minority population was black to one in which less than half that population is black." (Newhouse News Service, A)

The Wall Street Journal's analysis of federal equal opportunity records discovered that only blacks suffered a net job loss in the 1990-91 recession: there were signs that "employers might be laying off blacks while retaining or hiring other minorities to meet their affirmative action goals. The *Journal* study noted that blacks were hit hardest in California, New York, Illinois and Florida, which also happen to be the biggest immigration states." (Newhouse News Service, B)

"It is a subtle process. It is hard to find a smoking gun. Legally, hiring other minorities is no defense for not hiring blacks. But practically speaking, it happens." A former Labor Department solicitor and now consultant cited a client whose minority hires were way up, but "when you looked behind the minority numbers what you're seeing are a lot of Pakistani, [Asian] Indian and Vietnamese," leaving the employer with less pressure to hire blacks. A former director of an employment agency for Cambodian refugees in Chicago said he was "struck by the number of times employers said to me directly: 'We want to phase out our blacks and bring in Asians. It keeps us clear in EEO (Equal Employment Opportunity) and gets us better workers.'" (Newhouse News Service, B)

Black workers are not unaware of what is happening, thus explaining some of the anti-immigrant rage seen in situations like the Los Angeles riots in 1992. An editorial in the Mexican-American *La Prensa San Diego* spoke directly about this: "Faced with nearly a million and a half Latinos taking over the inner city, blacks revolted, rioted and looted. Whatever measure of power and influence they had pried loose from the white power structure, they now see as being in danger of being transferred to the Latino community. Not only are they losing influence, public offices and control of the major civil rights mechanisms, they now see themselves being replaced in the pecking order by the Asian community, in this case the Koreans..." (Mills, A)

"New immigrants have frequently acquired their power at the expense of native-born minorities." (Mills, A) Nowhere is this more apparent than in higher education. The University of Pennsylvania each year gives 30 full "Mayor's scholarships" to students from Philadelphia, boasting how many go to minorities. But half of them go to Asians, in a city that is 40% black and less than 3% Asian. A black student at Cornell University said she had been told the student body was more than 20% minority. When she arrived, she found it was 14% Asian, 6% Hispanic and 5% black. Cornell labor economist Vernon Briggs Jr. said of the national tendencies to use immigration in that way, "It is immigration as a tool of institutional racism." (Newhouse News Service, B)

CLAIM E: In the global marketplace, the U.S. needs citizens who immigrated from other countries so they can help us be competitive through better understanding of those country's cultures.

PRO-STABILIZATION RESPONSE:

♦ We can learn about other cultures without importing thousands of foreigners to practice their culture in the U.S.

"Some appear to believe that the U.S. and its national culture is perpetually on the brink of enervation and stagnation, and cannot persist without constant enrichment or revitalization from abroad. This seems an odd idea for a multi-racial society of more than 250 million people, especially when it is remembered that our principal economic competitor is an Asian island society with little cultural or ethnic diversity but quite abundant vitality and inventiveness." (Graham, A, p.16)

What made the U.S. the world's most advanced economy was not having citizens born elsewhere but usually having a "degree of labor scarcity that meant that a worker could expect a decent wage for his or her work. The scarcity encouraged experiments with labor-saving approaches and technologies, which in turn led to higher productivity, higher wages and a mass market that is still the center of the world trade." (Grant, A, p.150)

In order to compete, is every country in the world supposed to bring in workers from all other countries? "In the rush to create diversity, the nations would have created uniformity." (Stein, G)

CLAIM F: If we advocate a pro-family-values stance, a top priority has to be to help reunite families who have been separated.

PRO-STABILIZATION RESPONSE:

♦ Typically, the immigrant here in the U.S. who wants to "reunite" his family is the family member

who made the choice to break up the family in the first place by moving to the U.S.
(Population-Environment Balance, 15C)

Beyond dependent minor children and spouses, there is no justification for giving preference to relatives of recent immigrants. If the recent immigrants — except for the small percentage who face political danger — want to live near their siblings, parents, aunts, uncles, cousins, nephews and nieces — they can move back to their home countries.

In this age of reasonably priced international phone service and air travel, immigrants can get back to see their relatives about as often as many Americans see their parents, siblings, aunts and uncles. Immigrants in Los Angeles are closer to their relatives in Mexico City than are others in Los Angeles to their relatives in Boston.
(Bouvier, C)

If family reunification was limited to U.S. citizens bringing in their minor children and spouses, immigration numbers eventually would go so low that the U.S. could begin moving toward population stabilization. (Bouvier, C)

Argument No. 12

Tradition

GENERAL CLAIM: Despite pragmatic reasons to do so, we cannot limit immigration because . . .

WE MUST HONOR OUR IMMIGRANT PAST

GENERAL PRO-STABILIZATION RESPONSE:

♦ **"Traditions are to be honored, celebrated and remembered. But they are to be perpetuated only if they continue to serve some national purpose."** (Mehlman, B)

♦ **If we adopted a truly traditional immigration policy, we would cut present admissions by at least three-fourths. The average number of immigrants from 1776 to 1965 (when the present mass immigration period began) was 229,000 a year — contrasted to nearly 1 million now.** (INS; Briggs, A, p.41; Martin, Jack, B)

Americans have been reared on inspiring stories of our immigrant ancestors. It is not surprising that many — even those who understand the grave difficulties in maintaining high immigration — feel emotional barriers to changing what they perceive as an essential and defining national tradition. But much of what they think they know about that tradition is not accurate. And even the positive parts that are true should not bind a nation to make decisions that hurt its people today and in the future.

"James Reston has remarked that 'the history of mankind is strewn with habits, creeds and dogmas that were essential in one age and disastrous in another.' As a people, Americans have paid dearly, and continue to pay, for their devotion to the myths of the bountiful frontier, with its limitless resources and ever-fruitful land." (Tanton, H)

"The basic rationale for current

U.S. immigration policy was established in the 19th century, a time far different from our own era when the nation faced an unsettled continent of boundless resources, the task of industrial and urban development still ahead.... Historically, immigration policy was seen as part of 'nation-building' — to populate a relatively empty land. Are large numbers of immigrants now needed for a land that is built, or even, as many believe, overbuilt?" (Graham, A, pp.4-5)

"Lots of things worked in the past, but all institutions and practices must conform to new realities." (Mehlman, B)

New occasions teach new duties
Time makes ancient good uncouth
They must upward still and onward
Who would keep abreast of truth.

James Russell Lowell was thinking of slavery as he penned those words in 1845. But the universal and timeless truth of the need to re-examine traditions in each generation is attested by the singing of these words in churches across America today in the grand old hymn, "Once To Every Man and Nation." (Lowell, A)

CLAIM A: America is great because of immigrants. We should honor our ancestors by keeping the door open.

PRO-STABILIZATION RESPONSE:

♦ **"America is not great because it has had immigration; America is great because it was founded on the most enlightened principles of government ever experimented with in human history."** (Mehlman, B)

It in no way belittles our immigrant ancestors to protect the character and identity of nationhood that were the very attributes that attracted them and to which they contributed in so many ways. From the earliest to the most recent immigrants, their motivation was not to replicate the overcrowded, unstable conditions they had fled. It was not their intent that their descendants live in such conditions in America. "As a free and self-ruling people, we have the right to preserve that character and heritage. A nation of Americans can properly control immigration or set any other policies to guide its future and destiny." (Vinson, A, p.3)

Americans always should be humbled in their pride of nationhood by the realization that much success is due to the abundance of resources and space that greeted the nation's founders. Combined with enlightened government, those made it possible to incorporate so many migrants from other lands. "Immigrants came to America because this is a great country, not the other way around. Many immigrants indeed helped make America greater still, but they were not the cause of its greatness." (Mehlman, 12)

It only follows reason that once the abundance and open spaces were occupied, immigrants would not be as valuable to the country.

By the country's 100th anniversary in 1876, there were 46 million residents, "eight times the number who lived here when Lewis and Clark ventured into the heartland. By 1890, the director of the Census Bureau declared that a frontier no longer existed." The cities were undergoing explosive growth and were "nightmares of primitive sanitation and waste disposal systems." (Shabecoff, A, p.29)

With the passing of frontier conditions in 1890, the demographic rationale for continuing the tradition of mass immigration disappeared.

CLAIM B: We are a nation of immigrants; how can we pull up the drawbridge now?

PRO-STABILIZATION RESPONSE:

♦ **All countries were immigrant nations at one time, until they matured.** (Oberlink, A)

Although we have been an immigrant nation, we literally are not a nation of immigrants or the children of immigrants. Long before the country was constituted in 1776, the vast majority of people in the North American colonies were native-born. Our primary identity has never been where we came from, or that we came from somewhere else. "Our identity is what we have become first and foremost: a nation of Americans." (Vinson, A, p.3)

The fundamental flaw of the "nation of immigrants" argument is that it assumes the U.S. is different from other countries in that regard. In fact, this country is like all others in that its inhabitants are descendants of a variety of outside groups from some recent or ancient period.

Take the English. Even before

immigration into England over recent decades from their collapsing worldwide empire, the English were "a very mongrel group, being formed from ancient Britons, Romans, Angles, Saxons, Jutes, Celts, Danes, Normans, Huguenots and East European Jews. That's the English — the British are less exclusive." (O'Sullivan, A)

What makes the U.S. different from most countries is that it was settled later and its frontier did not disappear until relatively recently. If the U.S. decides that it has matured as a nation and should halt mass immigration, it simply will be following the pattern of other countries.

"Contrary to the false mythology about immigration today, America was not created to be a haven for all the peoples of the world. Its primary purpose, as stated in the Preamble of the Constitution, was to provide American citizens and their descendants with such blessings as unity, liberty and domestic tranquility." If continuing the immigration tradition interferes with the much more fundamental Constitutional tradition, it is time to choose the higher tradition. (Vinson, A, p.3)

CLAIM C: To meet population stabilization and environmental goals, immigration probably would have to be cut between 75% and 95%. That would so violate our traditions that we no longer would be America.

PRO-STABILIZATION RESPONSE:

♦ **The most profound violation of our immigration tradition has been the unprecedentedly high numbers of the last 20 years.** (INS)

♦ **If we honored tradition by matching the immigrant flows of the Colonial period that created this new nation, we would take 3,500 immigrants every *year*. Right now, we take about 3,500 every *day*.** (Ellis Island Museum)

Most people who talk about guarding our immigration tradition have no idea of the quantitative aspects of that tradition. If they did, they would know that most proposals now in Congress to slash immigration levels adhere to tradition far better than does the current level of immigration.

The U.S. currently allows some 1.3 million foreigners (including an estimated 300,000 illegal aliens) to settle permanently each year. (Martin, Jack, B)

The federal government has no plans to lower that number at any time in the future. The country never has had a sustained period of immigration anywhere near this level. Immigration in most years of nationhood ran more than 75% below the present level.
(INS; Briggs, A)

The confusion about tradition seems to rise primarily because most of us have been immersed through movies and literature in the stories of the Great Wave of 1880 to 1924. But we need to know that that period was a gross aberration and does not resemble any other part of our history, except what has occurred since 1965.

Even the Great Wave (with average annual admissions of 584,000) fails to measure up to the "tidal wave" of the 1990s (currently 1,300,000 annually).

U.S. immigration has been a constant repetition of waves and lulls. But the highs have been much higher in some periods than others. Prior to the present immigration era that began in 1965, there had been five major periods. The following annual averages give a feel for the overall effect during an era, although not the peaks and valleys:

No. 1: Colonial Era (1607-1775)
Annual Average: 3,500

These are the people who poured onto the Eastern Seaboard, drove out the indigenous inhabitants, rolled back the wilderness and created a new nation. During many of those years, the majority were involuntary immigrants from Africa.

The *combined* total of immigrants from Europe and Africa during the entire 169-year colonial era was less than arrive now in a mere six months. (Ellis Island Museum)

No. 2: New Nation (1776-1819)
Annual Average: 6,500

The legal slave trade came to an end in 1808, but the number of people annually making the journey to join the newly independent nation doubled. (Briggs, A, p.41)

No. 3: Continental Expansion (1820-1879)
Annual Average: 162,000

Immigration exploded during this era. Steamships made travel relatively safe and quick. Wars, purchases and treaties created a continental nation with vast expanses of sparsely-settled or empty territory. Businesses imported laborers; the government enticed land settlers.

At times the level of admissions passed the tolerance of natives. But even with an open frontier, still-bountiful natural resources, free land and other enticements, the U.S. had to accommodate a volume of immigrants that was only about 12% of the 1990s level. (INS)

No. 4: Great Wave (1880-1924)
Annual Average: 584,000

Just as the frontier was closing, the industrial revolution created a huge new labor market. Rather than hire poor, underemployed rural whites and freed slaves, industrialists commissioned flotillas of ships to bring back new workers from Europe. (Goldin, A)

"Contrary to some romanticized views of the Great Wave, its

numbers — although little more than half the levels of the 1990s — overwhelmed urban capacities of accommodation. In turn-of-the-century cities, the 'running sores of immigration' were sweatshops, paupers, drug abuse, and 'fetid slums,' according to Syracuse University's David Bennett, author of a book on nativism." America suffered the second of its three great waves of crime. Ugly ethnic and racial hatred against and among immigrants propelled the Ku Klux Klan to its greatest popularity ever. (*Newsday*, A)

The American people, and even Congress, could see that the level of immigration was far above the cultural, economic and environmental capacity of the country to absorb them. In 1897, Congress voted for the first of many measures to curb substantially the Great Wave. But a series of presidents — prodded by industrialists and ethnic political leaders — successfully blocked the action until immigration was limited greatly in 1917 and even more restricted in 1924. (Goldin, A)

No. 5: Era of the Rise-of-the-Middle-Class (1925-1965)
Annual Average: 178,000

America returned to the Continental Expansion levels of immigration that had proven so much more tolerable than the Great Wave. Immigrants who came during that wave were especially helped to assimilate because average annual flows were only 117,000 during the first half of this No. 5 era, rising to 241,000 during the second half. The KKK's power receded, and crime rates fell. After the Great Depression and beginning during World War II, labor markets tightened, sweatshops virtually disappeared, blacks were able to enter the industrial economy in major numbers, and middle-class economic status became the norm for most Americans. (Briggs, E)

It was that immigration tradition that Congress unintentionally violated and overturned with a new law in 1965 that attempted to end selection on the basis of national origin but which led to today's wildly nontraditional level of 1.3 million immigrants a year.

After reviewing our immigration tradition, let's take a look at the proposals for change now being offered. What tradition do they support?

One bill would return the U.S. to the tradition of the Great Wave.

Several pieces of legislation would cut annual admissions to the 325,000-350,000 level. It appears to be important to their sponsors to stay slightly above the level of 1965, which was 297,000. As we've seen, however, only one era in U.S. history sustained that level or higher.

Another bill would allow about 235,000 immigrants a year at first and gradually decrease admissions. Even that level is higher than four of the five eras of immigration. However, one could call it a return to tradition. The average influx from 1776 to 1965 (including the Great Wave) was 229,000 a year.

The U.S. Census Bureau provides yet another, more environmentally helpful, scenario. Based on current estimates of out-migration and of fertility, the U.S. could take in around 160,000 immigrants a year and still be able to level off population at around 300 million population at around 300 million shortly after 2050. (Census Bureau, E) One could argue that the 160,000 figure matches the best of America's immigration traditions. It reflects the level of generous admissions during the 19th-century Continental Expansion and the 20th-century Rise-of-the-Middle-Class eras, periods when immigration for the most part was viewed as a positive force in the country and enjoyed the support of the majority of Americans.

Finally, other chapters have shown and will show that — in order to keep the 1994 population of 260 million from being larger in 2050 and contributing to worse environmental conditions — immigration cannot possibly run above 100,000, unless fertility drops.

An immigration ceiling of 100,000 sounds radical. But it is not far from the average number during eras when immigration was considered by Americans to be positive. If one excludes the Great Wave and the post-1965 period — both eras in which Americans overwhelmingly opposed the levels of immigration — our tradition has been an average of only 119,000 a year.

If 119,000 a year was not too low during a time of far less congestion and environmental crisis, surely it is a tradition that is not too low for today.

CLAIM D: Why all the fuss? Even today's immigration is less than one-half of 1% of the total U.S. population. As a percentage of population, immigrants were a much larger presence in the past.

PRO-STABILIZATION RESPONSE:

♦ Immigration as a percentage of population is a valid consideration when weighing assimilation capacity; but what matters to environmental resources and infrastructure capacity — that are over, or close to, the edge of over-exploitation — is absolute numbers.

For the ailing Chesapeake Bay, the percentage of population that immigration adds each year is not particularly important. It could be 50% and not matter for now, if the watershed population were only a few thousand. But millions of people are taxing the watershed to its limits. It is the raw number of additional car-driving, toilet-flushing, dwelling-using, solid-waste-producing residents that means so much to the ability of the bay to survive.

Nuclear physicist Albert Bartlett has a special perspective on any argument that something should work now because it worked in the past. The attitude that "we have always had immigration, so we should always have immigration" is an example of the free-fall illusion, he says. "If one leaps from the top of the Empire State Building, the first five or six seconds of free-fall are so wonderfully exhilarating that one might be led to think, 'I have been falling for some time, I can enjoy this fall forever.' But after about eight seconds the free-fall is interrupted by the street pavement which makes all of the future very different from the past. In mathematical terms, the pavement is a boundary condition which determines that the equations describing the free-fall cannot describe it forever. The finite resources upon which we depend for survival are the boundary condition that limits the population which can be sustained." (Bartlett-Lytwak, A)

Even in terms of assimilation, an evaluation of immigrants as a percentage of total population is a bit misleading. When immigrants were a higher percentage, Americans had much higher fertility. Consequently, the population growth that caused the need for so much expansion of schools, services, streets and other tax-using infrastructure was not seen as primarily for the benefit of foreigners. Today, however, most growth requirements are attributable to immigration. Immigrants during the 1980s were a 32% higher portion of population growth than during the peak 1901-1910 period, according to the Urban Institute.That portion is projected to rise to double the amount by 2020s. (Brimelow, A)

Anyway, given the way Americans despised immigration during the Great Wave, it makes little sense to suggest we be happy with any comparability today.

CLAIM E: This country would be a far worse place if it were not for the masses of immigrants who came at the turn of the century and helped turn us into a world-class economy and power.

PRO-STABILIZATION RESPONSE:

♦ Romanticizers of the Great Wave are unfortunately guilty of an especially grievous case of Eurocentric myopia. From an African-American point of view, the Great Wave delayed economic opportunity for decades.

To criticize the Great Wave — or any period of immigration — is not to criticize the individuals who were part of it. "The world is made up of 5.5 billion mostly wonderful people. Being a wonderful person cannot be a reasonable qualification for migrating to the U.S." (Mehlman, B) And being wonderful people cannot compensate for what happens when too many of them arrive at once. Because immigration was drastically reduced in 1925, problems caused by having too many immigrants subsided and we now can look back positively and, of course, affirm the sizeable fraction of the current population who descended from that wave. None of that, however, should blind us to the reality of the damage the Great Wave level of migration did to this country at the time.

A famous series of paintings by the renowned black artist Jacob Lawrence poignantly captures the social cost of the Great Wave. A viewer of "The Migration Series" feels transported by the paintings as if by a movie into the realistic scenes of the southern rural culture in which families of freed slaves were trapped during the turn-of-the-century wave of foreign workers. If the government had not allowed the industrialists to fill their factories with European peasants, they would have been forced to make use of the great black labor resource at their doorsteps. The paintings chronicle how that is exactly what happened when the flow of immigrants dried up. If we had not had the Great Wave, the culture of low wages, economic and educational deprivation, injustice and even lynching could have begun to subside much earlier. Blacks could have gotten in on the bottom floor of an industrialization that raised its workers to middle-class status. (*The Social Contract*, A)

Would America be less of a world-class power today if its black citizens — whose American ancestry on average runs farther back than white citizens — had gotten a decades-earlier start on moving into the economic mainstream? Might not our intractable black-white race problems be far less intractable and the overall quality of life for all Americans more tranquil and fulfilling if immigration had been at a lower level?

CLAIM F: Must we dismantle the Statue of Liberty which has words like "huddled masses" chiseled into its base?

PRO-STABILIZATION RESPONSE:

♦ **The primary symbolism of the Statue of Liberty —**

that the U.S. should serve as a beacon of freedom to be emulated by other countries — remains valid regardless of the level of immigration.

♦ **The "huddled masses" symbolism is not chiseled into the statue but is part of a poem by Emma Lazarus added many years after the statue was erected. It is on a small plaque, placed inside by private individuals, not our government.**

♦ **The statue's official name is "Liberty *Enlightening* the World," not "Liberty *Inviting* the World."**

♦ **It's the Statue of Liberty, not the Statue of Immigration.**

♦ **Regardless of what symbolism people attribute to the monument, symbols should not drive public policy.**

Public policy should be developed on the basis of hard facts and analysis about a nation's current situation and future needs. Nonetheless, statues, poems and inspiring stories are important parts of the mythology that binds people into a nation. It is important to understand the symbolism of what may be our most emotion-inspiring monument. Hardly an editorial writer or graphics illustrator in America can resist referring to the Statue of Liberty when dealing with the subject of immigration. The confusion about its symbolism derives primarily from: (1) the happenstance that the main reception center for Great Wave immigrants was on neighboring Ellis Island in New York harbor; and (2) the unofficial placement of a small poem by Emma Lazarus on a plaque inside the statue nearly two decades after it was erected. (Koed, B)

Popular media in recent decades have turned Lady Liberty into a symbol of immigration, some presenting it as something akin to a scriptural basis for maintaining a national open door.

Edouard-Rene Lefebvre de Laboulaye conceived the idea of the statue in the mid-19th century as a way to highlight the preferability of the U.S. form of democracy to the government that then ruled his native France. There is no indication he ever nursed thoughts that the solution was for millions of the French to immigrate to the United States. The solution was for France to emulate the American ideals of governance. Neither Laboulaye nor Frederic-Auguste Bartholdi (the sculptor) ever suggested associating the statue with a promise of new life in the U.S. for the downtrodden of the Earth. (Blanchet-Dard, A)

Bartholdi wrote: "I will try especially to glorify the Republic and Liberty over there, hoping that I will one day find them back here..." (Koed, B)

During the erection of the statue, the fund-raising for its pedestal and the opening dedication in 1886, it was clear to everybody that the statue was to be a symbol for other nations to emulate America's republican form of government and the concept of individual liberties. The fact that Lady Liberty holds a book of law in one hand symbolizes the necessity of the rule of law — including enforcing immigration laws — in the maintenance of a free society. (Koed, B)

Except for a friend's fond gesture of homage to deceased New York City poet Emma Lazarus, the grand vision of the statue's designers might not have been as blurred in the public mind of today. Like multitudes of other artists — including Mark Twain and Walt Whitman — Lazarus had offered a poem to be auctioned in 1883 to raise money to build the pedestal for the statue. In her "The New Colossus," she used the unbuilt statue as a vehicle for expressing her passionate concern for Jews being persecuted in Russian pogroms after the assassination of Alexander II. "No one noticed the sonnet at the time. It was never mentioned at the inauguration, never printed in the press reports." It is known that James Russell Lowell commented favorably to Lazarus, "but no one else seemed to take it seriously.... Lazarus herself was in Paris when the statue was unveiled, and when she returned home the next year she was too ill with cancer to give it any attention. She died that year." (Koed, B)

Nearly two decades later in 1903, Georgina Schuyler — with no particular commitment to the "golden door" described in the poem — sought to honor her long-dead poet friend. She arranged to have a small plaque, engraved with the sonnet, placed inside the pedestal. "It was done quietly with no ceremony. The press ignored it." (Koed, B)

A visitor to the statue will note that Lazarus' words are not chiseled into the base. Rather, they are on one small plaque that is one among hundreds of other items exhibited in a museum. But the millions of immigrants who sailed into New York harbor during that period saw the poem when they visited the statue and helped make the poem a larger symbol than the statue in the public's mind.

Despite the passionate and grandiose sentiment in the poem, the ideals of the statue are far more grand. America as a refuge for the world's huddled masses could never aid more than a tiny fraction of a percent of the world's hapless people. But as a beacon of liberty, the idea and model of which might break the bonds of despotism worldwide, the U.S. could provide comfort to whole populations of hapless people otherwise left behind by their migrating countrymen. (*Daily Californian*, A)

To take in so many foreign citizens that education and other institutions and infrastructures begin to fail is to dishonor the statue. And that threatens the ability of the United States to remain a role model of successful democracy for the rest of the world. (Kennan, A, pp.151-156)

For many Americans, however, it doesn't matter what the statue was intended to symbolize. They cherish the poem as an integral part of what they think it means to be an American. For them, it may be important to acknowledge the statue as a symbol of our success at absorbing immigrants at another time in our history. "The Statue of Liberty ought to be placed in the same category as the arch in St. Louis. Just because we have chosen to commemorate the 'Gateway to the West,' does not elevate westward migration to the realm of the sacred, nor does it imply that we ought to continue to encourage movement to the West." (Mehlman, B)

Argument No. 13

Fear of Name-Calling

GENERAL CLAIM: It is frightening to agree to limit immigration because . . .

SOME LIMITATIONISTS ARE BIGOTED

GENERAL PRO-STABILIZATION RESPONSE:

♦ **There are self-serving people with ugly motives on both sides of the immigration issue, as there are highly principled people; like other issues, this one needs to be decided on its merits, not by name-calling.**

♦ **"There are undoubtedly bigots who want immigration stopped for racial reasons...But opposition to racial bigotry should not blind us to the facts: There are limits to population size, in a theater or in a state, in a phone booth or on the planet."** (Gilliam, A)

The argument that population stabilization supporters are bigoted must be addressed because it has had such a powerful ability to keep Americans from dealing with huge problems staring them in the face. With virtually every community in America looking at a population doubling in one lifetime while the environment already is overtaxed, why are there so few blue-ribbon panels and journalists studying how the growth is to be accommodated or whether it should be allowed? The answer is, "We are keeping quiet because we are afraid of being accused of racism.... As an Anglo, I have compunctions about closing the door on more immigrants, most of whom would be non-Anglo. Being anti-immigration is to risk being classified with 'hate groups,' despite the fact that I believe in racial and cultural diversity and their benefits to America." (Gilliam, A)

For many Americans committed to protecting the environment, as well as to principles of racial justice, the immigration issue is a deeply troubling one. Like *San Francisco Chronicle* environmental journalist Harold Gilliam, quoted above, they cannot look at the facts about population growth without realizing that current levels of immigration are connected directly to deteriorating environmental quality.

Yet, it seems to many that history teaches that the people behind restrictions are the sorts of people with whom they would never associate. This is an important concern because it relates to people's very sense of moral identity. When terms like xenophobia, nativism, scapegoating, immigrant-bashing and racism are connected to limitationism, many environmental and economic justice advocates choose just to avoid the issue altogether. As was shown in earlier chapters, though, avoidance is an option that only furthers environmental decline and economic disparity. Hence, the need to take a closer look at what many have been taught was "the ugly side" and follow historian Otis Graham's advice to be sure of what it is that history really teaches us.

CLAIM A: As long as immigrants came primarily from Europe, everything was fine. When Latin America and Asia became the primary sources, the attitude of Americans turned ugly.

PRO-STABILIZATION RESPONSE:

♦ Numbers, not national origin, are the main determinant of Americans' attitudes toward immigrants.

It is a myth that Americans have suddenly turned mean-spirited toward foreign workers because they now are primarily Latino and Asian. In the late 1960s and early 1970s, most immigrants also were from Latin America and Asia, but the numbers were relatively low; there was little opposition. On the other hand, during the 1880-1924 era when immigrants primarily were from Europe and the numbers were high, Americans' opposition was even more hostile than today's. (*The Social Contract*, G)

Doubtless, many Americans find it easier to accept immigrants whose culture, language, religion and race are similar to their own. But public opinion polls show that Americans have tolerated immigration, regardless of national origin, when the numbers were low, and that they increasingly opposed immigration as the numbers rose higher:

• When legal immigration stood at 297,000 in 1965, Gallup found the majority of Americans happy with the level, while 33% wanted reductions.

• As the annual number rose well above 400,000 by 1976, Gallup found the majority of Americans (52%) opposed the influx.

• By 1993, with the legal number approaching a million, a CNN/USA Today poll found 65% wanted immigration decreased generally, and 76% said immigration should be stopped or reduced until the economy improved. Sentiment is hardening. A 1994 CBS News poll found that half of Americans who want immigration reduced favor halting all in-migration. And a third of them even want to send back home all immigrants who arrived in the last five years! (*National Review*, B)

It is interesting that many advocates of high immigration have no trouble appreciating the desire of an Egypt, a Nepal, a Kenya, a Brazil, a Mexico, a Norway or a Jamaica to have the right of self-determination and to maintain their national cultures. But they consider it somehow illegitimate for the U.S., Canada, Australia and sometimes a few European countries to set immigration levels in the self-interest of their own citizens or to maintain their own cultures. (Nelson, A)

CLAIM B: The movement to reduce immigration is a movement of white people afraid that people of color will take over the country.

PRO-STABILIZATION RESPONSE:

♦ **"The majority of Americans and Californians of all ethnicities want to see legal immigration reduced and laws against illegal immigration strictly enforced."** (Oberlink, B)

One might think that at least Latinos would be supportive of immigration, which includes more Latin Americans than any other group. But they aren't. A 1993 survey found that a higher percentage of Latinos than non-Hispanic whites oppose current levels. (The Latino National Political Survey, A)

When opposition to current immigration is found throughout the ethnic mosaic of America, it should be apparent that the issue transcends questions of race.

African-Americans, whose roots go back further on average into America's history than do those of most Americans of European descent, are among the most passionate advocates of limitation. (Their attitudes are discussed in detail under CLAIM C.)

"One finds in (the immigration restriction movement) children of immigrants themselves, who admire the ability of America to assimilate immigrants and their children, but who fear that the assimilatory powers of America have weakened because of the legal support to bilingualism in education and voting, because of the power of multicultural trends in education. It is easy to accuse such people of wanting to pull up the drawbridge after they have gained entry. They would answer that they fear the U.S. is no longer capable of assimilating those now coming as it assimilated them." (Glazer, A)

National and state legislators are the ones who tend to make a racial issue out of immigration by consistently highlighting the opinions of those ethnic organizations that claim limitationism is a bigoted response from white Americans. But those very organizations are ones that support high immigration in contradiction to the anti-immigration sentiments held by the majority of the ethnic constituents for whom they purport to speak. (Oberlink, B)

The Latino National Political Survey discovered, for example, that 75% of Mexican-Americans who were U.S. citizens said there are too many immigrants. That compared to 74% of non-Hispanic white American citizens. (Latino National Political Survey, A)

Recent Mexican immigrants in the U.S. who are not yet citizens are even more opposed to present immigration (84%) than are Mexican-American and white citizens (Latino National Political Survey, A)

Although suggestions that the National Guard be deployed along the Mexican border have been decried by self-appointed ethnic spokesmen as a racist militarization of the border, a Field Poll revealed that 57% of Latinos in California favor this proposal. (Oberlink, B)

Why would recent immigrants be so interested in shutting the door? Most economic studies find that high levels of immigration are most harmful to the immigrants who recently arrived and who are in the most direct competition for entry-level jobs. (*Immigration 2000*, A)

When Fidel Castro began to encourage his disgruntled citizens to flee Cuba by boat in 1994, Cuban-American elected officials in south Florida pled with federal officials to prevent a boatlift that could destroy not just their economy but their community. (*Washington Post*, J)

Although immigration supporters try to divide Americans along racial and ethnic lines, citizens in this country are remarkably unified on this issue. U.S. Rep. Bob Stump of Arizona was the sponsor of the most restrictive of immigration bills in 1994. "My hometown is probably 80% Mexican-American. They aren't mad at me. They want legal immigration reduced." (*National Review*, B)

CLAIM C: At heart, limitationism throughout American history has been an attempt to preserve the economic status of natives at the expense of potential immigrants who were different racially or culturally. The hysteria and violence around the turn of the century exemplifies this.

PRO-STABILIZATION RESPONSE:

♦ **"It is in no sense anti-immigration ... to state that U.S. workers should have the first claim on U.S. jobs and that U.S. wages and working conditions should not be undermined by workers from other lands."** (AFL-CIO, A)

♦ **The history of post-slavery African-Americans in this country has been one of opposing the entrance of immigrants who competed for jobs. Have blacks been bigoted and selfish for refusing to quietly keep in "their place" as they watched masses of foreign workers move up the ladder ahead of them?**

It is an ironic and cruel twist of history that today's supporters of a labor oversupply that depresses wages and working conditions have been able to paint America's struggling labor classes from 1840 to 1924 as bigoted violators of the American heritage. These were the laborers who stood up to the Robber Barons' attempts to keep U.S. workers in near-servitude through the mass importation of competitive foreign workers.

The image of American workers violently meeting ships of Asians arriving on the Pacific Coast around the turn of the century shocks our late-20th-century sensibilities with its racial connotations. But it would be helpful for once to step into the shoes of those American workers. On the U.S. and Canadian West Coast, workers had finally begun to unionize and gain wage and benefits concessions from the powerful industrialists after long, hard battles. Big business counter-attacked by importing shiploads of Asian workers to undercut the unions. Although the workers often acted with inappropriate racial epithets and violence against the competitors, the basic issue was fighting to hold onto what little piece of the economic pie they'd wrested from the industrial class. Laws to bar Asian immigration during those times were liberal and progressive vehicles for the benefit of the working class, not primarily vehicles of racism. (Jarvis, A)

While Congress shut off only Asian immigration, the public clamored for an end to mass European immigration, as well. By 1897, citizens had persuaded the majority of both houses of Congress to approve the first of several pieces of legislation that would have reined in migration. But a succession of presidents vetoed this and subsequent bills, and a bare minimum one-third of Congress protected the vetoes. The Great Wave was kept alive until 1924 because of the influence of industrialists — who favored mass immigration as an effective tool in holding down wages — and immigrant political leaders, whose power was enhanced by a continuing influx. (Goldin, A)

Then, as now, the public grew frustrated with the federal government's blocking of the majority will. Unfortunately, many citizens focused their ire on the immigrants themselves, rather than on politicians responsible for the level of immigration. Immigrants became targets for ugly verbal and physical attacks. One of the most tragic aspects of the anti-immigrant agitation was that it enabled the Ku Klux Klan to grow to its greatest popularity ever, a phenomenon that at the same time increased cruelty against black citizens who themselves were more victimized by the foreign labor importation than others. (Bennet, B; Briggs, A, E)

Free blacks were complaining about immigration during the first mini-boom before the Civil War. "Every hour sees the black man elbowed out of employment by some newly arrived immigrant whose hunger and whose color are thought to give him a better title to the place," Frederick Douglass wrote. (Cook, A)

Immediately after the Civil War, freed slaves desperately needed land to establish themselves economically. Fortunately, incredible acreage was opening up in the West then. But the railroad companies instead recruited *immigrants* to settle the land. Few blacks got land. Most were stuck in the South where they could be used by the old slave masters as a continuing source of cheap labor. (Fuchs, A)

In 1895, Booker T. Washington beseeched the Atlanta Exposition audience of white industrialists to stop sending their worker-import boats to Europe and instead to open factory jobs to the underemployed freed slaves and their descendants. (Washington, A)

Most blacks stayed in the South as northern industrialists ignored Mr. Washington and kept importing Europeans. The competition was so intense that the black population in many northern cities actually decreased, as many blacks lost the higher positions they earlier had achieved. (Bodnar, A)

For 80 years, some of the most vitriolic attacks on immigrants came from black newspapers and leaders. They vigorously supported Chinese exclusion laws and leveled especially harsh criticism at Mexican and Filipino workers who were imported later. (Fuchs, A)

Throughout, African-Americans opposed immigrants because of their differing cultures and most of all because they threatened blacks' economic situation and were used "to press us further down the economic ladder." (Shankman, A)

Those black workers — and their white American laboring-class counterparts — indeed confronted immigration on the basis of what it did to them economically. Was — and is — it unduly selfish and bigoted for the workers of any nation to take such an approach? And how do we weigh the moral claims when the argument against workers' immigration concerns tend to come from America's professional class which is financially enhanced by immigration? (Foreman-Peck, A)

CLAIM D: Even if non-white Americans are part of the movement, limitationism is full of nativism, immigrant-bashing and scape-goating, unworthy of our national ideals of non-discrimination.

PRO-STABILIZATION RESPONSE:

♦ By definition, nativism, scapegoating and immigrant-bashing all have to do with hostility toward the foreign born in our midst, not about reducing the number of foreign citizens who might enter in the future.

American journalists have been quite careless in their use of the word "nativism," as if it described people who want immigration lowered. Because "nativism" is such a powerful word with very negative connotations, it is important to use it properly and carefully. Dictionaries show that "nativism" is not about limiting immigration; rather, it describes a policy favoring the native born over immigrants already in the country. As long as limitationists don't show hostility toward immigrants already here, they do not cross the line into nativism. (Barton, A)

The word "nativism" first appeared in the 1830s. (*Random House Webster's College Dictionary*) It described one part of the limitationist strain that ran through America for a century. Inherent in some nativist thinking was the belief that certain types of Europeans were genetically more disposed to certain traits that made them better candidates for U.S. citizenship. Even very progressive intellectuals endorsed those ideas. Major scientific advances in sociology and genetics in the 1920s and 1930s challenged such thinking by the late 1930s. (Bennett, A)

Historian David Bennett, an authority on nativist abuses, argues that nativism "declined in the '30s and virtually disappeared by the '50s until another kind of anti-alien fear reached a new height with McCarthyism.... Nativism hasn't really returned." Studying the limitation movement during the 1980s, Bennett found, "There didn't seem to be a nativist movement at all. This was a different coalition to curb immigration. A lot of the arguments were coming from American liberals and environmentalists. The activists were not coming from just one side of the political aisle. They weren't using nativist rhetoric." (Bennett, A)

As long as advocates do not suggest discriminatory treatment against immigrants already here, they could push for stopping all immigration forever and not be nativist. (Barton, A)

Although nativist rhetoric and attitudes still can be found among a small number of Americans, "nativist" is far too strong to be applied to most immigration opponents of today. It is "absurd," for example, for some pro-immigration activists in California to say that recent advocacy to stabilize the state's population to protect the state's environment is nativist. (Bennett, A)

"Scapegoating" can be a form of nativism. To make immigrants a scapegoat is to place blame where none is due or to suggest that they are the total cause of a problem when they are only part of the cause. The major California population stabilization group has commented to state legislators: "While CAPS is among those who believe that current immigration policy is a *contributing* factor in the state's economic malaise we have been unable in our research to find a statement by any leading political figure, or anyone else, who maintains that such is the *sole* or primary cause.... CAPS condemns racism and bigotry, particularly when they manifest themselves in acts of violence." (Oberlink, B)

CLAIM E: The country simply is experiencing just another in a long line of outbreaks of xenophobia in which fear of foreigners dulls Americans' judgment. When the economy improves, they get over it.

PRO-STABILIZATION RESPONSE:

♦ **"It's our job ... to have reasoned discourse. To say a particular policy position is xenophobic is not an invitation to debate. It is name-calling."** (Themstrom, A)

♦ **We have to acknowledge that for some**

immigration advocates, the use of such epithets as "xenophobia" and "racism" is an unprincipled effort to avoid having to face up to the environmental and other consequences of their position. It is a motion for cloture — to shut off debate. (Tanton, G)

The main cure for "xenophobia" has always been reducing the numbers. Americans entered into each "xenophobic" era because immigration went too high. Their agitation did not end with economic recovery but with removal of what agitated them in the first place, too much immigration. "Recovering tolerance and civic harmony depended ... on a period of relief from heavy immigration, during which an inclusive national enterprise could bring old and new Americans together." (Higham, A)

"Just as spelling [xenophobia] in a round of Scrabble scores so many points as to be a game-stopper, hurling it against a person in debate scores the kind of points that make it a discussion-stopper." (*The Social Contract*, G)

During much of the current public debate over immigration, there has been a remarkably uncontested assumption that history "teaches" that immigration limitationism in the past was always guided by xenophobia and therefore should be rejected for the present. "This is a misuse of history.... A misapplied past has made our national future more difficult.... As a case in point, take the restrictionist impulse of the 1890s to 1920s. It cannot simply be stigmatized as racist and alarmist, though there was far too much of that. Restrictionism attracted some of the best minds in America, including many liberal clergymen, spokesmen for organized labor and the black community, and socialists." (Graham, B)

"Xenophobia" is not misused as promiscuously as "nativism." Most users seem to know it has something to do with fear of foreigners, but not that the fear has to be irrational. Because it refers to motives, linguists find its use problematic. It ascribes a motive to a person "when you may not know the motive." (Levi, A)

Dictionaries defining "xenophobia," "xenophobe," and "phobia," distinguish between rational fear and exaggerated or irrational fear. A xenophobe is a person who is unduly, inexplicably or illogically fearful of foreigners.

Traditionally, Americans' xenophobia has taken three forms: fear of Catholics (particularly the power of the papacy), fear of radical philosophies being brought in by immigrants, fear of mongrelizing the Anglo-Saxon virtues of the country. (Higham, B)

Every one of those fears at various times in history could be expressed in a rational, legitimate and non-xenophobic way. Most had to do with concern about survival of the nation's culture. There is nothing illegitimate about that. At issue is not which culture is better but the effect on one's own culture. "The skinheads in Germany are a very ugly form, but that doesn't mean the German people don't have a serious concern about what it takes to maintain a German culture. Part of that requires excluding things from your culture." What turns those legitimate concerns into negative patterns is when a person stereotypes all immigrants or when a person's concerns are expressed "emotionally." (Keeley, A)

Along with the three "xenophobic" fears, there always has been a fourth: fear of numerical increase. One really cannot justify using the term "xenophobic" against people motivated out of this fear because it is not based on the composition of immigrants. Thomas Jefferson was an early exponent of the fear of numerical increase, worrying that more immigrants would create a congestion that would be incompatible with his ideal of an America of farms and small towns. The fear was a part of a lot of arguments at the turn of the last century that America couldn't handle more immigrants now that the frontier was closed and cities were overcrowded. It is continued today through the environmental movement. (Keeley, A)

Some immigration advocates use epithets freely against environmentalists. "They need a 'boo-word' — a word with such intensely negative connotations that, hopefully, no opponent in debate can shrug it off, yet so vague in its meaning that it can be applied to practically anyone who disagrees with them." If you are afraid of dealing with the very strong environmental reasons why present immigration cannot continue, and if you are unscrupulous in insisting on high immigration, you try to create "moral monopoly." The essence of the "moral monopolist tactic is to claim that you preeminently possess some virtue — which in reality is shared by almost the entire community — and that your opponents disgracefully lack it." Without throwing out labels like racism, nativism and xenophobia, immigration advocates would have to debate issues like the environmental carrying capacity of the nation. (O'Connor, A)

Many critics of Martin Luther King Jr. suggested that it was un-American to support his civil rights struggles because there were a number of Communists who also supported the movement. Had Americans gone along with that guilt-by-association reasoning instead of weighing the actual merits of the civil rights cause, one of the most significant shifts in our history would not have occurred. If indeed the bio-diversity and health of the environment in our country are dependent on population stabilization which at the moment cannot be achieved without a deep reduction in immigration, would it make any more sense to refuse to act because some people also supporting the reduction are racists?

Sen. Joe McCarthy was a master in the 1950s of using guilt-by-association to attack an opponent and avoid real debate. Sen. Eugene McCarthy fears a similar trait is apparent among some advocates of high immigration today. He was a co-sponsor of the 1965 bill that opened the way for the last three decades of high immigration. He says nobody who supported the bill intended for it to increase the numbers. The purpose of the bill was merely to make sure immigration quotas did not discriminate on the basis of race, religion or national origin. But now the *volume* of immigration desperately needs to be addressed, he says. Unfortunately, "many advocates of high immigration have tried to prevent public discussion by making personal attacks on the analysts. I hope the immigration debate has matured enough so that we can leave the *argumentum ad hominem* behind and stick to the issues. Critics [of proposals for limiting the volume] should present their own alternative suggestions for public critique and review." (McCarthy, B)

Argument No. 14

Humanitarianism

GENERAL CLAIM: No matter what the consequences of U.S. population growth, we cannot limit immigration because we have . . .

INTERNATIONAL OBLIGATIONS TO THE POOR

GENERAL PRO-STABILIZATION RESPONSE:

♦ **The current, historically high level of immigration will not appreciably improve conditions in the third world. But it is moving the U.S. itself toward third world conditions, "thus depriving the planet of one of the few great regions that might have continued ... to be helpful to much of the remainder of the world..."** (Kennan, A, p.154)

♦ **The moral priority for this nation is to address the needs of that segment of the descendants of slavery who remain mired in the underclass. To the extent that largescale immigration interferes, the poor in other countries must wait.** (McCarthy, C)

More than 99% of the impoverished people of the world will never have the opportunity to migrate to the U.S. even if it doubled present immigration levels. "Rather, they will have to bloom where they are planted if they are to bloom at all. They will have to work to change conditions they don't like rather than just move away from them. Helping make it possible for them to stay rather than leave is the proper focus for our efforts." (Tanton, B)

Mass immigration as a humanitarian policy fails on three counts: (1) it harms U.S. citizens as well as our country's ecosystems and biodiversity; (2) it does so without offering any significant relief to the poverty and overpopulation problems of the third world; (3) in many aspects, it actually brings harm to the very populations around the world it is supposed to help. (U.S. Senate Briefing, A)

A small but influential minority of Americans sincerely believes that current high levels of immigration are an essential form of international humanitarianism. To them, immigration is a key way for the U.S. to show compassion to the desperately impoverished and politically repressed peoples of the underdeveloped world. To these self-designated immigration humanitarians, this is a moral decision that supersedes the majority wishes of the American people. We should acknowledge that even many Americans who want immigration cut are a bit troubled by the thought that they might be reneging on a humanitarian duty. At heart, this is a moral matter that must be assessed by answering three questions: (1) Is U.S. immigration policy a net benefit to the targeted population? (2) If so, does the level of international benefit justify the negative effects of population growth on the U.S.? (3) To the extent that there is a moral claim to allow immigration, how does it relate to other conflicting moral claims that are made upon Americans? (U.S. Senate Briefing, A)

Geo-political analyst George Kennan's answers to the previous questions are that "even the maximum numbers we could conceivably take would be only a drop from the bucket of the planet's overpopulation" while having a devastating effect on the U.S. which is "rapidly consuming its own natural capital.... Surely, the present environmental crisis is essentially the reflection of a disbalance between human population — its sheer numbers as well as its way of life" — and dwindling natural resources. (Kennan, A, pp.151-156)

Humanitarian idealists, although doubtless sincere, are unrealistic. "The U.S. is a small part of the world — only 5% of the population of the Earth. We can voluntarily share the world's poverty; we cannot make the world rich by sharing our wealth." (Lamm, A, p.25)

What if the U.S. were to make the ultimate gesture of egalitarianism and share its wealth with all the "Less-Developed Countries" (LDCs)? In this look at an extreme case of humanitarianism, residents of each LDC and the U.S. would pool all their wealth, divide it equally and live at the same level. This done, we find that Americans' wealth is so diluted that on average it would fall below the current level of even some LDCs, the better off of which would suffer a drop in standard of living, too.

Using per capita gross national product figures as a method of comparison (Population Reference Bureau, C), here is the result: All Americans and all LDC residents would live like the average Iranian. To give a better idea of how much of a drop that would be, the average per capita GNP for residents of Mexico is about 50% higher than in Iran (and the Mexican standard is only 15% of the U.S. standard.)

"There will be those who will say, 'Oh, it is our duty to receive as many as possible of these people and to share our prosperity with them...' But suppose there are limits to our capacity to absorb. Suppose the effect of such a policy is to create, in the end, conditions within this country no better than those of the places the masses of immigrants have left...." Then the the third world would no longer have available a nation (the U.S.) that could have helped them, as it does now, "by its relatively high standard of civilization, by its quality as example, by its ability to shed insight on the problems of the others and to help them find their answers to their own problems." (Kennan, A, pp.153-154)

CLAIM A: Largescale immigration is a significant way for the U.S. to help the impoverished people of the world.

PRO-STABILIZATION RESPONSE:

♦ **Most analysts agree that current U.S. immigration probably is about as high as the American people would ever allow it to go. Yet, it is such a tiny fraction of 1% of the world's impoverished people that its positive effect is almost imperceptible. Besides, it is not the most impoverished who migrate.**

Does U.S. immigration make a significant improvement for the people of the third world? To answer that, we must use numbers that are so large that they need an illustration that gives us some ballpark perspective of their effect. Let's try this one, in one ballpark:

Suppose that the members of Congress — pressured by large numbers of constituents to cut immigration — wanted to put the humanitarian aspects to the test on TV for all Americans to appreciate this form of international aid.

Congress settles on a plan to allot current visas for about 1 million legal immigrants through a lottery drawing to be conducted at a baseball stadium. The 535 members walk two blocks from the Capitol to Union Station and board a train to the nearest ballpark — Camden Yards in Baltimore.

They have invited foreign guests from the world's impoverished countries. Each guest is a proxy for 100,000 impoverished third-world residents. The 10 guests whose ticket numbers are drawn can go immediately to a phone and each summon 100,000 immigrants to move to the U.S.

The losers are to be provided — before they set sail back home — with a chance to see an exhibition game of the national American pastime.

The 535 lawmakers humbly take seats in the left-centerfield bleachers and await the foreign proxies who have sailed up the Chesapeake Bay and disembarked at the Baltimore Harbor just a few blocks away.

The first proxies to enter the stadium and start taking seats near home plate are the ones from Mexico and all of Central America. There are 1,230 of them (representing 123 million people hoping to be among the million chosen for immigrant status).

It was not a simple task to decide which people could lay such a humanitarian claim on the collective U.S. conscience to deserve humanitarian immigration options. Finally, it was decided that Mexico would be a kind of benchmark. Indeed, if U.S. immigration policy is driven by humanitarianism, Mexico must be the standard because it supplied 23% of all immigrants 1981-1990. (*The World Almanac,* A) With the average resident living at about 15% the level of the average U.S. resident, Mexico certainly deserves our compassion.

So all the other foreign proxy guests coming into the ballpark are from countries with a standard of living below that of Mexico. (Based on per capita gross national product figures in *1994 World Population Data Sheet* by the Population Reference Bureau.)

Next come 300 proxies from Caribbean nations. Not represented are the Bahamas and a few other islands with income too high to qualify. (Puerto Ricans are not here because they have unlimited access to the U.S. already. If they were an independent people, though, they would be too wealthy to be a part of this humanitarian event.)

The senators and representatives watch as the baseline boxes fill up with 2,770 from South America (excluding Argentina and Suriname) and 3,100 from Eastern Europe.

Already, 7,400 seats are taken, and the representatives from the **really** poor countries are just starting to arrive.

From Africa, 6,990 proxies pour in, representing some 700 million people. The ones from Southern Africa live a bit better than the citizens of East Europe; the ones from North Africa live at about half that level; and the majority who live in the middle of the continent survive at a level below that of the Chinese.

Before the 11,920 Chinese representatives have finished looking for seats, every available place in the lower decks is taken and the upper decks start to fill. Having one of the 10 winning immigration lottery tickets is an especially tantalizing prospect for these proxies whose 1.2 billion fellow citizens live at one-ninth Mexico's level.

Representing even more desperately poor people — one-eleventh Mexico's level — are the 9,110 Indians. The procession concludes as another 10,820 proxies from the rest of the poor nations of the Mideast, East Asia and Southeast Asia fill the remaining seats of the upper deck and spill over into the bleachers.

The U.S. Representatives and Senators look out over the 47,000-seat stadium filled with the faces of the world's needy people. They marvel at the magnitude of the humanitarian task. There are 46,240 guest proxies at the ballpark. Fewer than 500 empty seats are left, scattered among the lawmakers in the bleachers.

The Speaker of the House of Representatives walks across the field to home plate and reaches into the big basket of ticket stubs. In the country's act of humanitarianism to the poor of the world, he pulls out 10 tickets, enough to fill this year's allotment of 1 million immigrants.

After the 10 winners disappear into the dugouts, the TV cameras pan the crowd. Many viewers notice that they can't even tell a difference — 99.98% of the deserving guests are still up in the stands. Who can spot the 10 empty seats?

After the ball game, the 46,230 disappointed proxies go back to their boat, empty-handed, and return to the 4.6 billion poor people who must live out their dreams at home.

The second year, the same 46,230 return and take their same seats. Just as the Speaker is about to draw this year's lucky 10 tickets, a terrible commotion can be heard at the gates behind the lawmakers' bleacher seats. The chairmen and ranking members of the Judiciary Committees and their subcommittees on immigration are sent back to see what is happening.

At the gate, the delegation finds 800 people saying they deserve entry. They explain that during the past year, the population of their countries has grown. There are some 80 million more impoverished people in the world than last year.

So 10 of those population-growth proxie guests take the seats of the 10 who won last year, and the other 790 new guests move into the bleachers, filling the empty seats, clogging the aisles and sitting on the lawmakers' armrests.

Each year thereafter, the 10 who win the immigration lottery are replaced by approximately 800 more proxie guests — representing yet another 80-million addition to the world's impoverished members. After only a few years, every step, aisle and walkway in the stadium is packed to the maximum, guests have been crammed into the press booths, and folding chairs cover every inch of foul-ball territory on the field.

The journalists and members of Congress, who can't even get a good view of the drawing or the annual exhibition game anyway, conclude that, numerically speaking, U.S. immigration is a futile and rather hollow gesture toward helping the poor of the world.

The next year, instead of shipping all the proxies to Camden Yards to help 0.02% of them while disappointing 99.98%, Congress begins finding more effective ways to help the masses make progress where they live — and without harming the U.S. in the process through exploding population growth.

That's a ballpark illustration, not a prediction.

CLAIM B: We must be careful in cutting our immigration numbers because we have a sacrosanct tradition of providing shelter to refugees under threat of death or persecution.

PRO-STABILIZATION RESPONSE:

♦ **Less than 5% of people now allowed to migrate to the U.S. are U.N.-certified refugees.** (Barnett, A)

♦ **We must be certain that our refugee programs do not undermine the forces for change in the refugees' home countries that could help the greatest number of people.** (Population Environment Balance, A)

If it were true that humanitarianism drives our immigration policy, one would think that all our admissions — or at least the majority — would be true refugees and legitimate asylum seekers. Nobody is in more need than they. But only about 10% of our visas are for refugees. Probably more than half of those are not true refugees but are granted refugee visas by special legislation. (Barnett, A)

A definition of refugees gradually emerged after World War II and an upper limit of 17,500 a year to the U.S. was established. The Refugee Act of 1980 prescribed a "normal flow" of 50,000 a year who could not return home "because of persecution or a well-founded fear of persecution on account of race, religion, nationality, membership in a particular social group, or political opinion." (Graham, A, p.17)

Each Congress and president has used the refugee policy to embarrass some regimes and win political points with some domestic constituencies. The number of "refugee" admissions has doubled. "The logic of the greatest good for the greatest numbers runs afoul of the political purposes of U.S. refugee policy." (Center for Immigration Studies, A)

The fact is, however, that even if the U.S. made sure it took only true political (and not economic) refugees, it could not make much of a dent in the worldwide need. The U.N. High Commissioner for Refugees lists around 20 million refugees outside their countries of origin and another 20 million or so displaced within their own countries. "The symbolic resettlement of a small number of true political refugees is surely desirable and consistent with the benevolent affection of our people, but refugee resettlement in the U.S. has ceased to be a practical option for most refugees. In an overpopulated world, the capacity to unleash disasters and to inflict suffering far exceeds this nation's capacity to absorb the victims." (Bikales, A)

The United Nations recognizes that the only course for most refugees will be to provide temporary refuge in nearby countries until they can be assisted to return home. (Center for Immigration Studies, A)

If the U.S. wanted to do the most good with its limited refugee budget, it would devote nearly all of it to helping refugees where they are. U.S. Committee for Refugees' director Roger Winter estimates that a day's worth of funding needed for U.S. resettlement of one refugee covers the needs of 500 refugees abroad for a day. (Center for Immigration Studies, A)

The U.S. also needs to consider that its taking of refugees may actually make matters worse in the home countries and lessen the chance for political and social change. Haiti is a good example. Despite wide publicity on U.S. interdiction efforts to stop the flow of Haitians, a sizeable portion of that small country's population has been admitted to the U.S. over the last decade — more than 200,000 out of a population of 6 million. Haiti's public and private schools three decades ago were the envy of the Caribbean. So many teachers and other educated Haitians have left that a whole generation of school children is growing up without much education at all, raising questions whether Haiti will have a citizenry capable of supporting a true democracy. (*New York Times*, F)

"It is often the politically dissatisfied or economically unfulfilled who decide to leave. Their feelings are understandable, but (we) believe that we should not encourage them to migrate. These dissatisfied people are precisely the ones who should stay at home because they are often the most motivated and best able to rectify the problems of their own societies. What, for example, would have happened to the Polish reform movement had Lech Walesa decided to emigrate to the U.S.?" (Population-Environment Balance, A)

"As we look at other countries that have overthrown communist or authoritarian governments in recent years, we find that in each case the revolution was sparked from within. With a domestic opposition in place, the forces of democracy were able to pick off, one by one, the rotting regimes of Eastern Europe and Latin America. But instead of an organized opposition in Havana, poised to overthrow the despot, Castro's opposition is comfortably ensconced 90 miles away in Miami. From there they are free to howl about what Fidel has done to their island, and little else." (Stein, A)

"This story was told to me by George Immerwahr who was teaching graduate students in Sri Lanka: He decided one day to pose for them some questions of Sri Lankan society and see what they thought the solutions might be. The response from the entire student body was, 'We don't know and we don't care since we're going to leave the country.' I've long felt that this attitude was one of the main defects in immigration policy, focusing attention as it does on emigration as a solution to personal problems, rather than staying and working on the problems of the home society to make things better." A confirmation of the attitude happened while entertaining long-time Dutch friends who were in the process of moving to the U.S. As [the husband] described defects in the Netherlands, "I pressed him for possible solutions. In exasperation, he finally said, and I quote him exactly, 'I don't know and I don't care. We're leaving.'" (Tanton, G)

In the case of true refugees whose lives may be on the line, it is not for others to judge whether they should seek refuge or courageously stay and fight for their people. But for the sake of their home countries — and in recognition of the reality of a crowded world — refuge should be a temporary, not a permanent solution. The point of providing safe haven to refugees should not be — as is now embodied in U.S. law — to make people citizens of new countries. Rather, it is to provide shelter in the midst of a life-threatening occurrence. When the threat to life is over, refugees need to return home to help rebuild their country and to make room in the U.S. for others when their lives are threatened.

Under present laws and administrative procedures, however, even those allowed into the U.S. expressly under temporary terms tend to never leave. People from nearly two dozen countries have been offered some sort of "temporary" stay in the last two decades. In not one case have most of a nationality returned home after conditions improved, according to INS spokesman Duke Austin. (*New York Times*, K)

One cannot help but wonder if the American unwillingness to temporarily shelter the fleeing Haitian boat people in 1992-1994 was influenced by the fact that the U.S. "guest house" already was full of hundreds of thousands of "temporary" refugees from Nicaragua and El Salvador who have refused to go home — a response accepted by Congress and the president — even though the civil wars there are over and democratic governments are in place. (*San Diego Union*, B)

CLAIM C: For gifted people unfortunate enough to be born in the underdeveloped world, immigration to the U.S. allows them to bloom to their full potential.

PRO-STABILIZATION RESPONSE:

♦ Highly qualified people who move abroad deprive "their own countries of needed skills" and add

another element to the South-North flow of "reverse assistance." (Sadik, A)

Immigration drains skills and energy needed to lift the third-world nations out of their misery. "It is short-sighted to encourage immigration of skilled and professional people.... Why should Pakistan train a doctor to come to America?" (Parsons, B)

Another sign that U.S. immigration policies are not really very humanitarian in their goals is that we do not take the world's most needy but some of the most energetic who have the ambition and drive to make such a move. And many of them are among their country's most educated. (United Nations Population Fund, A)

Africa has lost one-third of its highly educated manpower in recent decades. (United Nations Population Fund, A)

"Take Sierra Leone.... The literacy rate is 15%. The brain drain is almost complete: anyone with the wherewithal has left already." (Kaplan, A)

The immigrant success stories we commonly see in the press never seem to recognize that the person eulogized might have made an equally outstanding contribution at home — where their services are often much in demand. Consider in contrast Govindappa Venkataswamy, M.D. of Maduarai, Tamil Nadu, India. In 1992, the New York Lighthouse for the Blind awarded him its annual Pisart Vision Award for distinguished service in the prevention of blindness, *in his home region.* He had founded and directed the Aravind Eye Hospitals which perform some of the highest volumes of eye surgery in the world. He established a children's hospital in Madurai and a variety of satellite hospitals, clinics and rehabilitation services. Suppose that instead he had decided to emigrate to the U.S. in hope that his skills could bloom to their highest form? (Tanton, E)

CLAIM D: Immigration is a very important type of assistance to third world countries because of the remittances sent back home.

PRO-STABILIZATION RESPONSE:

♦ **The United Nations finds remittances to be of mixed value.** (United Nations Population Fund, A)

Migrants in 1992 sent back some $66 billion in

remittances. Only the sale of oil brings more money into the underdeveloped nations. But studies demonstrate that "remittances are used for current consumption" by the few people who are relatives of the migrants, and contribute almost nothing to the kind of national development that provides permanent improvements for the whole population. (United Nations Population Fund, A)

The Washington Post has reported that many Central American immigrants, for example, send remittances back home in the form of consumer goods — such as electrical appliances for houses without electricity — that are not particularly helpful. A new study published in the *Hispanic Journal of Behavioral Sciences* shows that Mexican communities that have sent large numbers of people to the U.S., "are now in a downward spiral" despite remittances. "Yes, they have raised their lives a bit economically, but it is a pity," said a priest in one town. "The people morally, psychologically, have many problems. The families lose control, they lose unity, they lose the sense of being families." The study described towns devoid of men, where tense and saddened women cope with the responsibilities of running a household alone, trying to earn money to supplement what their husbands send sporadically — or don't send at all." (*San Jose Mercury News*, A)

To some extent remittances improve the diet and health of the families receiving them. But studies in many countries have found that "fewer than one in five wives has received any remittances from husbands who migrate. And when remittances are received, they seldom account for as much as half of the family income." (United Nations Population Fund, A)

CLAIM E: U.S. immigration is an essential safety valve for the overpopulation of the underdeveloped countries.

PRO-STABILIZATION RESPONSE:

♦ **World population grows by some 170 per minute, 10,000 per hour, 250,000 per day. "Each nation has a solemn responsibility to provide for the health, education, employment and security of its own citizens. No nation can expect to solve deficiencies in these areas by exporting its surplus people."** (Tanton, C)

The only way to relieve third-world population pressures is for them to bring their fertility rates down into balance with their much-lowered (at least for now) death rates. Britain's leading medical journal, *The Lancet*, provided a morbid illustration of how impossible it is for immigration to be even a minor part of the solution. If a bomb as destructive as the one that destroyed Hiroshima on Aug. 6, 1945, had been dropped on a different population center of the world every day in every year since then, "it would not have stabilized human numbers." (Browne, A)

"I firmly believe ... that we do neither our homeland nor our planet (including its human members) a favor by acting as a continuing sponge for immigrants from other lands. In doing so, we retard the impetus behind population and economic reforms in other nations..." (Ervin, A)

The U.S. cannot be very credible in preaching environmental responsibility until we reduce consumption and stabilizes our population. Growing by nearly 3 million a year, the U.S. does not project a positive image as world leader. (Abernethy, D)

"We may feel a warm glow of satisfaction by allowing an immigrant to enter the U.S., but that immigrant will soon be consuming his disproportionate share of the world resources as well.... I believe the best role for America is as a model.... We must stabilize our [own] population.... This would require us to restrict immigration — not totally, but dramatically. America, in the 21st century, would be a much better beacon to the world if we developed new policies to face the world's new realities and urged other countries to follow us, rather than being a haven for a relative few abandoning their own countries." (Lamm, A, p.25)

"Fundamental to the concept of national rights and responsibilities is the duty of each nation to match its population with its political, social and environmental resources, in both the short and the long term." (Tanton, B)

CLAIM F: Even if it doesn't do anything for the rest of the impoverished people in the world, immigration at least is helpful to the ones who are able to come.

PRO-STABILIZATION RESPONSE:

♦ **A chance to immigrate to a wealthy country is not**

an unmixed blessing, and can be a curse. (United Nations Population Fund, A)

Not only does their numerical presence accelerate the deterioration of the environment in the U.S., but their immigration doesn't necessarily gain for the immigrants themselves a demonstrably better life.

Immigration often is harmful to the women making the journey, according to the United Nations. "Most educated women end up in the low-status, low-wage production and service jobs as unskilled female migrants... migrant women, especially refugees, are vulnerable to rape, abduction, sexual harassment and physical violence and demands for sexual favors in return for documentation or obtaining goods.... [Women migrants'] status may be improved by migration, but the advantages are not clear cut." (United Nations Population Fund, A)

"Illegal immigrants become indentured servants working in restaurants or sweat shops all day. Some women are forced into prostitution." (*Christian Science Monitor*, A)

Mexican congressmen have visited the U.S. to inspect the living conditions of Mexicans who have immigrated. They have made complaints to human rights organizations about *legal* immigrants who have worked in the U.S. for years but are paid such low wages that they can afford neither the food nor lodging for a "dignified life." Observing immigrants living on wooden pallets under plastic roofs, a Mexican official said: "It distresses us to see our people living under those conditions." (*San Diego Union*, A)

Thousands of immigrants move to big cities where they cram into tiny, illegal rooms. Many of them live in windowless 8 x 10-foot cells, which they share with other immigrants who work and sleep different hours. (*New York Times*, H)

And then there are the stories of immigrants who fled unrest in their countries only to live in urban precincts where the chance of violent death is even higher. When a man who had fled the Sudan was beaten to death while working in the U.S. capital as a pizza deliveryman, a friend noted that the man's father had asked him to forget about America and come back to the Sudan where there aren't as many crazy people. (*The Washington Post*, N)

Many immigrants would like to return home but don't, because of pride or new relationships in the U.S. that make leaving difficult. "Now I can't go back because I would have nothing to show for all the time I spent here," said one immigrant who came from Mexico six years ago. (*The Washington Post*, Y)

The kindest thing an industrial nation can do for a recent immigrant is to stop additional immigration, said Victor Foerster, an attorney in Germany. It is the constant influx of new immigrants that makes life for past immigrants so brutal. A recently enacted German law states: "It is only by applying a consistent and efficient policy of restriction that the indispensable commitment of the German population to the integration of aliens can be ensured. This is a prerequisite for safeguarding social peace." (*The Social Contract*, B)

CLAIM G: The U.S. is the cause of a great deal of pain around the world through its foreign policy, military interventions, multi-national corporate activity and rapacious appetite for natural resources. Allowing immigration from those countries is the least we can do.

PRO-STABILIZATION RESPONSE:

♦ If the U.S. is harming other countries, the prime remedy is to stop. U.S. immigration policies often further harm those nations through the "brain drain," etc.

Because of corrupt practices and disastrous borrowing by leaders of many third-world nations in the past, and loans willingly made by many affluent countries' banks, the underdeveloped world is saddled with debilitating debt. Payments of interest on that debt, combined with other factors, means that the poor nations send more money to rich countries than the poor receive in foreign aid. The net flow of wealth from the poor "South" to the rich "North" is estimated at $200 billion annually. (*Multinational Monitor*, A)

Some persons and organizations concerned about the justice of such economic relationships have suggested that economic refugees are fleeing problems made in the U.S.A.; they are simply following their "confiscated wealth." But it is unclear how taking immigrants from the poor countries addresses any problems in the international monetary and investment system. As contended earlier, emigration often worsens future prospects for the poor countries.

That U.S. policies have sometimes been harmful to other countries is undeniable. One could argue, however, that, on the whole, the U.S. has done more good than harm. (Mehlman, B)

CLAIM H: The immigration debate is between the moral high ground (generosity to striving and needy strangers knocking at our door) and the practical national interest (reduction in numbers).

PRO-STABILIZATION RESPONSE:

♦ **The immigration issue is not right vs. wrong, but right vs. right. The task is to assess costs and benefits for *all* parties concerned, and over the long run.** (Teitelbaum, A; *The Atlantic Monthly*, B)

"The intellectual class has bought the myth that those who support large numbers are generous and those who don't are selfish bigots..." (Betts, C) The morality in this debate is much more complex. "Who suffers as a result of high immigration levels? It is not the wealthy industrialist who realizes greater profits by keeping wage levels down. It is not the upper middle-class family who can afford private schools or the move to affluent suburbs where public schools do the jobs they are supposed to do. Those who suffer the most are our own poor, including recently-arrived immigrants, but especially hard-hit are inner-city blacks." (Oberlink, A)

"Excluding the kooks on the fringes, all sides advocate human rights and justice; none supports persecution and injustice. The disagreement is about which basic rights have precedence over which other basic rights; consensus in such a setting is, unsurprisingly, elusive." (Teitelbaum, A)

Albert A. Bartlett of the University of Colorado and Edward P. Lytwak of Carrying Capacity Network have assembled a list of what they consider morally valid reasons to limit immigration in order to stop U.S. population growth: (Bartlett-Lytwak, A)

- Reduce destruction of the environment.
- Reduce shortages of vital resources such as water, while increasing our margins of safety in times of shortage.
- Preserve resources for the use of future generations.
- Save our society from the large expenditures that are now used to support the increases in population, and allow the resources to be used instead to help achieve better lives for the millions of our citizens who now are largely excluded from the mainstream, and to improve our nation's flexibility in giving aid to the people of developing nations.

- Slow the rise in the cost of housing.
- Reduce the competition for jobs.
- Allow tax revenues to be used to repair our crumbling national infrastructure instead of having to add to it.
- Stop the growth in congestion, pollution, urban violence, and all of the other assaults on the lives and well-being of Americans that are the direct consequences of population growth.
- Slow the growth of big government, litigation, regulation and the ever more restrictive social engineering that is required to manage large growing populations.
- Preserve American representative democracy.
- Set an example for those parts of the world that are currently experiencing the devastation of rapid population growth.

Immigration represents a "raging river cutting its channels through an American society that rapidly is changed in the process. Demographers aren't being parochial when they proclaim that demography is destiny. No government planning could have anticipated the trends of the last 40 years without taking into account the pervasive influence of the Baby Boom bulge. The same now is true for planning without recognizing the enormous changes wrought by the unintended renewal of mass immigration." The prime moral principle of U.S. immigration policy should be that it "first, do no harm." Will adding more than a million immigrants (most of them from underdeveloped countries) move America toward a more egalitarian society or one more closely resembling underdeveloped nations with populations divided between the affluent and the barely-surviving? Will besieged school systems find it easier to provide sufficient building space and teaching resources for their children if the federal government imports hundreds of thousands more English-deficient students into their districts? Labor economist Vernon Briggs wrote recently in *The New York Times*: "Immigration reform is not a panacea. But unless our immigration policy is changed, any urban programs are doomed to failure." (Center for Immigration Studies, A)

It is important to note that among those who support high immigration and population growth are those who benefit directly: immigration lawyers, immigrant group power brokers, architects, real estate developers, landowners, banks, industrialists looking for a loose labor market. Although they have the democratic right to lobby for their self-interest, "let's be honest: the pressure to bring more people into the community comes from many sources, and it has more to do with making money than it does with kindness and sharing." (Hardin, E)

Katherine Betts, an Australian sociologist, has developed a theory in her book, *Ideology and Immigration*, that the elite classes of her country, Canada and the U.S. advocate high immigration — somewhat subconsciously — as a way to distinguish themselves as morally superior to the working and poor classes who overwhelmingly reject immigration. (Betts, C)

CLAIM I: The promotion of the idea of blacks as victims of immigration is a sad attempt to divide the people of color and distract them from their opportunity to forge a powerful coalition to win advances for blacks, Hispanics, Asians and other immigrants together.

PRO-STABILIZATION RESPONSE:

♦ **"All immigrants fight for jobs and space.... They displace what and whom they can. Although U.S. history is awash in labor battles, political fights, and property wars among all religious and ethnic groups, their struggles are persistently framed as struggles between recent arrivals and blacks."** (Morrison, A)

"The nation a generation ago, in rare unity, launched perhaps its greatest moral crusade: to eliminate racism and to bring blacks into the economic mainstream. Since then, by winking at the failure to enforce our immigration laws, we have inadvertently done the one thing that could most effectively sabotage that crusade. We have allowed the almost unfettered entry of competition for entry level jobs, at which the blacks could be starting their entry into the economy.... It is not enough to argue that the immigrant — hungry and fearful of deportation — will work harder. One must also answer the question: The blacks are Americans; how do we bring the increasingly alienated, restless and isolated ghetto blacks into the system?" (Grant, D)

Affirmative action — created to compensate for centuries of discrimination against blacks — now is being used by immigrant groups to gain jobs at the expense of black jobholders. (*Christian Science Monitor*, F; *Staten Island Sunday Advance*, A)

Blacks have been squeezed into a smaller segment of the economy, said Roger Waldinger, a UCLA sociologist who has studied competition for jobs between less-educated, less-skilled blacks and immigrants in Los Angeles County: "The census data show dramatic declines in African-American employment in fields where immigrants made big gains. Since

1980 while the number of black, U.S.-born bank tellers fell 39% to 3,555, the figure for foreign-born tellers climbed 56% to 15,679. Likewise, while employment of African-American hotel maids and housemen dropped 30% to 2,846, the immigrant total skyrocketed 166% to 32,273." (*Los Angeles Times*, B)

Businesses and hospitals, public schools and even the state government of California, are all routinely meeting their minority workforce goals by hiring foreign workers rather than blacks. (*San Jose Mercury News*, B)

Universities across the country show a clear preference for recruiting foreign-born professional-track students instead of working with American blacks. Doctoral-level funds go disproportionately to foreign students; blacks have to borrow. "Forty percent of doctorates are foreign born and 40% of them stay in the U.S." (Morris, B)

The U.S. has more physicians from India (22,312) than native-born black physicians (17,005). (Center for Immigration Studies, C)

One of the most significant effects of recent mass immigration is the way it appears to be driving lower-skilled blacks out of traditionally higher-paying urban centers and back to the South. (Frey, A)

For the last two decades of high immigration, the net flow has been out of major urban centers.

This reverse migration is historically troubling. Various economists and historians have shown that blacks' progress this century has come primarily when foreign immigration was low. When immigration numbers rose early this century, blacks — as now — were driven out of industrial centers. "When the rate of immigration declines, black migration to the North and West increases; when the rate of immigration increases, black migration (to high-paying centers) declines." (Frost, A)

It can be hypothesized with some certainty that had there been high immigration during the 1940s, '50s and '60s, there would not have been a successful civil rights movement. Consider:

- The main reason blacks' economic status rose during the first half of the 20th century was because of black migration out of the South. (Donohue-Heckman, A)
- That black migration was spurred by the cutoff of immigration from Europe. (Smith-Welch, A)
- At the end of the depression, with virtually no immigration for the previous 15 years, the migration of blacks from the South accelerated. "The outmigration of blacks from the South after 1940 was the greatest single economic step forward in black history, and a major advance toward the integration of blacks into the mainstream of American life." (Wright, A)
- Tight labor markets in the 1940s and 1950s, when there were few immigrants to interfere, helped blacks make extraordinary economic advances. (Donohue-Heckman, A)
- Impressive improvement in the relative economic status of blacks during those years of low immigration after 1940 "is largely an untold story that belies widely held views of black stagnation."

While the real incomes of white males expanded two-and-one-half-fold between 1940 and 1980, they quadrupled for black men! Even the wages of black college graduates grew 45% faster than those of white graduates during that 40-year period.
(Smith-Welch, A)

- The civil rights laws of the 1960s clearly helped boost blacks' economic opportunities for the next decade. But the racial wage gap narrowed just as rapidly prior to affirmative action as afterward. "This suggests that ... education and migration were the primary determinants..." of black wages rising toward the level of white wages. (Smith-Welch, A)

- Because of the massive loss of cheap black labor, southern industries after 1940 had to mechanize and improve the education and working conditions for the blacks who remained. "In 1940 the *raison d'etre* of southern state governments was the protection of white supremacy and social stability; 30 years later their central purpose was the promotion of business and industrial development. This change ... ultimately made possible the success for the civil rights revolution of the 1950s and 1960s." (Wright, A)

In short, having a low level of foreign immigration set in motion the chain of events that led to rapid economic advancement and full civil rights for the descendants of slavery.

Unfortunately, progress toward black/white economic equity stalled in the mid-1970s at about the same time as immigration levels began to rise to historically high levels. By 1964, the aggregate black earnings had risen to 62% of that of whites. They continued to rise until stalling at 72% in 1973. Since then they have fallen back to 69% in 1987. (Donohue-Heckman, A)

It is not surprising then that the black family structure suffered immensely in the three decades since the immigration law was changed in 1965. In the 1950s, black women married at higher proportions than did white women. "By 1991, the proportion of black women who do not ever marry had reached an incredible figure of 25%.... This figure is three times higher than the comparable percentage for white women. The major explanation for the disparity" is the shrinking pool of black men able to earn a living in the regular economy that is sufficient to support a family. This is especially true of 16-to-24-year-olds who cannot seem to get those all-important entry-level jobs. "The consequential effect on black family structure has been devastating. In 1990, 57.6% of all black births were out of wedlock." (Briggs, A, pp.214-215)

"Immigration policy was not purposely intended to harm black Americans, but it has done just that. The longer it is allowed to function as a political policy, the worse are the economic prospects for blacks." (Briggs, A, pp.214-215)

CLAIM J: It is selfish to put the needs of Americans ahead of more desperate people in other nations by denying them entry into our country, and it is especially offensive to the Judeo-Christian ethical tradition that continues to guide the majority of Americans.

PRO-STABILIZATION RESPONSE:

♦ **If our standard is to put our own poor aside in order to help the most needy people of the world, then virtually none of our current immigrants would qualify — because they are among the more energetic and resourceful of third-world citizens.** (Mishan, A)

♦ **Throughout history, acting in *self-interest* for one's own people generally has not been considered morally *selfish*.** (Lachs, A)

♦ **"The union and fellowship of men will be best preserved if each receives from us the more kindness in proportion as he is more closely connected with us."** (Roman: Cicero, *De Off.* I. xvi.)

♦ **"...every good man, who is right-minded, loves and cherishes his own."** (Greek: Homer, *Illiad*, ix. 340)

♦ **"I ought not to be unfeeling like a statue but should fulfill both my natural and artificial relations, as a worshipper, a son, a brother, a father, and a citizen."** (Greek: Epictetus, iii. 24)

♦ **The general rule is that the poor of your town come before the poor of any other town."** (Jewish: see Manson, A)

♦ **"If any provide not for his own, and specially for those of his own house, he hath denied the faith."** (Christian: I Timothy 5:8)

Philosopher John Lachs of Vanderbilt University has reflected on ethical thought into antiquity and concluded that there is a near universal standard that people's moral obligations generally are heaviest toward people who are the most connected. That is not to say that one should have no concern for people in other lands. "Morality would be vastly simplified if we could assert that all human beings are equally worthy of respect and leave the matter at that. Of course, this would place vast duties on us, for we would end up owing everybody everything." Since such a moral standard would be so impossible it could lead to people taking no responsibility at all for others, civilizations have assumed a hierarchy of responsibility not unlike that of Epictetus above. "One's own children cannot be told to get in line with all those needing to be fed; the fact that they are ours gives them priority and imposes overriding obligations on us. Similarly, citizens of a nation stand in a special relation to one another, and that relation is the source of special duties. The mutuality of our burdens and benefits as citizens is what justifies the duty to pay taxes and to contribute to the national defense.... Open immigration is incompatible with the welfare and educational benefits offered in this (U.S.) country.... The moral course does not consist of following high-minded principles wherever they may lead, but of doing what good we can, given the costs and consequences of available actions." (Lachs, A)

Americans are an exceptionally generous people. It is a tribute to their sensitivity to others that many feel a need to help some of them by allowing immigration to the United States. The impulse is both humanistic and religious. The majority of Americans hear strong messages from holy texts and religious leaders encouraging generosity to foreigners who might be passing through or perhaps wanting to stay. But religious adherents also "recognize the difficulty of converting isolated scriptural passages into complex public policy. For (them), immigration laws no less than police forces, armies, tax collectors, and prisons are regretable but necessary expressions of our search for a measure of security and order in our human community flawed by sin. Prudence — the virtue that requires us to 'count the cost' — like love, has high standing in the Christian tradition." (Simcox, B)

Religious advocates of immigration often marvel that in the midst of the narrow legalisms of the Levitical Code for the ancient Israelites, there is this call for a kind of universalism: "When an alien settles with you in your land, you shall not oppress him. He shall be treated as a native born among you, and you shall love him as a man like yourself, because you were aliens in Egypt. I am the Lord your God." (Leviticus 19: 33-34, [NEB]) Some immigration advocates interpret that as a requirement to grant permanent residency in the U.S. with all rights of citizenship to whomever can make a case of strong need.

For Christians, there additionally are many teachings of Jesus to love one's neighbor, to love one's enemy, to emulate the behavior of the "good Samaritan" and give assistance to those in need even when it is inconvenient or breaks taboos. Perhaps the strongest humanitarian teaching comes in Jesus' Parable of the Last Judgment. Matthew writes that he offered the parable just before his trial and crucifixion. In the illustration, all nations are gathered, with the people separated into the blessed and the damned. The king banishes the damned into eternal fire for having failed to feed him when he was hungry and to give him shelter when he was "a stranger." The damned say they never remember having seen the king in such straits. To that, the king answers, "Truly, I say to you, as you did it not to one of the least of these, you did it not to me." (Matthew 25:31-56, [RSV])

Most Christians, and adherents of other religions, consider such teachings of values and principles to be essential ingredients in what it means to be a good person and to behave ethically. Nonetheless, most see the principles as ones that must be weighed and balanced in some complexity with other worthy principles before dictating an individual action, let alone public policy for a whole society. Michael Josephson, a teacher of ethics, reminds his listeners that some values can "trump" others. Presbyterian minister Robert Kyser comments: "One might teach a child to never tell a lie but when the storm trooper is asking the whereabouts of Anne Frank, the value of preserving a life trumps the value of not telling a lie. It seems to me that the value of opening America's doors to those who come to escape persecution trumps the value of providing for those who seek economic betterment, and that stabilizing America's population to preserve the blessings of liberty as well as the integrity of physical resources trumps the value of feeling good about having extended the welcome mat." Church people sometimes take on humanitarian projects of bringing foreign citizens into their community without thinking far enough ahead. "The burden of support often falls on the schools and the social service establishment, perhaps even the criminal justice system — an obligation that the wider community may not have wished to undertake..." (Kyser, A)

From ethical philosophy, Lachs suggests that although individuals can legitimately choose a self-sacrificial path of action, it would be inappropriate for them to insist that the entire community has a moral obligation to do the same. "The moral injunction is to take due account of others, not to refuse to take ourselves into account. Self-sacrifice reaches beyond the sphere of ethics; if we demand it as an element of basic decency, it erodes moral resolve.... Self-interest in such cases is not narrowly selfish. We are, after all, looking out for *our* good, not each for his or her grubby self. And the people we wish to benefit are fellow citizens with whom we share the enterprise of life..." (Lachs, A)

Gerda Bikales, a Nazi Holocaust survivor, notes: "The appeal to our conscience is not for us to share the misery of the most miserable on this Earth, but to improve their lives through our acts of compassion and generosity.... The wise sharing of our possessions, rather than their renunciation, is the paradigm we seek." A nation of good-hearted mendicants who met every need they encountered could not long sustain itself and very quickly would be unable to help anybody. (Bikales, A)

To the degree that Americans do not harm other nations, they need not be apologetic about taking seriously the needs of their own country. (McConnell, A)

Said the Rev. Jesse L. Jackson during the debate over the free trade agreement with Mexico: "How can we push for relief in the jobs situation in Mexico when we haven't addressed the unemployment problem facing people of color in this country?" (*Washington Post*, G)

Many Hispanic-American elected officials also opposed the agreement, saying the country's priority responsibility was to help poor Hispanic Americans before people in Latin American countries. "It shows we care about our Latin American brothers and sisters, but we also care about ourselves and about the country that adopted us," said U.S. Rep. Robert Menendez, D-N.J. (*New York Times*, B)

Those black and Hispanic American leaders were in keeping with the old Jewish law: "As between relatives and poor strangers, relatives come first..." (Manson, B)

What do Americans owe the poor in other nations besides doing them no harm? Through religious and other private charities and through taxes distributed in the form of foreign aid, Americans attempt to assist the rest of the world. Perhaps the amount should be higher. Perhaps it should be given more efficiently and directed in ways that are more helpful. But there is no clear moral or ethical teaching that suggests that taking large numbers of immigrants is a requirement.

"We cannot think clearly about ... ethical problems if we begin by asserting the moral irrelevance of nations.... (they) exist and (provide) the defining context and the structuring elements of the moral problems that surround immigration." The plight of people in other countries unable to improve themselves by moving to the U.S. causes some Americans discomfort and makes them feel "embarrassed at our undeserved good fortune." But even with the best of intentions, Americans cannot revise the moral structure of the world. They can be fair, forthright, avoid discrimination and be helpful where possible. (Lachs, A)

"Prudence is the quality that leads men and women to organize themselves into nation-states in their common search for peace, order and justice. Civic prudence requires each member of a national community to give the first claim on his concern to fellow members. Prudence is that quality that makes us realize that, while the love that we owe all other human beings should be without bounds, the means we have to give expression to that love have limits. It is with prudence that even churches lock their doors at night." (Simcox, B)

Even by allowing the current unprecedented level of immigration, the U.S. still refuses entry to most of the world's needy people who are hungry, naked and without shelter and would like to come in. And thus it always will be — a continuous process of line-drawing choices, saying yes to some and necessarily no to others, and balancing one moral claim against many others. (The Forum, National Presbyterian Church, A)

CLAIM K: Those countries with lots of land and moderate population are obligated to share space with countries with little land and big populations. Or if environmentalists insist that every country is overpopulated, what does it matter if people move freely from one overpopulated country to another?

PRO-STABILIZATION RESPONSE:

♦ **"To globalize the economy by erasure of national economic boundaries through free trade, free capital mobility, and free, or at least uncontrolled migration, is to wound fatally the major unit of community capable of carrying out any policies for the common good."** (Daly, A)

♦ **"And they shall build houses and inhabit them, and they shall plant vineyards and eat the fruit of them."** (Isaiah 65:21)

An important part of Lutheran "two-kingdom" theology is that the civil kingdom has the responsibility for maintaining "good order in society." The Southern Baptists evaluate government with the understanding that God ordained governments to reward and protect moral behavior. (*Prophets and Politics*, A) If there are no boundaries, and if anybody in the world can harvest the benefit of somebody else's sacrifice — indeed if citizens of one country are not allowed to "eat the fruit of the vineyards they have planted" — then we will have irradicated most incentives for environmentally responsible behavior, and probably, soon after, environmental quality itself.

"There exists no right to be able to move into and occupy someone else's country.... The right to control immigration is an important one, since immigration can become a form of conquest... It is not right that future generations should be doomed to live in continuous turmoil and confrontation." (Thomay, A)

"To try to admit all who want to come here because others fail to stabilize their populations within their carrying capacity limits would ultimately create world-wide poverty..." (Population-Environment Balance, A)

By limiting fertility, a nation manages to keep its environment attractive. If that obligates the nation to take another nation's excess population, "all cultures and societies will be threatened with obliteration unless they enter into a competitive breeding contest. Those cultures that reproduce the most would be presumed to have the moral authority to take over other societies. (Mehlman, B)

Argument No. 15

Demographic Transition

GENERAL CLAIM: Immigration will decline naturally if we . . .

HELP DEVELOP THE THIRD WORLD

GENERAL PRO-STABILIZATION RESPONSE:

♦ **Here is yet another "if" proposition. With millions of people on the U.S. immigration backlog list and with indications that millions more would sign up if they thought there was any hope of getting in, limitation by natural forces is a pipe dream for now.**

The "demographic transition" and related theories are the "silver bullets" that everybody would like to find for America's environmental and social problems. The demographic transition theory itself hypothesizes that if we just devote enough resources to help develop some 150 poor countries, their residents will automatically lower their fertility. Related theories hold that with improved economic status and lowered fertility in those nations, residents will be so content that they won't want to come to the U.S., and our population will stabilize. This is a wonderful thought for generous-hearted people who don't want to confront the conflict between their humanitarian ideals about immigrants and their ideals about the survival of our nation's environmental resources. Conservatives and liberals alike embrace the theories because it helps them avoid tough decisions. (Linden, B) The theories are great ideas — if only they could work in the next few decades before the U.S. moves toward China-like density.

CLAIM A: We won't have to reduce the level of legal immigration if we help raise the standard of living in the sending countries. Current immigration slots will go unfilled as people decide to stay home.

PRO-STABILIZATION RESPONSE:

♦ **"The statement reflects unconscious hubris. The U.S. cannot save the world."** (Grant, E)

♦ **Forty years of development assistance to the third world has not decreased immigration pressure but increased it.** (Zurcher, A)

While advanced nations may wish to continue offering assistance to improve the lot of third-world citizens, the advanced nations cannot afford to wait for the immigration push factors to cease, in the view of Peter Thompkins, former chief of British Immigration Service. The developed nations have no choice but to act decisively now if they are to protect the civilization of their own citizens. (Thompkins, A)

Any serious assessment of the world situation will show that even under the very best of scenarios and the most extravagant aid possible, standards of living in under-developed nations cannot become competitive with advanced nations for many decades, according to professor Antonio Golini of the Institute for Population Research in Italy. Thus, the immigration push factors will remain in place. If the advanced nations were to relax immigration controls until the push factors disappeared, their populations likely would multiply several times over. (Golini, A)

The prognosis is even more dismal, according to Professor H. J. Hoffman-Novotny of Zurich: If living conditions by some miracle did rise high enough in underdeveloped nations so that their residents would stop fleeing, the world environment would be devastated by the additional resource consumption and pollution. (Hoffman-Novotny, A)

Prospects for such economic success, however, are unlikely, in the dark view of *New York Times* correspondent Malcolm Browne: Anybody who actually thinks foreign aid can soon eliminate "push" factors in the third world doesn't know the hopelessness overpopulation has created. "The third world is not a 'developing' culture. It is a putrefying state of existence perpetually in the grip of a plague deadlier than anthrax: the burgeoning human race.... For the past dozen years I have devoted most of my reporting to science.... I have become convinced that until population growth can be controlled, all other environmental problems will remain insoluble." (Browne, A)

CLAIM B: The demographic transition theory explains that if the standard of living were improved in immigrant-sending countries, fertility would automatically fall and the countries no longer would have an overpopulation problem driving people away.

PRO-STABILIZATION RESPONSE:

♦ **In at least some instances, economic improvement actually has increased fertility in the third world. And societies denied the escape valve of sending immigrants, often lower their fertility.** (Abernethy, B)

♦ **Even if enough aid could cause the "demographic transition" to occur tomorrow and all third-world countries adopted replacement-level fertility, it still would be another half-century before those countries stopped creating excess population. World population would have grown another 50% by then.** (McCarthy, B)

Since World War II, wealthy countries have been pouring aid into underdeveloped countries. The aid has reduced mortality dramatically. Far fewer children die. The aid introduces miraculous-appearing technology into pre-modern societies. "Trouble is, it often turns out that people have more children as their sense of well-being increases, particularly when technological advance or government largesse give them the idea that the old limits no longer apply." (Linden, B)

The phrase "development is the best contraceptive" is by now rather worn, having been touted vigorously by delegates from developing countries at the 1974 World Population Conference. The rationale for this phrase was that Europe and North America over the previous two centuries had experienced marked decline in fertility as they became more prosperous. But cause and effect are difficult to sort out, and there is strong evidence that declining fertility helps lead to prosperity. (Ryerson, A)

"For decades we believed — and some still believe — that the answer to high fertility was better education, lower infant mortality and a higher standard of living. We were assured that these developments would lower families' preferred number of children, and that fertility rates would fall as modern contraception became available. Unfortunately, clues that the model did not work started to accumulate early on." (Abernethy, E)

"If development does work as a contraceptive, it appears to have a high failure rate." (Ryerson, A)

Africa received three times as much foreign aid per capita as any other continent. Health care availability increased. Literacy for women rose. General economic optimism pervaded more and more sectors of society. But African fertility rates climbed to where they surpassed all other continents. (Abernethy, E)

Perhaps these results should not have been so surprising. Americans, giddy with post-war optimism, promptly accelerated their fertility to create the famous Baby Boom of 1947-1964.

"Family-size targets stay high or rise when people think that limits that formerly operated have been relieved." Traditional cultures around the world for centuries had restrained fertility to keep it in balance with the resources at hand. Any windfall of resources — such as industrialized societies bearing gifts — frequently results in a population explosion in the society being helped. More water wells for the pastoralists of the African Sahel promoted larger herd size, earlier marriage (because the bride price is paid in animals), and much higher fertility. Land redistribution in Turkey promoted a larger family size among formerly landless peasants. The introduction of the potato into Ireland in about 1745 increased agricultural productivity and caused a baby boom. (Abernethy, B)

Few, however, would advocate using poverty as a sure-fire method to reduce fertility, although examples abound of poverty's ability to do that. When Mexican unemployment rose 40-50% during the 1980s, fertility fell significantly. Sudan's fertility dropped 17% during the late 1980s at a time of extreme deterioration of the economy. Brazil experienced a similar trend in the 1980s. Despite those examples, "improved economic conditions in many societies may actually lead to reductions in fertility levels." But there is no clear understanding of the length of time that must elapse. (Ryerson, A)

The primary demographic answer for the poor nations is to help them reduce their fertility long before their economic situation improves. A society simply does not need rising income, better education, increasing urbanization and improved status for women to lower fertility — a change that then will make it easier to improve income, education and status of women. In every country studied, the average woman wants fewer children than she is having. "Of all the foreign aid that flows from rich to poor countries, a mere 1% goes to family planning.... Of all the mistakes we've made in family planning, the

worst has been not keeping up with the contraceptive demand. Because of this... the world's population growth is on a faster track than it otherwise would be."
(Potts-Campbell, A)

Allowing a community to export its excess population raises the likelihood that a nation's fertility will remain high or increase. (Abernethy, B)

It is extremely important for Americans to seek the most effective ways to help the third-world countries that send so many of their citizens to our doorstep. But no such effort should be considered a substitute for protecting the U.S. from being overwhelmed by those immigrants in the meantime. If the people of the underdeveloped world stopped having babies today, their nations still would have excess workers to export for decades to come. "Based on persons already born, the work force in the third world will see a net increase by 2010 of 800 million — a third more than all those currently employed in the developed world. Unemployment and under-employment rates in the less-developed countries are already 40% or more in many instances. The developed countries are cutting jobs left and right.... The future will see more and more people seeking to fill a job base that already is not broad enough to provide decent employment for existing applicants."
(McCarthy, B)

Argument No. 16

Fatalism

GENERAL CLAIM: We cannot stabilize population by limiting immigration because . . .

IMMIGRANTS CAN'T BE STOPPED

GENERAL PRO-STABILIZATION RESPONSE:

♦ **A country that concedes it cannot control who enters, abdicates its existence as a sovereign nation.**

♦ **Over the last three years, European countries have demonstrated numerous actions at the national level that can control immigration.** (Jenks, A)

If true, the "fatalism" argument would render meaningless any discussion of the previous arguments. If you can't do anything about it anyway, why bother? We might as well grab our share of happiness while we can as the population marches on toward a half-billion. But before conceding that future, we had better take a closer look. It is difficult not to wonder if some fatalists benefit from inaction and are merely trying to avoid dealing with all the other issues surrounding immigration.

The "fatalism" premise is based primarily on America's experience over the last 25 years with illegal aliens. It seems that no matter how many national commissions study the problem, how much national debate and media exposure and how much legislation, foreign citizens continue to pour across our border with impunity. The TV news footage of aliens scaling fences, charging through crossing check-points, wading rivers, making amphibious landings, and of TV personalities buying fake ID cards on streets corners creates an understandable impression that immigrants simply can't be stopped, if they really want to move here. And if that is true, what's the point of limiting legal immigration? Perhaps this argument should have been placed at the front of the book. If the reader is convinced after this chapter that there is no possibility that the U.S. can control its borders, the discussion in the rest of the book doesn't really matter.

Probably unconsciously, policy-makers and the media routinely operate as though they believe the "fatalism" argument. Rarely do stories about mounting traffic congestion, for example, mention the immigration component. Of course, reporters rarely hear public policy people make the connection, either.

"Politicians, planners and concerned citizens in my state of California keep debating how to solve such worsening problems as urban sprawl, environmental degradation (including the paving over of prime agricultural land), traffic congestion and bulging school enrollments. They correctly identify the growth of the population from 10.6 million in 1950 to 20 million in 1970 to 30 million (in 1992) as the major underlying factor. But the debate never rises above 'managing growth' to the more global questions: is population growth an eternal 'given' and, if not, what is needed to stop it?" (Burke, B)

Despite all the study, talk and legislation, however, there really has been relatively little action aimed at curbing illegal immigration into this country.

CLAIM A: Reducing the number of people who enter legally will just increase the number who, in desperation, come illegally.

PRO-STABILIZATION RESPONSE:

♦ The inverse — that fewer legal admissions will result in fewer illegal entries — may very well be the case. Legal immigrants, by sending home cash, goods and information, encourage others to migrate.
(Tanton, G)

In 1994, Greece, Italy, Portugal and Spain acted on the proposition that legal immigration accelerates illegal immigration. All four essentially shut down their legal entry programs as a method of controlling illegal aliens.
(*Migration News*, A)

A profound change can happen in a third-world community when its first resident migrates to the U.S. Letters describe marvelous affluence and contain remittances of what must seem like large amounts of money. These encourage other members of the community to consider emigrating. The more who go, the more relatives and acquaintances there are in the U.S. to house new migrants and ease their way into the new society. Once the pull of stories from America enters a community and the migration stream is established, legalities become a minor consideration for people in foreign communities. The migration accelerates with or without legal permission; a large community of legal immigrants in the U.S. makes it easier for the illegal aliens to avoid detection and to operate in the underground economy. (Tanton, G)

Federal statistics since 1965 indicate that illegal immigration has increased nearly every year that legal immigration has increased.
(Center for Immigration Studies, D)

CLAIM B: We can never control a 2,000-mile border with Mexico, a third-world country next to the world's most prosperous.

PRO-STABILIZATION RESPONSE:

♦ **Most of the U.S.-Mexico border is such harsh and desolate desert and mountains as to be impassable to all but the toughest of aliens. Only 200 miles need heavy patrolling.** (Federation for American Immigration Reform, C)

Efforts to fortify the border over the last few years have shown what is possible along the busiest sections. One gauge of effectiveness is the number of apprehensions — fewer arrests are generally considered a sign that fewer illegal aliens are crossing the border. Better fencing in the San Diego sector resulted in a 6% decline in illegal alien apprehensions the first year while nationwide apprehensions were going up by 5%. (High, A) An increased-manpower effort, Operation Hold The Line in El Paso, has reduced apprehensions by nearly three-quarters. (Center for Immigration Studies, D)

About 90% of all illegal alien crossings occur near 10 cities along 200 miles of the U.S.-Mexico border. (Federation for American Immigration Reform, D)

In 1993, the border patrol had only 3,700 officers for the entire country, about 3,400 of them on the Mexican border. (INS)

By contrast, Germany — only the size of the states of Washington and Oregon — has 4 400 Border Police patrolling just its eastern boundary. (Jenks, A)

Recent Border Patrol experiments have shown that by

adding officers, the border really can be sealed against illegal entry by undocumented workers, organized crime functionaries, terrorists and drug smugglers. An increase in the border officers to 9,900, along with structural measures, should be enough to essentially stop large-scale illegal crossings. (Federation for American Immigration Reform, D)

"Silvestre Reyes, chief of the Border Patrol (in El Paso), accomplished something no other officer of the Immigration and Naturalization Serve ever had. He got the border in his sector under control. Not just for a brief, flashy demonstration, but permanently. El Paso had been the nation's second busiest border crossing for illegal aliens. Every day, 8,000 or more people waded across the Rio Grande, then melted into the city's Hispanic neighborhoods. But in September 1993, Mr. Reyes devised a new border-control tactic. He positioned 400 of his officers right on the border, forming a blockade of sorts. It brought illegal immigration to a virtual halt. The strategy has been in effect for a year now, and the border here remains generally quiet. With that, Mr. Reyes is dispelling the widely held belief that the nation's borders cannot be controlled without Draconian, police-state tactics." (*New York Times*, I)

The new preventative deployment of the Border Patrol in El Paso is both more humane and more effective. Besides dramatically curbing illegal entry, it also has decreased complaints against the Border Patrol by Hispanic residents and citizens of the U.S., reduced car theft and petty crimes, and shown long-term benefits for legal job seekers and the conditions of unemployment.
(Martin, Jack, C)

CLAIM C: Proposals that might be successful in controlling the southern border would be prohibitively expensive.

PRO-STABILIZATION RESPONSE:

♦ **The El Paso experiment demonstrates that the Border Patrol is able to sustain an effective,, continuous front-line border control presence within available resources.** (Center for Immigration Studies, D)

A beefed-up border presence as at El Paso does deplete officer ranks for other interior functions, suggesting the need for more officers. Where additional resources are required, the cost could easily be covered by a proposed border-crossing fee and by better collection of fees already authorized. (Federation for American Immigration Reform, D)

The overall Immigration and Naturalization Service is so poorly supported by Congress that it doesn't even have personnel to open all of its mail. "Many of the envelopes contain checks and cash — application fees that could be fed into the I.N.S. budget.... Airlines and cruise ships collect $6 from each passenger arriving in the U.S., and they are supposed to turn that money over to the I.N.S. But the Justice Department found that the agency was failing to collect the fees from 22 airlines and six cruise lines — a loss of as much as $23 million a year.... Nationwide, the Justice Department found, the immigration service failed to collect about $38 million in bond money in the last six years." (*New York Times*, J)

Additional money could be collected through various congressional proposals for border fees of between $1 and $3 per pedestrian per crossing and around $5 for each private vehicle. Some fee money could be used to create more and better border inspection lanes so that people crossing legally would be able to move more easily and faster, improving commercial and personal relationships among the people on both sides of the border.

Reduced fees for frequent border crossers could minimize or eliminate any hardship for people who routinely cross the border legally for their livelihood.

CLAIM D: Even if borders are totally sealed against illegal entry, it must be remembered that more than half of illegal aliens in this country arrived lawfully but failed to leave when their time was up. As a democracy with a high regard for human rights, the U.S. never will be able to take the draconian measures necessary to keep track of legal visitors and deport them when their visas expire.

PRO-STABILIZATION RESPONSE:

♦ **In the past three years, European democracies have taken major steps to rid themselves of unwanted guests. Their methods have included specific protections to prevent violations of civil rights or privacy.** (Jenks, B)

Immigration expert David North in a paper for the Organization for Economic Cooperation and Development in 1991 called attention to the dilemma facing industrialized democracies. The democratic traditions and rule of law that make these nations attractive to illegal aliens also make it difficult for the nations to withstand the migrating masses, he wrote. But he included an important qualifier: "It is not that immigration control is impossible. I suggest that democracies do not control well because they are reluctant to ... be tough-minded enough to inflict pain on otherwise law-abiding disadvantaged persons in order to manage international migration effectively." (*The Social Contract*, B)

North's paper was much-discussed and debated by immigration officials throughout Europe. Within a year, Europeans were in such an uproar about uncontrolled illegal immigration, that their governments acted quickly and decisively, proving North correct in saying it *is* possible for a democratic nation to reassert its sovereignty.

Asylum claimants have been the largest source of illegal immigration for the affluent European nations. As in the U.S., the pattern was to claim asylum and then get lost in the populations of the country while their cases were pending. Tens of thousands of Eastern Europeans entered this way, seeking jobs, as did millions from the former Yugoslavia and Soviet Union. The following actions helped Western European nations regain control (although not absolute control) of their borders. Thus far, there has been no public outcry that the European people have lost any essential ingredient of a democratic and humane society. (Jenks, A) The following items, compiled by immigration researcher Rosemary Jenks, detail some of the successful actions:

- Governments allocated more resources for border guards and other border control efforts.

- "Most European governments consider employer sanctions against hiring illegal aliens to be an integral component of national labor policy. Sanctions have been more effective in Europe than in the United States for three main reasons: (1) sanctions have been in force, in most cases, since the 1970s, so they have been fine-tuned and standardized to a greater degree; (2) sanctions are generally enforced by the labor department, rather than immigration authorities, as a routine part of labor inspections; and (3) most European countries have a single, standard identification system to establish work eligibility. These systems include national identity cards, as in France; national population registries, as in Scandinavia; tamper-resistant social security cards for work authorization purposes, as in Germany; and national alien registries, as in the Netherlands. Welfare agencies and other public service offices are often linked to these systems to prevent welfare abuse and identify illegal aliens... There has been very little concern that civil rights or privacy are being violated."

- All European Union countries except Greece, Ireland and Luxembourg have overhauled their asylum policies since 1992. Most have shortened the decision-making process so that rejected asylum-seekers are returned to their country of origin almost immediately. A $20-million investment in personnel and computer equipment enabled the French asylum office to reduce processing time from up to five years to an average of two months. Its backlog of applications was reduced from 50,000 to 15,000 in the first year.

- Austria, France, Germany, the Netherlands, Sweden, Switzerland and the United Kingdom summarily eject asylum-seekers who have come directly from a third "safe" country. Even if they are from a country in turmoil, they are rejected if they have come through a country in which persecution does not exist. After all, the purpose of asylum is to protect against death or persecution. As soon as a person arrives in a safe country, there is no legitimate asylum reason to travel on to yet another safe country and ask for asylum there.

- "European governments have recognized that it is not feasible to attempt to manage immigration solely from the national level." They are in the process of creating a computerized fingerprint system for asylum seekers and legally-resident aliens that will enable them to know when they are dealing with somebody who has abused the system previously or who has been rejected by another country. Such persons in all EU countries automatically are to be rejected.

- In many European countries, asylum seekers awaiting decision about whether they may remain must stay in government-run "reception" centers so they can be easily deported if denied entrance. Asylum seekers generally are not granted permission to work (unlike the U.S.) until their application is approved.

- All European Union countries have agreed to admit no foreign workers unless they will be doing tasks for which there are no available workers in all EU nations. Furthermore, the workers can be granted only temporary permission to enter the countries.

- Chain family migration has been halted. Family reunification in most countries is limited to spouses and minor children — no parents, adult children, siblings, etc., though there are some exceptions. Austria, France and the Netherlands stipulate that a sponsor for family members must have lived in the country legally for a designated period (ranging from two to seven years) and have adequate income and housing to provide for the new immigrants. Such a measure in Denmark reduced the number of family-based immigrants by 50%.

In addition to all those European measures not yet adopted by the U.S., various members of Congress have proposed the following measures: (Federation for American Immigration Reform, D)

- Remove the profit motive for alien smuggling. Add the crime to those covered by the Racketeer Influenced and Corrupt Organization (RICO) Act. Arrested smugglers could have to forfeit all property in any way connected to their trade.

• Make the owners of boats, buses, trains and planes that bring people into the country accountable for making sure nobody gets on board without proper documentation and permission to come to the U.S. One proposal would establish a maximum ratio of document violators to total passengers. When that ratio was exceeded, the fine would be $10,000 to $20,000 for each alien brought in violation of the law. Carriers averaging more than two violations per arrival would forfeit landing rights in the U.S. for the next year.

• State and local law enforcement agencies would be required to notify the INS when they arrest an alien, whether legal or illegal. Courts would begin deportation hearings at the time aliens are sentenced for their crimes so they can be shipped directly from prison to their home country when they are released.

• Any foreigner convicted of a crime of assault, guilty of violating any immigration law such as visa provisions or caught entering the nation illegally, would forever lose the privilege of getting in line for legal admission.

• Local and state governments that failed to screen out illegal aliens for specified social services and that didn't cooperate fully with federal authorities in apprehending illegal aliens would suffer severe losses of federal financial assistance.

• Persons granted asylum would have to leave the U.S. if during their first three years in the country, (1) conditions in their home country that justified asylum are eliminated; (2) another safe country indicates willingness to accept them; or (3) the alien returns to the home country for a visit.

CLAIM E: Too much of enforcement against illegal immigration is based on employer sanctions and a national worker identification system. That subjects all citizens to more Big Brother invasion of privacy tactics. Such a Gestapo-like solution still couldn't prohibit fraud.

PRO-STABILIZATION RESPONSE:

♦ **"Gestapo talk is nothing but a scare tactic. All that is needed is a counterfeit-proof ID that a person would show only when applying for a job. A computer system would do nothing more than verify that the person seeking the job is who he claims to be."** (Stein, C)

"The phrase 'national identity card' conjures up the image of police stops, race and nationality coding and various abuses that have occurred in other countries. That's not what is being considered here." Barbara Jordan, the chairwoman of the National Commission on Immigration Reform that is recommending a reliable work-authorization system, notes that all workers already have to provide a Social Security number upon taking employment. The proposal merely is to create a system that ensures that people are who they say they are. (*Washington Post*, I)

Employer sanctions — penalties against employers who hire illegal aliens — were supposed to be the key weapon in discouraging foreign workers from entering the country or remaining in the country illegally. Since most come for jobs, the theory went, most would leave or not come in the first place if they found it virtually impossible to get a job. When the sanctions law was passed in 1986, apprehensions of illegal border crossers dropped sharply. But as the word got out that it was easy to obtain fraudulent documents, the flow of illegal aliens went up higher than ever.

"If America were more adult about this issue, like some Western European nations, we might save ourselves endless inconvenience by establishing a single official ID." (Kuttner, A)

Indeed, Europe operates secure identification systems with few problems. (see CLAIM 16-D)

American civil liberties organizations protest that such a system would threaten personal privacy and lead to discrimination against foreign-looking persons. In fact, it would reveal no private information not already exposed today and, by making the same initial Social Security check of all potential employees, it would reduce the chances of discrimination. "Employers would no longer have a reason to ask if any applicant was an immigrant or to reject all foreign-looking applicants out of hand. And American workers at the bottom of the economic ladder would benefit from more effective ways of discouraging the hiring of illegal immigrants." (*New York Times*, D)

"I have spent my career protecting the constitutional and civil rights of Americans," said Jordan upon proposing the national identification system. She said she never would support any move that created "an unwarranted intrusion in private lives." (*Washington Times*, B)

Right now, "Membership cards from a video rental shop have more safeguards built into them than do our vital national records and documents.... There is no reason to believe that having the ability to verify whether a prospective employee is a legal resident of the U.S. will lead to discrimination against minorities. Any system will be universal.... Merchants don't just run a check on some people's credit cards. They sweep everyone's card through the same device and within seconds they know whether the card is valid, whether the customer has a credit line or if the card has been reported lost or stolen.... What the opponents of the ... proposal are really afraid of is that a verifiable Social Security card might actually be successful in controlling illegal immigration." (Stein, C)

An essential element of any system to guard against fraud is the establishment of a program that will electronically link the birth and death records of every state. Social Security cards would be issued upon that network's verification that the applicant truly was born in the U.S. or had entered illegally. The Social Security card would need a photo or something like a fingerprint to ensure that it belonged to its bearer. Employers should be able to electronically check the card as is done for credit cards to verify the person's legal right to work in this country. (High, A)

Such verification is performed tens of millions of times a day in shops and restaurants around the country handling credit card purchases. (FAIR, D)

This type of verification is being used in Mexico — at a cost of nearly $800 million — to ensure that people showing up at polls have the right to vote and haven't voted already. Their cards include a photograph, signature, hologram and fingerprint. (*Christian Science Monitor*, B)

"Privacy is really more of a myth than a reality today. The government and countless private databases have reams of information on all of us. We have voluntarily surrendered much of our privacy for the conveniences of modern society. If the government was inclined to abuse our civil liberties, it could do so already." (Mehlman, B)

CLAIM F: No matter how many ways you thwart the entry of illegal aliens, you are dealing with desperate people who have very little to lose by continuing to try to come here. Even a job in the underground economy with no benefits, low pay and no legal protections would still look good to much of the world.

PRO-STABILIZATION RESPONSE:

♦ **True, there always will be some illegal immigration. But Europe — by adopting only some of the measures now proposed in the U.S. — has achieved significant reductions in the illegal flow.**

♦ **The federal government itself inspires fatalism about controlling illegal immigration because of its**

half-hearted efforts. (*New York Times*, J)

Germany provides a good example. By sending non-eligible asylum seekers home almost immediately, Germany provided quick signals to others in those countries that an effort to immigrate for economic reasons was futile. From just 5,583 asylum seekers deported in 1990, Germany sent home 35,915 in 1993. The number of new asylum seekers dropped 72% in the first portion of 1994, compared to that period of the previous year. (*Washington Post*, E)

It is ludicrous to use the last two decades' experience to suggest that the U.S. can't control illegal immigration, because each Congress and administration has made so few concerted efforts to do so. A devastating investigative series by *The New York Times* in September, 1994 conclusively showed that the system remains tipped in favor of illegal aliens.

The *Times*' investigation "found that the Immigration and Naturalization Service, an arm of the Justice Department, is broadly dysfunctional. Hobbled by understaffing, underfinancing, conflicting mandates from Congress and widespread mismanagement failures, it is an agency in disarray. It lurches from one immigration emergency to the next, its employees demoralized, its mission unrealized. On the most mundane level, the agency cannot even find a way to open its mail and answer its phones. On a more serious one, it does not make a concerted effort to find and deport most aliens with criminal records.... No agency of the government is more vulnerable to corruption than the I.N.S.... Deportation officers seldom deport anyone... 'We have no mission, no tools, no leadership, so where are we?' complained Juan Bustos, a deportation officer in San Francisco." (*New York Times*, J)

The effect of bumbling by Congress, the White House, and the Justice Department in immigration enforcement (with El Paso being a notable exception) is that, in the *Times*' words, it "fosters a numbing fatalism." (*New York Times*, J)

For those Americans who accept the fatalism that immigrants never can be stopped, they need to know the source of their fatalism: Congress, the White House, and the Justice Department. If the U.S. would aspire toward the resolve and competence of Western Europe in these matters — modified for special American circumstances — there is no reason we could not drastically cut admissions of legal immigrants while at the same time halting most illegal immigration.

Argument No. 17

Freedom

GENERAL CLAIM: Limiting immigration and stabilizing population would require . . .

TOO MUCH GOVERNMENT INTERFERENCE

GENERAL PRO-STABILIZATION RESPONSE:

♦ **It was government interference — federal laws beginning in 1965 — that forced mass immigration on the American people.** (High, B)

♦ **Population growth inevitably circumscribes freedoms, while it multiplies governmental interference.** (Parsons, A)

John Locke recognized that true Liberty is not the absence of restrictions on freedom but the result of the most creative use of restrictions on some freedoms to enhance others: "The end of law is not to abolish or restrain but to preserve and enlarge freedom: for in all states of created beings capable of laws: where there is no law there is no freedom." (Locke, A) Without social control, there is anarchy, "which most of us reject" because it allows freedom only for the powerful and offers "uncertainty, fear and trembling for everybody else." The question is not whether efforts to stem population growth would reduce some individual freedom but whether it would reduce Liberty more than would unrestricted population growth. (Parsons, A p.97)

Throughout the country, industrialists and common folk alike chafe at being told increasingly by government that they must change some form of behavior in order to lessen their impact on environmental resources or on their fellow citizens.

Many losses of freedom are related to population growth. "Amenities and freedoms diminish in direct relation to the number of people trying to enjoy them." (Brownridge, A)

Population growth has pushed California so close to the brink of ecological disaster, the only solution eventually may be to force the abandonment of the private automobile as a primary form of transportation, of detached single-family homes to meet housing needs, and of swimming pools and lawns as private amenities. (*Time*, A)

Population pressures have so limited the options for the salmon of the Northwest that extraordinary efforts are underway to save the region's last wild salmon runs. But apparently the only way to do it is to restrict the freedom of a lot of people in the Northwest. For a huge aluminum company, it will mean the loss of freedom to pay cheap prices for hydroelectric power. For gill-net fishermen, it will mean a reduction in the salmon take from a fishery that has sustained families for generations. For farmers, the cost of irrigation will rise. For grain shippers, it can mean annual temporary shutdown of barge traffic that links the area to Pacific Rim markets. (*The Washington Post*, P)

Other restrictions that population congestion already has forced on some parts of the country include:

- Prohibitions on driving on certain highways during rush hours without pooling of riders.
- Restrictions on the use of a fireplace at home, a charcoal grill or mower in the yard, or use of certain kinds of perfumes, laundry starch and lighter fluid — even the baking of bread in bakeries!
- Restricted use of water.
- The inability to buy a favorite car model because air pollution requirements have pushed it out of one's price range.
- The loss of a job because an industry cannot shoulder the costs necessary to meet environmental standards.
- Numerous curtailments of individual freedoms in cities because a large part of the citizenry finds certain behaviors obnoxious. (Samuelson, A; *Christian Science Monitor*, E; *Washington Post*, P)

"More crowding means more people will bump into one another; and to mitigate these bumps, people nowadays demand that government interfere ever more. The more a population is culturally and linguistically divided, the more irritating the bumps will be — hence the louder the demands for government-determined outcomes.... An unintended consequence of growth will be more government." (Ikle, A)

The sociologist Georg Simmel wrote: "Qualitatively speaking, the larger the group is, usually the more prohibitive and restrictive the kinds of conduct which it must demand of its participants in order to maintain itself..." (Wolff, A)

The right to swing your fist stops at the other fellow's nose — and the noses will be much closer together with denser population.

CLAIM A: We must guard against any curtailment of personal freedom, no matter how small, lest we set ourselves on a slippery slope that will lead to major losses of freedom for our descendants.

PRO-STABILIZATION RESPONSE:

♦ Each generation must restrain itself from insisting on all possible freedoms so as not to cut off options for children and grandchildren.

The 1972 presidential-congressional Commission on Population Growth and the American Future concluded that "population growth limits our options.... With less land per person and more people to accommodate, there are fewer alternatives, less room for diversity, less room for error.... Population growth forces upon us slow but irreversible changes in lifestyle. Imbedded in our traditions as to what constitutes the American way of life is freedom from public regulation — virtually free use of water; access to uncongested unregulated roadways; freedom to do as we please with what we own.... Clearly, we do not live this way now. Maybe we never did. But everything is relative. The population of 2020 may look back with envy on what, from their vantage point, appears to be our relatively unfettered way of life." (Commission on Population Growth and the American Future, A)

The U.S. government's continued stimulation of population growth would deny to our grandchildren even the limited freedoms we still cling to today: being able to experience wilderness and the magnificent natural shrines that are our National Parks. Even today, recent population growth has robbed us of being able during most times to enjoy those parks without being jostled by crowds, fighting traffic and struggling to find a place to stay. "The greatest freedom of all is found in wilderness — a place to experience the world without being manipulated by other humans.... There are so many people and so little wilderness that visits are often rationed with computerized permits.... In some areas you must reserve space months in advance. To raft some rivers you must apply years in advance. Because of overuse, onerous restrictions have become necessary. Campfires are often prohibited. Lakes and streams are often polluted. Solitude is difficult to find. And it is almost impossible to escape the noise of aircraft." (Brownridge, A)

What now may seem to us to be significant restrictions on our freedom will be seen by our grandchildren and great-grandchildren as the glorious, never-to-be-recaptured past if our immigration policies force them to live in a country with 100% more human beings — all competing for use of static or dwindling resources. Our descendants surely will be bewildered to read that we willed that lifestyle to them on the basis that we did not want to restrict the freedom to immigrate.

"The point is that the way we behave now creates the boundary conditions within which those coming later must live. If we allow the country or the world to become grossly over-populated, the people of later epochs will not have the freedom to do anything constructive about it..." (Parsons, A, p.115)

CLAIM B: The only way to stop desperate third-world people from coming to the U.S. is to adopt measures that cut into Americans' personal privacy. That is too great a price to pay.

PRO-STABILIZATION RESPONSE:

♦ **Nothing is more invasive of Americans' privacy or creates a more frightening sense of loss of freedom than the rise of crime. High immigration is one of the factors in the current crime wave.** (Gurr, A)

♦ **Hundreds of thousands of hunters and fishing enthusiasts in this country long have understood that they had to suffer the inconvenience of licenses, restricted seasons and "take" limits to ensure their ability to hunt and fish in the future. The unwillingness of Congress to place more restrictions on immigration has led to population growth that has eradicated much outdoor freedom over the last two decades, with 68% in one survey reporting that their favorite outdoor recreational area "no longer exists."** (Izaak Walton League, E)

Each effort to gain better control over U.S. borders or to discourage illegal aliens from obtaining U.S. jobs and social benefits is met with howls of protest from groups saying the measures would at least indirectly limit legitimate American residents in some way. To the extent that the measures turn out to be effective but also somewhat inconvenient to Americans, would citizens nonetheless consider the inconvenience to be a small price in exchange for forgoing the many more losses of freedom from continued population growth? (see General Pro-Stabilization Response)

Population growth forces many restrictions on personal freedom. Since more than 50% of U.S. population growth in the years 1970-1990 was caused by immigration (*The Social Contract*, I) it is reasonable to link immigration with many of the restrictions forced by population growth. It is important to note, however, that it is not individual immigrants who are responsible for population problems (except to the extent they have above-replacement-level fertility). Rather, it is immigrants' collective numbers, determined by Congress, that causes most population growth and, thus, it is those immigration numbers that are at least partly responsible for the freedom restrictions we experience in our everyday lives.

One example in California could be seen during the recent drought. Immigration-induced population growth was responsible for water rationing being more severe than it would have been without immigration. When that linkage was made publicly, some people said it was "immigrant-bashing." But to say immigration made matters worse was not to say immigration was the cause of the drought or the shortage, or that immigrants used and wasted more water than Americans. It simply was to note that the higher population created through immigration meant less water available per person. Once the link between immigration numbers, population growth and the pressure to restrict freedoms is understood, it is easier to weigh how much inconvenience Americans may be willing to accept in order to restrict immigration.

Some of the personal-freedom losses of immigration-fueled population growth have to do with aesthetics and quality of life. While the U.S. population grew by some 60 million in the last 20 years, American lovers of outdoor recreation have found their opportunities greatly reduced. In a 1993 survey, they were asked how their outdoor recreational areas changed over the last two decades. Their responses were: less game (64%), no longer exist (68%), fewer fish (69%), been developed (84%), more people (93%). (Izaak Walton League, E)

Population growth also robs many rural Americans of their freedom to live non-urbanized lifestyles. "Urban refugees" are spilling out of their overpopulating cities to seek respite in the countryside and small towns. But they bring with them expectations that change life for the very people they join. "In the city, the municipality orders life in great detail.... Newcomers from the city bring with them a belief in control and regulation.... The popular remark about urban arrivals is that they flee the city in disgust, then try to make the rural community like the place they abandoned." To support the metropolitan areas, the countryside is "criss-crossed with transmission towers and power line right-of-ways, sectioned and re-sectioned by barbed-wire fences, dotted and striped with incinerators, leaky landfills, billboards, pipelines, junk cars, mine tailings, gravel pits, clearcuts, noisy with small planes, chain saws, skimobiles..." (Proulx, A)

The most incendiary freedom-reduction charge against immigration-fueled population growth is that it results in more crime. Certainly, most immigrants are not criminals. There is no reason to suspect that immigrants have a lower moral character than Americans that would lend them susceptible to criminality. But when looking at the mass effect of additional millions from foreign cultures on our already deeply troubled society, problems emerge. In part, this is because immigrants disproportionately are uneducated, unskilled and do not fully assimilate into mainstream society. Like native-born Americans with the same characteristics, those immigrants encounter grave economic difficulties and pressures on their families that often are factors behind criminal behavior. In addition, high immigration seems to increase the prevalence of crime, not because of the immigrants themselves but because of their contribution to population growth which itself can be a factor in increasing crime. Crime historian Ted Robert Gurr of the University of Maryland is among those who have studied the links. He writes:

"Many streets in America's big cities are in a state of anarchy. Too often the police are overwhelmed. In some cities and neighborhoods, people are afraid to go outside.... The reason is that the United States is in the grip of the third of three great crime waves ... [each] linked to immigration, economic deprivation and war, which all interfere with the civilizing process..." (Gurr, A)

The three great crime waves have coincided with the first surge of mass immigration before the Civil War, with the much larger Great Wave of immigration at the beginning of this century and with the return of mass immigration since the 1960s.

First of all, high immigration has a direct effect on crime. When large numbers of people arrive from a single country, it is easier for foreign crime syndicates to transport their operations into the United States. Proliferation of nationality-based organized crime activity happened during the other great waves of immigration, and it is happening now, according to federal agency reports. (Lutton-Tanton, A, pp.62-74)

Most immigrants, of course, do not come to steal their way to the American Dream. But a sizeable minority for various reasons — perhaps disenchantment with an economy that doesn't need or reward large numbers of low-skill foreign workers — turns to crime once here. More than 25% of the felons in federal prisons are immigrants. (Lutton-Tanton, A, p.61)

Then, there is the indirect impact immigrants have on crime. By pushing population size upward, they encourage social disintegration. "The American psychologist Cattel did a study of the dimensions of various cultures correlating significant variables.... It is of interest that many political assassinations, riots and local rebellions, and a high ratio of divorces to marriages are positively associated with size of country." (Parsons, A, p.106)

California, the primary recipient of immigrants, tells us something of our national future if we continue high immigration and population growth. "It may be that the nation's largest state has simply become ungovernable, with a population too large, too diverse and too contentious.... 'We have to face the possibility that we're no longer a state, meaning one people willing or able to be governed for the com-mon good,'" said Sherry Bebitch Jeffe, political analyst at the Clare-mont Graduate School. (*Washington Times*, A)

A study of individuals' public behavior in several U.S. cities concluded that civility declined as density of population increased. (CNN, A)

The fate of many in urban black communities — suffering from disproportionate levels of high crime — is instructive. When freed slaves and their descendants could have gotten in on the ground floor of the industrial revolution, captains of industry imported immigrant workers instead. (Washington, A, pp.217-221)

Blacks "lacked the chances of immigrants to participate in an economy that produced a growing middle class. Since the best jobs were closed to them, a disproportionate number turned to gambling, prostitution and dealing in alcohol and drugs." All of that created a fertile climate for crime and homicide. (Gurr, A)

But the curtailment of immigration between 1924 and 1965 caused U.S. industry to turn to black Americans. Standards of living improved greatly after World War II and again after passage of the Civil Rights Act of 1964. (Briggs, A) Homicide rates among blacks declined dramatically until the early 1980s. By then, immigration had been increasing for almost two decades with a disproportionate number of immigrants settling where black Americans lived. Wages and job opportunities for lower-skilled blacks declined, and homicides surged. (Briggs, A; Gurr, A)

The first and second great waves of crime subsided after immigration levels were lowered and the earlier entrants were assimilated into the economy and society. "Today's epidemic will not go away without similar concerted action." (Gurr, A)

CLAIM C: Reducing legal immigration and deporting illegal aliens cheapens our commitment to democratic ideals.

PRO-STABILIZATION RESPONSE:

♦ **A chief ideal of democracy is that on most**

occasions the majority rules. Current immigration policy is a distortion of the democratic process.

"The demographic transformation of American society is occurring without the consultation or consent of the American electorate.... We can detect a central theme — that immigration policy's effective goals ... are to a remarkable degree established by decisions of private persons rather than elected-appointed officials. Because of the heavy emphasis on family reunification, the government's decisions have devolved to private individuals. The vast majority of them [are] either foreign-born citizens or permanent-resident aliens.... Immigration is not primarily about national purposes or national anything. It is about the rights of immigrating peoples and their sponsors in the U.S." (Graham, A, pp.13-14)

When the size of the U.S. House of Representatives was fixed at 435 seats in 1910, each member represented approximately 211,000 Americans.

Today, each member has to serve approximately 598,000 constituents. Each American's access to Congress has diminished accordingly.

"The size of constituency is clearly not the sole factor in determining excellence in government.... But it cannot be denied that the individual's voice and access will be diminished under such circumstances. No increase of Congress's ability to communicate with constituents by mass media can disguise or make up for that diminution." (Simcox, C)

As government grows more and more distant from the individual in a densely populated society, and as income disparities widen (see Argument No 10), legitimate concerns may well up about the capacity of democracy as we know it to survive.

"Australia's egalitarian culture has depended in part on the assumption that there was enough to go around for anyone who was prepared to do their share of the work. The fate of several South American countries suggests that inequality (leading even to dictatorship and death squads) can rapidly set in once a sizable middle class recognizes that it is quite impossible to extend their standard of living to all members of an ever-increasing populace." (O'Connor, B)

In the U.S., the freedom to live in a society where most people have a chance at a middle-class lifestyle without fear of a raging, criminal underclass is becoming increasingly a freedom of the textbooks only.

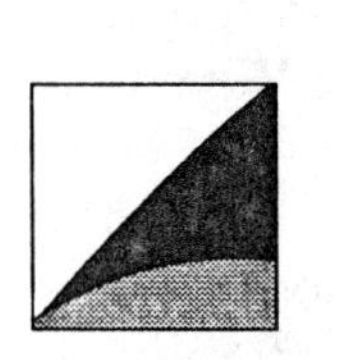

Summary

Our Choices

What then shall we Americans do about that chart on the front cover of this book? Do we leave the status quo of current immigration and fertility unchanged so it can hurtle us toward the doubled population size portrayed in the chart?

Or shall we re-chart the future?

The population decisions before us are not extremely complicated. Using the information in the previous 17 chapters, we can create a "decision tree" that fairly quickly shows us our options. It is a process that Congress might want to consider soon — the time for decisive action appears to be now.

No. 1: Do we have major environmental problems?

Yes.

Current per capita environmental impact, multiplied by U.S. population size, endangers human health, bio-diversity and our aesthetic natural heritage. If continued, current trends will grossly limit the quality-of-life options for our grandchildren.

It is not difficult to see the signs of environmental violation. Any one of the following is sufficient to confirm that the present combination of population size and per capita environmental impact is too high. Any increase in population or consumption just makes matters worse. (see Arguments No. 2 & 4)

- With about 50% of our wetlands already gone, development destroys 300,000 additional acres of these bio-diversity incubators every year.

- In 35 states, we currently draw out more ground water each year than is replenished naturally.

- There were 500 plant and animal species listed as endangered in 1988, 15 years after passage of the Endangered Species Act. By 1993, the number had increased to more than 700.

- We still pollute our lakes and streams so much that half of these resources cannot meet the goal of being fishable and swimmable.

- The air for 40 percent of Americans does not meet health standards.

- About half of all Americans live in major metropolitan areas in which their quality of life continues to decline due to transportation and other congestion.

- Energy-intensive, maximum-production agriculture results in the loss of topsoil 16 times faster than replacement, while soil productivity declines. Erosion and urban development destroy around 1.5 million acres of arable land per year.

- The oceans are over-fished. The global marine catch has been declining since 1989.

- Our national parks — the "crown jewels of America" — are overcrowded and endangered even at today's population size.

- A survey of outdoorsmen found that six of every 10 reported that their traditional hunting and fishing areas no longer exist.

Now, imagine the report on each of those items if our present population were doubled — which it is projected to do by late next century under current congressional policies.

It is true that, by many measures, the U.S. natural environment is far healthier than it was at other times of history. But during the past 25 years of concerted effort, the nation has used up most of the easy and relatively inexpensive cleanup solutions. Protection efforts on many fronts have stalled well short of reaching goals. In some areas — particularly in the protection of habitat, bio-diversity and farmland — things are getting worse.

No. 2: Do we just let our environment continue to deteriorate or change the factors causing the problem?

The choice belongs to the people.

Americans tell pollsters that saving the environment and having a lifestyle with high environmental quality is very important to us. We have made a major change in our fertility rate and modest changes in consumption to try to achieve those goals.

But we elect federal officials who lately have shown little interest in new laws to bring about further major decreases in environmental contamination. And every year, our officials force significant population growth through untraditional immigration policies.

If our choice as a nation is to double the intensity of damage to our environment, then we can be content with what we and our federal officials are doing. There is no reason to go through the following questions.

If, however, we want to keep matters from getting worse — if not actually to improve environmental protection — we need to move on to Question No. 3.

No. 3: Can we solve our environmental problems through population stabilization alone?

No.

All those problems are occurring at our present population level. If we never grew by another person, they still would occur.

Any plan to protect, preserve and restore our nation's environmental resources must include reduction of per capita impact on the environment.

No. 4: Can we rescue our nation's natural resources by focusing entirely on reducing per capita impact?

Not likely.

Per capita environmental impact can be lowered further by:

- Voluntary reductions in personal consumption, especially in the use of energy and automobiles, and choices to live in higher urban densities.

- Voluntary recycling and other waste-reduction efforts.

- The development of new technologies that make our lifestyles less harmful to the environment.

- Laws that force greater cuts in consumption and waste, and that halt residential and commercial development in natural habitats and agricultural land. It is here that preserving the environment comes in conflict with preserving individual liberties.

- Tougher enforcement of environmental laws.

Each of those measures has constituency groups to champion them. Each also has major detractors who have succeeded in keeping them from achieving enough per capita environmental reduction to reach our goals.

The combination of those reduction measures has not been

sufficient to stop the environmental destruction (witness the litany at the beginning of this chapter). If population continues to grow, the efforts behind each measure must be more intense each year just to keep the destruction from getting worse. Any claim that America has plenty of room for more people is spurious as long as the earlier-mentioned signs of environmental violation continue.

No. 5: Can we hold off on population measures until we find out the success of efforts to reduce per capita environmental impact?

No.

To delay dealing with population would be irresponsible, quite simply because those further per capita reductions are not now in place, nor do we have any assurance they ever will be.
(see Argument No. 3)

It is up to the American people in their personal lifestyle decisions and compliance with such laws as their elected officials may enact to decide how and how much to limit their per capita impact. Until those decisions are made and results achieved, any encouragement of population growth is tantamount to encouraging environmental destruction.

There is no environmentally valid reason for the federal government to force population growth as long as the aforementioned signs of environmental destruction continue.

If we decide we want to save the environment, and if any of those destruction signs continue, we have to answer Question 6.

No. 6: Do we restrain population growth by reducing fertility or immigration?

Both.

Our fertility level, however, has to determine the level of immigration. Congress can lower immigration numbers by simply passing a law. It doesn't have the same power over Americans' fertility. It might choose to provide incentives for smaller families or disincentives for larger ones, but no official would propose enforcing a fertility rate. (Increasing life expectancy also boosts the population size and decreases room for immigration. We'll assume nobody will object to that goal.)

As long as efforts — to reduce consumption and waste, to pass new laws, to toughen enforcement and to improve technology — are insufficient to do away with the environmental violation signs, the government needs to set a population-size goal that is compatible with our environmental needs. Immigration numbers would have to be set each year on the basis of the latest reported American fertility rate — so that the combination of the two would enable the attainment of the population goal.

No. 7: Can we have a national policy that will stabilize the population immediately?

Highly unlikely.

Even if Congress lowered immigration to zero, American women would need to have 54% fewer births next year than this year. The effective fertility rate of 2.05 children per woman would have to plummet to 0.96, less than a one-child-family average. (Bartlett-Lytwak, A)

Since nobody is going to advocate forcing women to adopt *any* fertility rate, we have to come up with a more realistic plan.

No. 8: How should we choose a population goal?

As long as environmental standards are not being met, we should aim, at a minimum, for a population-size goal no larger than current size — 260 million — and probably lower.

Because of population momentum — which causes growth for some 50 years after attainment of replacement-level fertility and zero-net immigration — perhaps the numerical goal should be pegged to a later date, such as the year 2050.

With that goal, the number of immigrants accepted each year would be based on current fertility and current total population. A computer program easily could be set up to identify the immigration level each year that — combined with current population size and fertility — would cause population to return back to 260 million by 2050. The size unavoidably would first rise another 20 to 40 million because of population momentum. (see Argument No. 1)

Ideally, the country needs to come up with a concept of a maximum sustainable population. That would be a level which could continue far into the future without diminishing the ability of later generations to live at the same lifestyle. That's different from the optimum number of people, which would be less than the maximum and enough to ensure that everybody was able to gain maximum enjoyment out of their lifestyle.

Different scientists have come up with various estimates of what the U.S. population goal should be for the end of the next century. Here are some: Paul Werbos of the National Science

Foundation (125-250 million); Robert Costanza of the University of Maryland (170 million or fewer "until technical breakthroughs happen — if they happen"); Cornell University professors David and Marcia Pimentel (less than 100 million — our size early this century); political scientist George F. Kennan (a maximum of 200 million).

Leon Bouvier and Lindsey Grant in their Sierra Club Books offering, *How Many Americans?*, show that hopes of moving our population-size to below the current 260-million level by 2050 probably are unrealistic. Their optimistic/realistic scenario indicates a population size of 278 million by 2050 and finally below the 1970 level of 203 million by the year 2100.

Their scenario allows for a rather liberal level of 200,000 immigrants per year (down from 1 million) and imagines that native-born Americans would reduce their fertility to 1.7 (the record U.S. low) by 2000, to 1.6 (Europe's low average) by 2025, and to 1.5 by 2050. Fertility of post-2000 immigrants and their descendants would have to drop from the current estimated 2.7 to 2.5 in 2000, to 2.0 in 2025 and to 1.5 by 2050.

No. 9: To reach a goal of 260 million in 2050, how many immigrants could we take under current conditions?

None.

Under present fertility and lifestyle, the only way we can keep from worsening that abysmal list of environmental atrocities noted earlier is to end all immigration. (Bouvier)

However, if Americans — particularly high-fertility recent immigrants — lower their fertility toward the 1.7 level, we could start taking in some new immigrants and not harm the environment.

This option, like all others, remains for the American people to decide. If we choose to lower our already-below-replacement-level fertility still further, we'll know it through the annual reporting of the fertility rate. We can adjust immigration upward when fertility goes down, and downward when fertility goes up.

No. 10: Is it realistic to think Congress would make the health of the environment a top priority and end all immigration for now?

No.

The nation's army of immigration lawyers — perhaps the most powerful and diligent of advocates for high immigration — would go out of business at a zero-admission level. They will be formidable foes of putting the environment first, but their personal cause will be self-interested and with little moral weight. Most of them should be able to find other jobs.

Businesses that rely on cheap, compliant foreign labor no doubt also will fight an immigration policy that is based on our nation's environmental needs. As we have seen, a lowering of immigration would cause some short-term, isolated dislocations; but our overall economy does not need immigration, and less-skilled American workers probably would be better off without it. There is no reason why skilled foreign workers have to be granted permanent occupancy in this country. If companies can't find Americans for a position, they could be allowed to hire foreign workers for just enough years (on temporary visas) until colleges or vocational schools were able to train Americans for the jobs. (see Argument No. 10)

Advocates for refugees, however, will have a stronger argument for why the environment should be made to suffer from population growth due to admissions of foreign persons. But as we have seen, resettlement could never help more than a tiny percentage of refugees around the world. Nonetheless, there surely will be a need to provide refuge for several thousand, if not tens of thousands, each year. Very few refugees, however, need be granted permanent residency. The point is to save their lives, not make them U.S. citizens. The U.S. should put most of its efforts and resources into helping the bulk of refugees in the settlement camps near their home countries and into making it possible for them to return home safely. We should bring refugees into this country only as a last resort and only until they can return home. As one set of refugees returns home when their lives no longer are in danger, there will be room in the U.S. for more temporary refugees. (see Argument No. 14)

The vast majority of immigrants today are allowed because they have relatives here. Although much is made of the value of family re-unification, it must be remembered that more than 90% of the immigrants doing the inviting of their relatives were not refugees. They made an economic decision to separate themselves from their families when they decided to move to the U.S. If annual visits back home aren't sufficient, they can move back permanently to be near their brothers, sisters, aunts, uncles, cousins and parents. (see Argument No. 11)

Re-unification of immediate family members with their immigrant father or mother, who is now a U.S. citizen, however, poses a more difficult decision. It is the author's view that no matter how upset Americans may be about immigration, it is unlikely that they will pressure Congress to delay reunification of spouses and minor, dependent children. Because of the massive admissions of the last two decades, immigrants who are immediate family members of U.S. citizens number nearly 200,000 a year. Any congressional action is likely to compromise environmental quality in order to continue to allow that flow.

The good news for the environment, and for Americans relying on the environment, is that the number of immigrants each year who could claim to be immediate relatives of citizens probably would decline fairly rapidly to well below a hundred thousand after a couple of decades of cutting off most other immigration.

An immigration level allowing unlimited admission of immediate relatives of citizens and, say, 25,000 permanent refugees, asylees, special-classification workers, etc., each year would bring in approximately 225,000 newcomers a year at first, but the number would decline over time — and so would the impact on population growth and the environment.

No. 11: How do we decide on the right number?

Democratically.

This is a democracy. We can choose not to change immigration enough to fully stop environmental destruction. But we need to be clear and honest that we have made a decision that immigration, or some of it, is more important than clean air, wetlands and other eco-systems, bio-diversity, fishable and swimmable lakes and rivers, sustainable agriculture and natural spaces for recreation and psychological nurture.

Most Americans, however, do not seem to favor such a choice. Although many of us may have an emotional or nostalgic reason to want to see immigration continued at fairly high levels, it would seem that:

- shutting off immigration might entail minor difficulties for some foreign countries but, on the whole, would tend to benefit the impoverished residents of those countries — especially if we were more creative and careful in assistance to them. (see Argument No. 14)

- the end of population growth in the U.S. would create opportunities for new kinds of vitality rather than stagnation in the society (see Argument No. 5), and would make it easier to preserve our traditional culture of bountiful individual liberty; (see Argument No. 17)

• the rich diversity of our cultural fabric does not require high immigration to keep it from becoming monochromatic and, indeed, domestic tranquility and appreciation of diversity might be enhanced with a cutoff of immigration; (see Argument No. 11)

• greatly reducing immigration to protect the environment, or to improve economic possibilities for lower-income Americans, is not xenophobic, nativist or racist; there are strong indications that continued high immigration may heighten institutional racism against America's historic minority, the African-Americans; (see Argument No. 13)

• a reduction of immigration to under 200,000 would not violate our immigration tradition but would constitute a return to levels common during most of our history, certainly the most positive parts of it. (see Argument No. 12)

The general choice before us is described well in a recent conservationist publication:

> *Traditionally, this country has supported national population growth to provide labor for expanding industries, settle territories and increase government revenues. But we no longer are a frontier nation. Manifest destiny has been replaced by a stark realization of the environmental and social costs of population growth: expanding urban blight, accelerated natural resource depletion, and increased pollution are just a few examples.*
>
> *The U.S. faces the choice of continuing on this path or charting a sustainable future, one that recognizes and respects the limits imposed by the environment.* (Izaak Walton League, F)

Shall we continue on this path of environmental degradation? Or shall we set immigration each year at a level based on population stabilization goals that will allow us to re-chart America's future — a future in which we "enjoy the fruit" of our natural heritage without "harming the tree" that produces it?

Sources

Abernethy, Virginia. Anthropology professor, Vanderbilt University; editor, *Population and Environment: A Journal of Interdisciplinary Studies.*
A - *Population Politics* (N.Y. and London: Insight Press, 1994).
B - "First Do No Harm," *Current World Leaders*, Dec 1993.
C - "How Julian Simon Could Win the Bet and Still Be Wrong," *Population and Environment*, Fall 1991.
D - Author summary of her book, *Population Politics*, Apr 1993.
E - Letter to William Ryerson, 1993.
F - Correspondence, Jun-Sep 1994.

Adams, James Truslow
A - *The Epic of America* (Boston: Little, Brown, and Company, 1932).

AFL-CIO
A - "U.S. Workers Should Have First Claim On American Jobs," Thomas Donahue, AFL-CIO Sec-Treas, *Interface*, Sum 1990.

Alliance for a Paving Moratorium
A - "The Problem with Paving; An Economic Dead-End," Fact-Sheet #1, 1993.

American Demographics
A - "Hispanics Take Miami," Jun 1, 1994.

American Friends Service Committee
A - "Borders and Quaker Values," *The Social Contract*, Spring 1991.

Associated Press
A - "Conditions Worsen for Hired Hands," Jennifer Dixon, Apr 2, 1992.
B - "UN Names 17 Nations as 'Potential Somalias'," Edith Lederer, Jun 3, 1994.
C - "Air in 43 Urban Areas Fails to Meet Federal Standards," Oct, 21, 1994 (Washington Post)

Atlantic Monthly
A - "The Ordeal of Immigration in Wausau," Roy Beck, Apr 1994.
B - "745 Boylston Street," editorial, Oct 1992.

Audubon Society
666 Pennsylvania Ave. SE, Suite 200, Washington, D.C. 20003, (202) 547-9009.
A - "Austin: Where Boom Can Mean Bust," Victor Chen, Jul-Aug 1994.
B - "Special Report: Cairo Conference on Population & Development," Victor Chen, Jul-Aug 1994.

Auster, Lawrence
A - *The Path to National Suicide: An Essay on Immigration and Multiculturalism* (Monterey, VA: The American Immigration Control Foundation, 1990).
B - "Avoiding the Issue," *National Review*, Feb 21, 1994.
C - "The Forbidden Topic," *National Review*, Apr 27, 1992.
D - "Not An Open-And-Shut Case," *The Social Contract*, Summer 1992.

Australians for an Ecologically Sustainable Population, P.O. Box 1875, Canberra ACT 2601.
A - *Future Directions*, Jul 1991 and Apr 1993.

Barnett, Don
A - "Their Teeming Shores," *National Review*, Nov 1, 1993.

Barrera, Mario
A - *Beyond Atzlan: Ethnic Autonomy in Comparative Perspective* (New York: Praeger, 1988).

Bartlett, Albert. Professor of physics, University of Colorado.
A - "Reflections on Sustainability, Population Growth, and the Environment," *Population and the Environment*, Sep 1994.
B - Quoted in "Discounting the Future," *The Social Contract*, Fall 1991.

Bartlett-Lytwak. Albert Bartlett and Edward Lytwak, coordinating editor, Carrying Capacity Network.
A - "Zero Growth of the Population of the United States," scheduled for *Population and Environment*, May 1995.

Barton, Josef. Northwestern University professor of history.
A - Quoted in "Xenophobia: Scrabble Winner, Debate Stopper," Roy Beck, *The Social Contract*, Spring 1992.

Becerra, Xavier. Democratic Congressman from California and a member of the Judiciary subcommittee on international law, immigration, and refugees.
A - "Move Over, Rodney Dangerfield," *Roll Call*, Apr 22, 1994.

Beck - Bouvier. Roy Beck and Leon Bouvier, demographer.
A - "Projected Growth If Congress Leaves Immigration Unchanged," *The Social Contract*, 1993.

Bennett, David. History professor, Syracuse University.
A - Quoted in "Xenophobia: Scrabble Winner, Debate Stopper," Roy Beck, *The Social Contract*, Spring 1992.
B - Interview, Feb 1992.
C - *The Party of Fear: From Nativist Movements to the New Right in American History* (Chapel Hill: University of North Carolina Press, 1988).

Berriozabal, Manuel P. Professor of mathematics, University of Texas (San Antonio).
A - "Importing Brains Does Not Solve Sortage of Technical Personnel," *Vista*, Feb 3, 1991.

Berry, Wendell
A - "God and Country," *Christian Ecology*, proceedings from the first North American Conference on Christianity and Ecology, Apr 1988.
B - "The Futility of Global Thinking," *Resurgence*, No. 139, 1990.

Betts, Katharine. Senior lecturer in sociology, Swinburne Institute of Technology, Australia.
A - *Ideology and Immigration: Australia 1976 - 1987* (Melbourne Univ. Press, 1988).
B - "Sydney and the Bush: No Growth and Some Hope," *Migration Action*, Nov 1990.
C - Quoted in "Challenging Immigration Fatalism," Roy Beck, *The Social Contract*, Winter 1991-92.

Bikales, Gerda
A - "The Golden Rule in the Age of the Global Village," *Arguing Immigration*, Nicolaus Mills, ed (N.Y.: Touchstone, 1994).

Binkin, Martin. Senior fellow in the Foreign Policy Studies program at the Brookings Institution.
A - "Manning the American Military in the Twenty-First Century," *Elephants in the Volkswagon*, Lindsey Grant, editor (New York: W.H. Greeman and Company, 1992).

Binores-Egger, Debbie. Analytical psychologist, Switzerland.
A - Interview, Aug 10, 1994.

Blanchet - Dard
A - *Statue of Liberty: The First Hundred Years* (Boston: Houghton Mifflin, 1986).

Bodnar, John E.
A - "The Impact of the 'New Immigration' on the Black Worker: Steelton, Pennsylvania, 1880-1920," *Journal of Labor History*, 1976.

Bogan, Elizabeth
A - *Immigration in New York* (N.Y.: Praeger, 1987).

Borjas, George. Professor of economics, University of California (San Diego).
A - "Learning to Love Welfare," *Taxi Magazine*, Apr 1994.
B - "Tired, Poor, on Welfare," *National Review*, Dec 13, 1993.

Boulding, Kenneth. Late economist at the Univ. of Colorado, served with Amer. Friends Service Comm. border study group.
A - "Borders and Quaker Values: Further Reflections," *The Social Contract*, Spr 1991

Bouvier, Leon. Demographer; retired vice president, Population Reference Bureau; adjunct professor, Tulane University.
A - *Fifty Million Californians?* (Washington: Center for Immigration Studies, 1991).
B - *Peaceful Invasions: Immigration and Changing America* (N.Y.: University Press of America, 1992).
C - Correspondence, Jun - Sept 1994.
D - *New York Newsday*, op-ed page, Aug 22, 1994.

Bouvier - Grant. Leon Bouvier and Lindsey Grant
A - *How Many Americans,* (San Francisco: Sierra Club Books, 1994).
B - "The Issue is Overpopulation," *Los Angeles Times*, Aug 10, 1994.

Briggs Jr., Vernon. Labor economist, School of Industrial and Labor Relations, Cornell University.
A - *Mass Immigration and the National Interest* (N.Y.: M.E. Sharpe, 1992)
B - "Political Confrontation with Economic Reality," *Elephants in the Volkswagon*, Lindsey Grant, editor (N.Y.: W.H. Freeman, 1992).
C - Quoted in "Native-Born Blacks Lose Out to Immigrants," Jonathan Tilove, *Portland Oregonian*, Dec 20, 1993.
D - "Immigration Policy and Workforce Preparedness," *ILR Report*, N.Y. State School of Industrial Relations, Cornell University, Fall 1990.
E - Article, *Clearinghouse Bulletin*, Oct 1992.

Brimelow, Peter
A - "The Closed Door," *The Social Contract*, Fall 1993.
B - "Does the Nation-State Exist?," *The Social Contract*, Summer 1993.
C - "Controlling Our Demographic Destiny," with Joseph Fallon, Feb 21, 1994.

Brown, Lester. Chief executive, World Resources Institute.
A - *State of the World 1994* (1994).

Browne, Malcolm W. Pulitzer Prize-winning journalist and a correspondent for *The New York Times.*
A - "Beware the Third World," *Muddy Boots and Red Socks* (N.Y.: Times Books: 1993).

Brownridge, Dennis. Former geography professor, University of California (Santa Barbara), now teaches at The Orme School in Arizona.
A - "You Can't Go West: Stress in the High Country," *Elephants in the Volkswagon*, Lindsey Grant, editor (N.Y.: W.H. Freeman, 1994).

Buffett, Warren E. Investor.
A - Quoted in *Living Within Limits*, Garrett Hardin (Oxford: Oxford University Press, 1993).

Burke, Meredith. Demographer and economist who has consulted to the World Bank and the U.S. Agency for International Development.
A - "It's Just Getting Too Crowded," *San Jose Mercury News.*
B - "The Most Politically Incorrect Topic," *Newsweek*, Feb 24, 1992.

Bustamante, Jorge A. Mexican sociologist.
A - "Immigration Ethics," *World Issues*, Center for the Study of Democractic Institutions, Feb/Mar 1978. At the time, Bustamante was professor at the Colegio de Mexico in Mexico City.

Business Week
A - "Enough Already with the Huddled Masses," Michael J. Mandel, Jun 20, 1994.

Cable News Network
A - "Decline of Civilization," reported by Morton Dean, Aug 1994.

California Department of Education
A - "California Schools Bursting At The Seams," Sep 3, 1991.

Carrying Capacity Network, 1325 G Street, NW, Suite 1003, Washington, D.C., 20005-3104, phone (202) 879-3044.

A - *Clearinghouse Bulletin*, Jun 1994.
B - *Clearinghouse Bulletin*, Jul 1994.
C - "Calls to Action," *Clearinghouse Bulletin*, 1992.
D - "Carrying Capacity Checkup & Connections," *Clearinghouse Bulletin*, Aug 1994.
E - "Costs of Growth," *Clearinghouse Bulletin*, Aug 1994.
G - "Living Within Our Environmental Means: Natural Resources and an Optimum Human Population," *Clearinghouse Bulletin*, Jun 1994.
H - "Vermont in Danger from Sprawl," Julie Bomengen and Michael Murphy, *Clearinghouse Bulletin*, Sep 1993.
I - "Water Divides Westerners," *Clearinghouse Bulletin*, 1992, reports of stories in *USA Today*, Jan 29, 1992, and the *Christian Science Monitor*, Feb 21, 1992.
J - "Why We Can't Go West," *Clearinghouse Bulletin*, Feb 1992.

CATO Institute, 1000 Mass. Ave., N.W., Washington, D.C. 20001.
A - "The Earth Is Alive and Well, New Book Argues," May 25, 1993.

Census Bureau
A - "Baby Boomers Contribute to the 'Graying' of the Voting Age," Lynne Casper, June 29, 1994.
B - "Population Projections of the U.S. by Age, Sex, Race and Hispanic Origin," Nov 1993.
C - "Current Population Reports", Series P-20, No. 454, Fertility of American Women, Jun 1990.
D - "U.S. Census of Population: 1950," Volume IV, Special Reports, Part 5, Chapter C: Fertility, 1955.
E - "Population Projections of the U.S. by Age, Sex, Race and Hispanic Origin: 1993 to 2050," p-25, 1104, Sep 1993.

Center for Immigration Studies, 1815 H St. NW, Suite 1010, Washington, D.C., 20006, phone (202) 328-7228.
A - "Immigration: A Test of Clinton's Commitment to the National Interest," Roy Beck, *Scope*, Winter 1993.
B - "Unemployment in Major Areas of Immigrant Settlement," May 1992.
C - "Foreign Born Professionals in the U.S.," Leon F. Bouvier and David Simcox, Apr 1994.
D - Interview, Sep 1994.

Christian Life Commission. Southern Baptist Convention, 901 Commerce Street, #550, Nashville, TN 37203-3696.
A - *The Earth is the Lord's* (Nashville: Broadman, 1992).

Christian Science Monitor
A - "Asian-American Cops Battle Gangs in N.Y.'s Chinatown," Sam Walker, Jul 25, 1994.
B - "High-Tech Welfare IDs," Jul 19, 1994.
C - "Rising Immigration Exacts a Heavy Toll On the Environment," Brad Knickerbocker, Jul 19, 1994.
D - "UN Urges Humanitarian Use of 'Peace Dividend'," Brad Knickerbocker and Peter Grier, Jun 8, 1994.
E - Article, Jan 14, 1993(Excerpt printed in the *Clearinghouse Bulletin*).
F - "Pendulum of Affirmative Action Swings Both Ways," Clemence Fiagome, Mar 11, 1994.

Commission on Population Growth and the American Future. Jointly appointed by President Nixon, Congress.
A - Report, 1972.

Conservation Biology
A - "On Reauthorization of Endangered Species Act," Mar 1994.

Cook, Adrian
A - *The Armies of the Streets: The New York City Draft Riots of 1863* (Lexington, KY: University Press of Kentucky, 1974).

Cutler, Rupert. Conservationist. Director, Explore Park, Roanoke, VA.
A - Quoted in "Who Will Feed China?" *World Watch*, Sep-Oct 1994.

Council of Economic Advisors.
A - "1993 Annual Report to the President," Feb 4, 1994.

The Daily Californian
A - "Lady Liberty's Torch Meant to Enlighten the Oppressed," Roy Beck, Aug 15, 1993.

Dallas Morning News
A - "INS Helping to Create Jobs, Fill Them With Legal Residents," Frank Trejo, Mar 25, 1994.

Daly, Herman E. School of Public Affairs, University of Maryland (College Park).
A - "Farewell Lecture," Jan 14, 1994 after six years of service in the World Bank.

D'Elia, Christopher. Vice president for Academic Affairs, University of Maryland Bio-technology Institute.
A - Spoken at conference of Society of Environmental Journalists, National Press Club, Aug 8, 1994.

Detroit News
A - "A Grass-Roots Effort Tries to Shut California's Door to Illegal Immigrants," Jun 12, 1994.

Dockery, David S. Dean, School of Theology and associate professor of theology, Southern Baptist Theological Seminary.
A - "The Environment, Ethics, and Exposition," *The Earth Is the Lord's* (Nashville: Broadman Press, 1992).

Donohue - Heckman. John J. Donohue III, Northwestern University; James Heckman, University of Chicago.
A - "Continuous Versus Episodic Change: The Impact of Civil Rights Policy on The Economic Status of Blacks," *Journal of Economic Literature*, Dec 1991.

The Economist
A - "Sin and the Devil," Sep 18, 1993.

Ehrlich, Paul. Professor of biological sciences, Stanford University.
A - *The Population Explosion*, with Anne H. Ehrlich (NY:Simon and Schuster, 1990).
B - "The Most Overpopulated Nation," Paul R. and Ann Ehrlich, *Elephants in the Volkswagon*, Lindsey Grant, editor (N.Y.: W.H. Freeman, 1992).
C - Response to questions from *Audobon Activist* magazine, Nov 1993.

Elyria Chronicle-Telegram, (Ohio)
A - "Stagnant-Growth, Smaller Cities have Much-Sought Qualities," Roy Beck, Mar 31, 1992.

Environmental Action
A - "Coming to America: Immigrants and the Environment," Babara Ruben, Summer 1994.

Erickson, Millard. Research Professor of Theology, Southwestern Baptist Theological Seminary.
A - "Biblical Ethics of Ecology," *The Earth Is the Lord's* (Nashville: Broadman Press, 1992).

Ervin, Nick. Conservation chairperson, San Diego Sierra Club.
A - "Immigration and the Environment," *Arguing Immigration*, Nicolaus Mills, editor (N.Y.: Touchstone, 1994).

Federation for American Immigration Reform, 1666 Connecticut Ave., Suite 400, Washington, D.C. 20009, phone (202) 328-7004.
A - *Immigration 2000: The Century of the New American Sweatshop* (1992).
B - Newsletter, cited in *The Social Contract*, Spring 1994.
C - *10 Steps To A Secure Border.*
D - "Backgrounder, Immigration Stabilization Act of 1993."

Federalist Papers
A - No. 2, John Jay.

Fleming, Thomas
A - "America, From Republic to Ant Farm," *Chronicles*, Oct 1991.

Foreman, Dave
A - *Confessions of an Eco-Warrior* (N.Y.: Harmony Books, 1991).

Foreman-Peck, James. St. Anthony's College, Oxford.
A - "A Political Economy of International Migration, 1815-1914," *The Manchester School*, Dec 1992.

The Forum, National Presbyterian Church, Washington, D.C.
A - Presentation, Roy Beck, Jan 17, 1993.

Fox - Mehlman. Robert Fox, sociologist and demographer, and Ira Mehlman, writer.
A - *Crowding Out the Future* (Washington: Federation for American Immigration Reform, 1992).

Fresno Bee
A - "Growers Angry About Preliminary Findings of Farm Labor Commission," Michael Doyle, Mar 31, 1992.

Frey, William. Professor, Population Studies, University of Michigan.
A - "Black College Grads, Those in Poverty Take Different Migration Paths," *Population Today*, Feb 1994.

Fromm, Erich
A - *The Fear of Freedom* (1942).

Frost, Raymond
A - Article in *Challenge*, Nov/Dec 1991.

Fuchs, Lawrence H. History proffessor, Brandeis University.
A - "The Reactions of Black Americans to Immigration," part of Virginia Yans-McLaughlin's *Immigration Reconsidered: History, Sociology and Politics*, 1990.

General Accounting Office
A - "Legal and Illegal Workers' Wages and Working Conditions," GAO/PEMD-88-13BR.

Geyer, Georgie Anne. Nationally syndicated columnist and author.
A - "Border Control Dilemma," *The Washington Times*, Jul 3, 1994.

Gilliam, Harold
A - "Bursting at the Seams," *The Social Contract*, Summer 1993.

Glazer, Nathan. Coeditor of *The Public Interest*.
A - "The Closing Door," *The New Republic*, Dec 27, 1993.

Goldin, Claudia. Harvard University economist.
A - Abstract, "The Political Economy of Immigration in the United States, 1890 to 1921," Apr 1993.

Golini, Antonio. Professor, Institute for Population Research, Italy.
A - Quoted in "Challenging Immigration Fatalism," Roy Beck, *The Social Contract*, Winter 1991-92.

Graham Jr., Otis. Historia, University of California (Santa Barbara).
A - *Rethinking the Purposes of Immigration Policy*, Center for Immigration Studies, May 1991.
B - "Cultural Carrying Capacity: A Biological Approach to Human Problems," *Focus*, Volume 2, No. 3, 1992.
C - "Uses and Misuses of History in the Debate Over Immigration Reform," *The Social Contract*, Winter 1990-91.

Graham - Beck. Otis Graham and Roy Beck.
A - "Immigration's Impact on Inner City Blacks," *Los Angeles Times*, May 19, 1992.

Grant, Lindsey. Deputy Assistant Secretary of State for Environment and Population Affairs (retired).
A - *Elephants in the Volkswagon*, Lindsey Grant, editor (New York: W.H. Freeman, 1992).
B - "Into The Wind: Unemployment and Welfare Reform," *The NPG Forum*, Mar 1994.
C - "The Two Child Family," *The NPG Forum*, Jul 1994.
D - Article in the *The NPG Forum*, Oct 1989.
E - Correspondence, Jun 1994.
F - "The Cairo Conference: Feminists vs. the Pope," *The NPG Forum*, Jul 1994.

Green, Ronald M.
A - "Immigration Ethics," *World Issues*, Center for the Study of Democratic Institutions, Feb/Mar 1978. At the time, Green was assistant professor of religion, Dartmouth College.

Gurr, Ted Robert. Professor of political science, University of Maryland (College Park) and the editor of the two-volume *Violence in America: The History of Crime*, 1989.
A - "Drowning in a Crime Wave," *The Social Contract*, Spring 1993.

Hardin, Garrett. Ecologist, University of California(Santa Barbara).
A - *Living Within Limits* (Oxford: Oxford University Press, 1993).
B - "Conspicuous Benevolence and the Population Bomb," *Chronicles*, Oct 1991.
C - "The Ethics of Population Growth and Immigration Control," *Crowding Out the Future*, 1992.
D - "How Diversity Should Be Nurtured," *The Social Contract*, Spring 1991.
E - "Sheer Numbers: Can Environmentalists Grasp the Nettle of Population?," *E Magazine*, Nov/Dec 1990.
F - "There Is No Global Population Problem," *The Humanist*, Jul/Aug 1989.
G - Correspondence, Jun 1994.
H - Quoted in "Rising Immigration Exacts a Heavy Toll On the Environment," Brad Knickerbocker, *The Christian Monitor*, Jul 19, 1994.

Harrison, Lawrence. Former official of U.S. Agency for International Development.
A - *Who Prospers* (N.Y.: Basic Books, 1992).
B - *Underdevelopment Is A State of Mind: The Latin American Case* (Madison Books, 1985).

Harvey, Joseph. Mechanical engineer, Princeton University.
A - "Outgrowing Growth," *Clearinghouse Bulletin*, Aug 1994.

Hern, Warren M. University of Colorado anthropologist.
A - "Why Are There So Many of Us?" *Focus*, 1992.

High, George B. Executive director, Center for Immigration Studies.
A - Testimony before the Task Force on Illegal Immigration of the House Republican Research Committee, Apr 13, 1994.
B - Correspondence, Aug-Sep 1994.

Higham, J. Historian
A - Quoted in "Not An Open-And-Shut Case," Lawrence Auster, *The Social Contract*, Summer 1992.
B - *Stranger in the Land* (1955).

Hoffman-Nowotny, H.J. Professor Sociological Institute, University of Zurich.
A - Quoted in "Challenging Immigration Fatalism," Roy Beck, *The Social Contract*, Winter 1991-92.

Holdren, John. Acting Chair of the Energy and Resources Group, University of California(Berkeley).
A - "Population and the Energy Problem," *Population and Environment*, Spring 1991.

Huddle - Simcox. Donald Huddle, economist, Rice University. David Simcox, fellow, Center for Immigration Studies.
A - "The Impact of Immigration on the Social Security System," Carrying Capacity Network, Jul 20, 1993.

Ikle, Fred Charles
A - "Growth Without End, Amen?," *National Review*, Mar 7, 1994.

Immigration 2000
A - Federation for American Reform, 1992.

Interfaith Coalition on Energy
A - Passage from the *Ice Melter Newsletter*, May 1992.

Izaac Walton League, 1401 Wilson Blvd., Level B, Arlington, VA 22209-2318, phone (703) 528-1818.
A - *Environments for Life*, Spring 1994.
B - "Exploring the Limits of Carrying Capacity," Special Report.

C - *Environments for Life*, Winter 1994.
D - "Grassroots Action Planner," World Population Awareness Week, Oct 23-30, 1994.
E - 1993 Survey of Members.
F - "National Focus: The Rebirth of Interest in U.S. Population Policy," *Environment for Life*.

Jarvis, Robert
A - "The 'Komagata Maru' Incident: A Canadian Immigration Battle Revisited," *The Social Contract*, Spring 1994.

Jenks, Rosemary. Senior analyst, Center for Immigration Studies, and editor, *Immigration Review*.
A - "European Immigration Reform: A Model for the U.S.?" *The Social Contract*, Summer 1994.
B - Correspondence, Sep 1994.

Joint Appeal by Religion and Science *for the Environment*, 1047 Amsterdam Ave., New York, NY 10025, phone (212) 316-7441.
A - "Statement of Religious Leaders at the Summit on Environment," Jun 3, 1991.
B - "Statement, May 12, 1992.

Kaplan, Robert
A - "Continental Drift," *The New Republic*, Dec 28, 1992.

Kasun, Jacqueline
A - "A Nation of Davids: Population Control and the Environment," *Chronicles*, Oct 1991.

Keeley, Charles. Professor of international migration, Georgetown University.
A - Quoted in "Xenophobia: Scrabble Winner, Debate Stopper," Roy Beck, *The Social Contract*, Spring 1992.

Kennan, George F. Former U.S. Ambassador to the Soviet Union.
A - *Around the Cragged Hill* (N.Y.: W.W. Norton and Company, 1993).

Kirschten, Dick
A - "Immigration and Rancor Are Soaring," *National Journal*, Jun 1994.

Koed, Elizabeth. Ph.D. student, Department of history, University of California(Santa Barbara).
A - "The Loss of Cheap Labor and Predictions of Economic Disasters: Two Case Studies," *The Social Contract*, Spring 1991.
B - "A Symbol Transformed," *The Social Contract*, Spring 1992.

Kosh, Ronald W. General Manager of AAA Potomac.
A - "The Commuter's Marriage of Inconvenience," *Washington Post*, Aug 28, 1994.

Kunofsky, Judith
A - "Is Immigration an Environmental Issue?," memo, Apr 26, 1990.

Kuttner, Robert. Economics correspondent, *The New Republic*.
A - "Illegal Immigration: Would a National ID Card Help?", *Business Week*, Aug 26, 1991.

Kyser, Robert. Presbyterian Church (U.S.A.) minister.
A - Correspondence, Jun 1994.

Lachs, John. Professor of philosophy, Vanderbilt University.
A - "Some Moral Problems in Immigration Policy," address to "Ethics and Immigration Conference," Los Angeles, Nov 1993.

Lamm, Richard D. Former governor of Colorado; professor, University of Denver.
A - "The Ethics of U.S. Immigration Policy in an Overpopulated World," *Crowding Out the Future*, 1993.
B - "The New Wealth of Nations," *Chronicles*, Oct 1991.

Lamm - Imhoff. Richard Lamm and Gary Imhoff.
A - *The Immigration Time Bomb* (N.Y.: Dutton, 1985).

Land, Richard. Executive director, Southern Baptist Convention Christian Life Commission.
A - "Overview: Beliefs and Behaviors," *The*

Earth Is the Lord's, edited by Richard Land and Louis Moore (Nashville: Broadman Press, 1992).

Latino National Political Survey
A - "The Latino National Political Survey," by University of Texas professor Rodolfo de la Garza, Dec 1992.

Levi, Judith. Northwestern University professor of linguistics.
A - Quoted in "Xenophobia: Scrabble Winner, Debate Stopper," Roy Beck, *The Social Contract*, Spring 1992.

Linenthal, Arthur, M.D.
A - "Past and Present: Always the Sweatshop," *The Pharos*, Fall 1990, Alpha Omega Honor Medical Society.

Linden, Eugene
A - "Gobbling Up the Land," *Time*, Nov 18, 1991.
B - "Population: The Awkward Truth," *Time*, Jun 20, 1994.

Locke, John
A - *Second Treatise of Civil Government*, 1690, Bk 2, Ch. 6, para. 57.

Los Angeles Times
A - "Extend Benefits to Non-Citizens, Mahony Urges," Sep 30, 1993.
B - "Job Market a Flash Point for Natives, Newcomers," Stuart Silverstein, Nov 15, 1993.

Lutton, Wayne. Historian.
A - "Reality Check: A Video Review of *Foreign Aid & the Reality of Overpopulation* by Professor Garrett Hardin," *The Social Contract*, Spring 1994.
B - "The Right Books," *National Review*, Oct 23, 1987.

Lutton - Tanton. Wayne Lutton and John Tanton, editor-publisher, *The Social Contract.*
A - *The Immigration Invasion* (Petoskey, MI: The Social Contract Press, 1994).

Luttwak, Edward N.
A - *The Endangered American Dream: How to Stop the United States From Becoming a Third World Country and How To Win the Geo-Economic Struggle for Industrial Supremacy* (N.Y.: Simon & Schuster, 1993).

Martin, Jack. Senior analyst, Center for Immigration Studies.
A - "Pushing Diversity," *Immigration Review*, Fall 1994.
B - "Immigration Statistics: 1993," Center for Immigration Studies.
C - "Operation Blockade: A Bullying Tactic or a Border Control Model?," Center for Immigration Studies, Dec 1993.

Martin, Philip. Professor, University of California(Davis).
A - "Illegal Immigration and the Colonization of the American Labor Market," Center for Immigration Studies, 1986.
B - "Supplementary Views to the Commission on Agricultural Workers," Nov 1992.
C - Interview, Sep 29, 1994.

Lowell, James Russell
A - "The Present Crisis," Stanza 18, 1844.

Mathews, Jessica
A - "Malthus's Warning," *Washington Post*, Jun 7, 1994.

Matloff, Norman. Professor of computer science, University of California(Davis).
A - "Easy Money, Lost Traditions," *National Review*, Feb 21, 1994.

McCarthy, Eugene. Former U.S. Senator.
A - *The Colony of the World* (N.Y.: Hippocrene Books, 1992).
B - Foreword, *The Immigration Invasion*, Wayne Lutton and John Tanton (Petoskey, MI: The Social Contract Press, 1994).
C - Address, briefing to immigration of U.S. Senate, Dec 1993.

McConnell, Robert, Ph.D. Associate professor of Geology, Mary Washington College.
A - "Conference: Ethics of Immigration," *The Social Contract*, Winter 1993-94.
B - "Population Growth and Environmental

Quality in California: An American Laboratory," *Population and Environment*, Sep 1992.

McNeill, William. Historian.
A - "Population Growth and the Clouds of War," *The Social Contract*, Fall 1993.

Mehlman, Ira. Director of writers' support, Federation for American Immigration Reform.
A - "Tax Ledgers Will Never Balance," *Los Angeles Times*, Aug 9, 1994.
B - Correspondence, Jun 1994.

The Miami Herald
A - Article, Aug 11, 1992 (cited in FAIR Florida Facts).

Migration News
A - Article, Jun 1994.

Miles, Jack
A - "Black vs. Browns," *The Atlantic Monthly*, Oct 1992.

Miller, Monique. Executive director, Carrying Capacity Network.
A - "High-Density Living: Salvation or Delusion?" *Clearinghouse Bulletin*, Sep/Oct 1993.
B - Correspondence, Jun 29, 1994.

Mills, Nicolaus
A - *Arguing Immigration* (NY: Touchstone Books, 1994).

Mishan, Ezra
A - "Immigration Ethics," *World Issues*, Center for the Study of Democratic Institutions, Feb/Mar 1978. At the time, Mishan was visiting environmental studies professor, University of California (Santa Barbara).

Moffett, George
A - *Critical Masses* (NY: Viking Penguin, 1994).

***Money* Magazine**
A - "Escape from America," Gary Belsky, Jul 1994.

Morris, Frank. Dean of Graduate Studies, Morgan State University.
A - Congressional testimony, U.S. House Judiciary Subcommittee on Immigration, Refugees and International Law, Mar 13, 1990.
B - Press conference, National Press Club, Apr 15, 1994.

Morrison, Toni. 1993 Winner of the Nobel Prize for Literature.
A - "On the Backs of Blacks," *Arguing Immigration*, Nicolaus Mills, editor (N.Y.: Touchstone, 1994).

Multinational Moniker
A - Aug 1992.

Myrdal, Gunner. Swedish sociologist.
A - Quoted in "The Ethics of U.S. Immigration Policy in an Overpopulated World," Richard Lamm, *Crowding Out the Future*, 1993.

National Assoc. of Home Builders
A - "Home Building Industry Still Poised for a Solid Year," newsrelease, Jun 3, 1994.

National Commission on the Environment
A - Quoted in *Choosing a Sustainable Future*, (Washington, D.C.: World Wildlife Fund, 1992).

Immigration, Refugee and Citizenship Forum, 220 "I" St., NE, Suite 220, Washington, D.C. 20002, phone (202) 544-0004.
A - "U.S. Immigration Policy: Rational, Regulated, and Beneficial," Jul 1, 1993.

National Geographic
A - "The Colorado: A River Drained Dry," Jim Carrier, Jun 1991.

National Review
A - "Controlling Our Demographic Destiny," Peter Brimelow and Joseph Fallon, Feb 21, 1994.
B - "Right of Silence," Roy Beck, Jul 11, 1994.

National Wildlife Federation
A - "Putting the Bite on Planet Earth," *International Wildlife*, Sep/Oct 1994.

Negative Population Growth, 210 The Plaza, P.O. Box 1206, Teaneck, N.J., 07666-1206, phone (201) 837-3555.
A - "Refugee and Asylum Policy: National Passion versus National Interest," *NPG Forum*, David Simcox and Rosemary Jenks, Feb 1992.

Nelson, Brent
A - "Downsizing the American Dream," *The Social Contract*, Spring 1994.
B - *America Balkanized* (Monterey, VA: American Immigration Control Foundation, 1994).

Newhouse News Service
A - "Immigration Alters Politics of Civil Rights," Jonathan Tilove, *Portland Oregonian*, Dec 19, 1993.
B - "Native-born Blacks Lose Out to Immigrants," Jonathan Tilove, *Portland Oregonian*, Dec 20, 1993.

Newsday
A - "A Moratorium For Cities' Sake," Roy Beck, Apr 8,1994.

The New York Times
A - "Essays Detail Why," William Stevens.
B - "Hispanic Legislators Are Surprise Hurdlein Trade Pact's Path," Clifford Krauss, Oct 12, 1993.
C - "Immigrants' Advocates Push for Vote," Deborah Sontag, Aug 3, 1992.
D - "A National Registry for Work," Aug 8, 1994.
E - "Study Ties Schizophrenia to City Life," Jul 18, 1992.
F - "Turmoil in Haiti Dims Future of Its Students," Garry Pierre-Pierre, Jul 6, 1994.
G - "Severe Ancient Drought: A Warning to California," William K. Stevens, Aug 1994.
H - "Crammed in Tiny, Illegal Rooms, Tenants at Margins of Survival," Sara Rimer, Mar 23, 1992.
I - "A Success at the Border Earned Only a Shrug," Joel Brinkley, Sep 14, 1994.
J - "At Immigration, Disarray and Defeat," Joel Brinkley, Sep 11, 1994.
K - "Temporary Sanctuary Tends to Get Permanent," Roy Beck, Mar 7, 1992.

Nowak, Mark. Executive director, Population - Environment Balance, 1325 G St. NW, Suite 1003, Washington, D.C. 20005-3104, phone (202) 879-3000.
A - Correspondence, Sep 1994.

Oberlink, Ric. Executive director, Californians for Population Stabilization, 926 J St., Suite 915, Sacramento, CA 95814, phone (916) 446-1033.
A - "The Effects of Massive Immigration," submitted to the Santa Cruz County Board of Supervisors, Apr 8, 1994.
B - Testimony by Ric Oberlink to the Assembly Select Committee on Statewide Immigration Impact, Jan 12, 1994.

O'Connor, Mark. Poet, member of Australians for an Ecologically Sustainable Population.
A - "Immigrationism, Racism, and Moral Monopoly," *The Social Contract*, Winter 1993-1994.
B - Letter to Professor Glenn Withers, head of the National Population Council, an Australian government-supported study group, *The Social Contract*, Fall 1992.

Orlando Sentinel
A - "Study Says Population Limit Vital," Jun 11, 1994.

O'Sullivan, John
A - "Nationhood: An American Activity," *National Review*, Feb 21, 1994.

Papademetriou, Demetrios
A - "Immigration's Effects on the United States," *Interpreter Releases*, Jan 3, 1994.

Parikh, Jyoti. Senior professor, leader of the energy and environment group, Indira Gandhi Institute of Development Research, Bombay.
A - "Restructuring Consumption Patterns for Sustainability," *The Network*, Oct 1992.

Parsons, Jack. Lecturer, social sciences, Great Britain.
A - *Population versus Liberty* (London: Pemberton, 1971), now available from The Social Contract Press.
B - Quoted in "Challenging Immigration

Fatalism," Roy Beck, *The Social Contract*, Winter 1991-92.

Peart, Wendell
A - Letter to the Editor, *The Social Contract*, Fall 1992.

Philadelphia Inquirer
A - "Refugees Increasing, Study Says," David Briscoe, Jun 16, 1994.

Pimentel, David
A - "Land, Energy and Water: The Constraints Governing Ideal U.S. Population Size," *Elephants in the Volkswagon*, Lindsey Grant, editor (N.Y.: W.H. Freeman, 1992).
B - "U.S. Carrying Capacity Overview," panelist, Carrying Capacity Network conference, Washington, D.C., 1993.

Pope, Carl. Executive director, Sierra Club.
A - "All Things Considered," National Public Radio, Sep 13, 1994.

Population Action International, 1120 19th St. NW, Suite 550, Washington, D.C. 20036.
A - "Challenging the Planet: Connections Between Population and the Environment," 1993.

Population Communication International, 777 U.N. Plaza, Suite 7C, New York, NY 10017.
A - "Myths About Population Growth," William Ryerson, 1994.

Population-Environment Balance, 1325 G St. NW, Suite 1003, Washington, D.C. 20005, phone (202) 879-3000.
A - "Know the Facts: The United States' Population and Environment," Sep 1993.
B - "Why Excess Immigration Damages the Environment," *FOCUS*, Vol. 2, No. 3, 1992.

Population Reference Bureau, 1875 Connecticut Ave. NW, Suite 520, Washington, D.C. 20009-5728.
A - "Public Is Concerned About World Population Growth," *Global Stewardship*, May/Jun 1994.
B - "The Religious Community and Population Concerns," For the Pew Charitable Trusts' Global Stewardship Initiative, Sep 20, 1993.
C - *1994 World Population Data Sheet*.

Potts - Campbell. Malcolm Potts, professor of family planning, and Martha Campbell, visiting scholar, School of Public Health. Both at the University of California (Berkeley).
A - "Debunking Myths About Family Planning," *Rocky Mountain Institute newsletter*, Summer 1994.

Prophets and Politics
A - *Prophets and Politics: Handbook on the Washington Offices of the U.S. Churches*, Roy Beck (Washington, D.C.: Institute on Religion and Democracy, 1994).

Proulx, E. Annie
A - "Urban Bumpkins," *Washington Post*, Sep 25, 1994.

Rawlings, Steve
A - *Household and Family Characteristics: March 1993*, Census Bureau news release, Aug 10, 1994.

Ray, David. Field coordinator, Federation for American Immigration Reform.
A - Interview, Aug 25, 1994.

Reder, Melvin W.
A - "Chicago Economics: Permanence and Change," *Journal of Economic Literature*, Mar 1982, summarized by Briggs in *Mass Immigration and the National Interest*.
B - "The Economic Consequences of Increased Immigration," *The Review of Economics and Statistics*, Aug 1963, summarized by Briggs in *Mass Immigration and the National Interest*.

Reisner, Marc
A - *Cadillac Desert* (1986).

Religious Action Center. The Washington public advocacy arm of Reform Judaism.
A - Quoted in "Religions and the Environ-

ment," *The Social Contract*, Winter 1992-1993.

Robertson, JM
A - *The Evolution of States* (1912).

Reuters
A - Jun 20, 1994.

Ryerson, William. Executive vice president, Population Communication International, 777 United Nations Plaza, Suite 7C, N.Y., N.Y. 10017-3521.
A - "Myths About Population Growth," Population Communication International.

Sadik, Nafis. Executive director, United Nations Population Fund.
A - "Where Are We Now: The Earth Summit," speech to the Population Council: 40th Anniversary Celebration, 1992.

Samuelson, Robert
A - "The Joys of Mowing," *Washington Post*, Apr 24, 1991.

San Diego Union
A - "Mexican Delegation Pleads for U.S. Aid to Migrants," Lola Sherman and Fernando Romero, Jun 8, 1992.
B - "Could Haitian refugees be granted merely a 'temporary' haven?" Roy Beck, Dec 29, 1991.

San Francisco Examiner
A - "Population is New Hot Topic in California," Jim Mayer, Mar 28, 1993.

Sanger, Margaret. Founder, Planned Parenthood Federation of America.
A - Quoted in *Audubon*, Jul/Aug 1994.

San Jose Mercury News
A - "Exodus of Men Haunts Mexico," Esther Schrader, Aug 15, 1993.
B - "Foreign Workers Skew Data on Minorities," Steve Johnson, Oct 11, 1993.

Shabecoff, Philip. Former environmental editor, *New York Times*.
A - *A Fierce Green Fire* (New York: Hill and Wang: 1993).

Shankman, Arnold
A - *Ambivalent Friends: Afro-Americans View the Immigrant* (Westport, CT: Greenwood Press, 1982).

Sierra Club, 730 Polk St., San Francisco, CA 94109, phone (415) 776-2211.
A - "Addressing California's Total Population Growth," *The Sierra Club California Green State of the State Report*, 1991.
B - "Defusing the Population Bomb," Sierra Club pamphlet.
C - *The Population Squeeze*, Sierra Population Program pamphlet.
D - Sierra Club Population Program statement, Oct 1990.

Simcox, David. Fellow, Center for Immigration Studies.
A - "The Commission on Population Growth and the American Future, 20 Years Later: A Lost Opportunity," *The Social Contract*, Summer 1992.
B - "Sanctuary, Immigration Law and Christian Conscience," *Engage Social Action*, Mar 1986.
C - "Sustainable Immigration: Learning to Say No," *Elephants in the Volkswagon*, Lindsey Grant, editor (N.Y.: W.H. Freeman, 1992).
D - *Scope*, No. 12, p6, Center for Immigration Studies.
E - Quoted in "Rising Immigration Exacts a Heavy Toll On the Environment," Brad Knickerbocker, *Christian Science Monitor*, Jul 19, 1994.

Smith, Joseph Wayne. Philosophy Department, Flinders University of South Australia.
A - *The Remorseless Working of Things*, available from The Social Contract office.

Smith-Welch. James P. Smith, RAND Corporation; Finis R. Welch, University of California (Los Angeles).
A - "Black Economic Progress After Myrdal," *Journal of Economic Literature*, Jun 1989.

The Social Contract, 316 1/2 E. Mitchell St., Petoskey, MI 49770, phone (616) 347-1171.

A - "Art Exhibition Portrays U.S. Blacks' Move North After Immigration Cuts," Roy Beck, Winter 1993-94.
B - "Challenging Immigration Fatalism," Roy Beck, Winter 1991-92
C - "Ford Study: Communities Tense, But Immigration Not Real Cause," Roy Beck, Summer 1993.
D - "Problems On the World Frontier," Roy Beck, Winter 1993.
E - "RAND: Urban Schools Reeling from High Immigrant Levels," Roy Beck, Summer 1993.
F - "Religions and the Environment," Roy Beck, Winter 1992-1993.
G - "Xenophobia: Scrabble Winner, Debate Stopper," Roy Beck, Spring 1992.
H - "Projected Growth If Congress Leaves Immigration Unchanged," Roy Beck, 1993.
I - "Immigration: No.1 in U.S. Growth," Roy Beck, Winter 1991-1992.
J - Editorial, *The Social Contract*, Spring 1991.

Southern Baptist Convention
A - National Convention Resolutions: 1970, 1983, 1990.

Sparks, Phil. Co-Director, Communications Consortium Media Center, Global Stewardship Initiative Project.
A - Speaking at the Society of Environmental Journalists' conference "Covering Population: Local and Global Dimensions," Aug 8, 1994.

Spear - White. Dr. Speare, professor of Sociology, Brown University. Dr. White, associate professor of Sociology, Brown University.
A - "Optimal City Size and Population Density for the Twenty-First Century," *Elephants in the Volkswagon*, Lindsey Grant, editor (N.Y.: W.H. Freeman, 1992).

Staten Island Advance
A - "At a Hospital in Watts, It's Latino vs. Black," Jonathan Tilove, Jan 9, 1994.

Statistical Abstract of the U.S.
A - 1980 Table 1116; 1990 Table 1028; 1993 Table 1037.
B - 1975 Table 967; 1993 Table 1017.

Stein, Dan. Executive director, Federation for American Immigration Reform, 1666 Connecticut Ave. NW, Suite 400, Washington, D.C. 20009, phone (202) 328-7004.
A - "Blanket Acceptance of Cubans is an Idea 3 Decades Out of Date," *Palm Beach Post*, Jul 28, 1991.
B - "Overwhelmed by Our Generosity," *Los Angeles Times*, Aug 8, 1994.
C - "Social Security: Trust but Verify," *New York Newsday*, Aug 16, 1994.
D - Letter to Don Collins, editor of *Money* magazine, regarding the article "Escape from America," Jul 20, 1994.
E - Letter to the Editor of *The Wall Street Journal*, Jul 6, 1994.
F - Letter to the Editor of *The Wall Street Journal*, Aug 4, 1993.
G - Interview, May 1994.
H - Speech before New York University Law School, Journal of Human Rights, Apr 8, 1994.
I - Quoted in "Immigration and the Clean Air Issue," Jun 23, 1994.
J - "Population, Migration and America: Is Immigration a Threat to National Security?" speech to the National War College, Aug 24, 1994.

Tanton, John. Editor-publisher, *The Social Contract*; opthomologist; founding chairman, Federation for American for American Immigration Reform; former national leader in the Sierra Club and Zero Population Growth.
A - *Rethinking Immigration Policy*, FAIR, 1979.
B - "End of the Migration Epoch?," *The Social Contract*, Spring 1994.
C - "The Metronome As A Population Teaching Tool," *The Social Contract*, Winter 1990-91.
D - "A New Decalogue For An Increasingly Crowded World," *The Social Contract*, Spring 1994.
E - *The Social Contract*, Fall 1992, p72.

F - Letter to Editor, *E Magazine*, Nov 1990.
G - Correspondence, Nov 1992, Jun-Sep 1994.
H - Letter to the Editor of *USA Today*, Oct 18, 1991.

Teitelbaum, Michael S.
A - "Right Versus Right: Immigration And Refugee Policy In the United States," *Foreign Affairs*, Fall 1980.

Thernstrom, Stephen. Professor of history, Harvard University.
A - Quoted in "Xenophobia: Scrabble Winner, Debate Stopper," Roy Beck, *The Social Contract*, Spring 1992.

Thomay, Laszlo
A - *The Natural Law of Race Relations* (Scott-Townsend Publishers: 1993).

Thompkins, Peter. Former chief, British Immigration Service.
A - Quoted in "Challenging Immigration Fatalism," Roy Beck, *The Social Contract*, Winter 1991-92.

Time
A - "The Endangered Dream," Jordan Bonfante, Nov 18, 1991.
B - "The Cultural Defense," Richard Lacayo, *Time*, Special Issue: "The New Face of America," Fall 1993.

Train, Russell E. Chairman, World Wildlife Fund and the Conservation Foundation.
A - Remarks at the North American Conference on Religion and Ecology, May 18, 1990.

Tyson, Ann Scott
A - "Ethnic, Economic Divisions of US Growing," *Christian Science Monitor*, Jul 7, 1994.

U.N. Environment Program
A - "Two Decades of Achievement," 1992.

United Nations Population Fund
A - "State of the World Population 1993," U.N. Population Fund annual report.

USA Today
A - "Having Babies Often More Than a Woman's Decision," Margaret Usdansky, 1994.
B - "Millions Live Life in the Slow Lanes," Haya El Nasser, Jun 16, 1994.
D - "Suburbs Swallow Farmland," Jul 15, 1993.

U.S. Department of Energy
A - "Energy Consumption and Conservation Potential: Supporting Analysis for the National Energy Strategy," Dec 1990.

U.S. National Academy of Sciences and the British Royal Society
A - Joint Statement, Feb 1992.

U.S. Network for Cairo 1994
A - Newsletter, May 1994.

U.S. News & World Report
A - "Living with Nature: E.O. Wilson argues that species extinction threatens the human spirit," Betsy Carpenter with Bob Holmes, Nov 30, 1992.

U.S. Senate Briefing
A - Address, Roy Beck, to immigration staffers, U.S. Senate, Dec 1993.

Vinson, John. President, American Immigration Control Foundation, P.O. Box 525, Monterey, VA 24465, phone (703) 468-2022.
A - *Immigration Out of Control* (AICF, 1992).

Wagenbichler, Hermann
A - "The Yugoslav Tragedy: Why Multicultural Societies Are Unlikely to Work," *The Social Contract*, Summer 1983.

Washington, Booker T. The foremost black spokesman of turn-of-the-century America and founder of the famed Tuskegee Institute.
A - *Up From Slavery* (N.Y.: Viking Penguin, 1901).

The Washington Post
A - "Baby Boom's Urban Cradle Braces for Future Rocked by Crime," Malcolm Gladwell, May 26, 1994.
B - "Black Teens Facing Worse Job Prospects," Steven Pearlstein and DeNeen

L. Brown, Jun 4, 1994.
C - "Climatology: California in the Middle Ages," Boyce Rensberger, Jun 20, 1994.
D - "Drivers' Tempers 'Seem to Be Running Awfully Hot'," Patricia Davis, Aug 16, 1994.
E - "German Churches Aid Refugees," Steve Vogel, Jun 17, 1994.
F - "Germany's Cure for A Boy Named Sue," Marc Fisher, Mar 25, 1991.
G - "Latino-Black Rivalry Grows," Gary Lee and Roberto Suro, Oct 13, 1993.
H - "Muslims Join Vatican In Critizing U.N. Population Document," Aug 12, 1994.
I - "Panel Urges U.S. Worker Registry," Roberto Suro, Aug 4, 1994.
J - "Resistance to New Boatlift Surging in Florida," Aug 11, 1994.
K - "Sacrificing for Salmon: Pacific Northwest to Feel Diverse Impact," Tom Kenworthy, Jan 14, 1992.
L - "Some Water Cleanups Not Feasible, Study Says," Gary Lee, Jun 24, 1994.
M - "Study Warns of Growing Underclass of the Unskilled," Catherine Manegold, Jun 3, 1994.
N - "Sudanese Student Working Toward American Dream Dies After Street Attack," Avis Thomas-Lester and David Leonhardt, Jun 11, 1994.
O - "Theologians Endorse Aims of Population Conference," Aug 25, 1994.
P - Article of Feb 9, 1992, cited in Carrying Capacity Network Newsletter, 1992.
Q - Letter to the Editor, Brian M. Harney, Chairman, Steering Committee Eastern States Petroleum Advisory Group.
R - "Net Losses: Fishing Decimating Oceans' 'Unlimited' Bounty," Anne Swardson, Aug 15, 1994.
S - "Reich Identifies 'Anxious Class' of Workers," Frank Swoboda, Aug 13, 1994.
T - "Emissions Goal May Be Out of Reach," Gary Lee, Sep 3, 1994.
U - "Redoubled Cleanup of Bay Called For," D'Vera Colin, Jun 13, 1991.
V - "Warnings Sought for D.C. Waters," D'Vera Cohn, Sep 1, 1994.
W - "Iowa, Where the Living Is Easier," Laura Sessions Stepp, Sep 5, 1994.
X - "Measuring Growth," Sep 4, 1994.
Y - "Immigrants Crowd Labor's Lowest Rung," Roberto Suro, Sep 13, 1994.
Z - "Reich Redefining 'Competitiveness'," Frank Swoboda, Sep 24, 1994.

The Washington Times
A - "California May Just Be Too Big To Be Managed," Valerie Richardson, Sep 1, 1992.
B - "Proposal targets illegal Aliens," Michele Kay, Aug 8, 1994.
C - " "Senate Approves Education Money with Strings Added," Carol Innerst, Aug 3, 1994.

Werbos, Paul
A - "Energy and Population," *Elephants in the Volkswagon*, Lindsey Grant, editor (N.Y.: W.H. Freeman, 1992).

Williamson, Jr., Chilton
A - "Flat-Earth Theories," *Chronicles*, Oct 1991.

Williamson, Jeffrey
A - "Inequality and the Industrial Revolution," *The Kuznets Memorial Lecture 1991* (Harvard University Press, 1991).

Wolff, K.H.
A - *The Sociology of Georg Simmel* (1950).

Wong, Linda
A - Quote from the EDGE Conference Summary, "Redefining the California Dream: Growth, Justice, and Sustainability," Jan 15-17, 1993.

Woodward, Herbert N. Chairman of the Board, Intermatic, Inc. and Monroe Industries, Inc.
A - "Discounting the Future," *The Social Contract*, Fall 1991.

The World Almanac
A - *The World Almanac and Book of Facts* (N.Y.: Pharos Books, 1992).

World Resources Institute
A - "The 1993 Information Please Environmental Almanac," 1993.

Wright, Gavin
A - *Old South, New South* (N.Y.: Basic Books).

Zero Population Growth, 1400 16th St. NW, Suite 320, Washington, D.C. 20007, phone (202) 332-2200.
A - "Are We Loving Our Parks to Death?", Laura McCarty, *ZPG Reporter*, Aug 1994.
B - "In Troubled Waters," Summer 1990 Fact Sheet.
C - "Major Population Initiative Launched," May 22, 1991.

Zurcher, Gottried. Vice director, Switzerland's Federal Office for Refugees.
A - Quoted in "Challenging Immigration Fatalism," Roy Beck, *The Social Contract*, Winter 1991-92.

Index of Topics

Advocates of Growth and Immigration: see Growth Advocates
Affirmative Action: 109-110, 151-153
African Americans: see Black Americans
Aging Population: 61-62, 88-90
Agriculture: 15-17, 19-21, 25-30, 45, 53-54, 94-95
Asylum: 170-172
Australia, comparisons: 35

Bigotry: 125-135
Birth Rates: 1-2, 8-13, 56-57, 84-86, 105, 162-164, 188-193
Black Americans: 92-94, 97-98, 100, 109, 120-121, 128-131, 134, 136, 151-153, 182, 193
Borders, enforceability: 165-175
Borders, legitimacy: 76-77, 79-83, 157-159
Brain Drain: 143-144

Carpooling: 37-39
Carrying Capacity: see Environment
Catholic Positions: 67-68
Charity: see Ethics of Helping
Childcare Workers: 97
Civil Rights: 109-110, 152-153, 169-174
Congestion: see Crowding and Traffic
Congress: 1-7, 12-13, 54, 118-119, 128, 130, 134-135, 141-143, 171-175, 179, 183, 186-193
Consumption: 32-42, 186-190
Crime: 181-182, see Domestic Tranquility and Freedom
Crowding and Sprawl: 17-19, 23-25, 30-31, 37-41, 57-61, 114, 177
Culture: 103-105, 107-108, 111, 126-128, 193

Defense: see National Security
Distribution of Population: 24-26, 38-40
Diversity: 103-112, 193
Domestic Tranquility: 79-82, 105-108, 121, 133, 158-159, 179-182, 193
Domestic Workers: 97

Economic Disparity: 3, 34-35, 40, 87-88, 92-94, 97, 101-102, 107, 120-121, 129-131, 146-149, 151-153, 182-183
Economic Justice: see Economic Disparity
Economic Need for Growth: 60-64, 87-102, 120-121, 129-131, 191-193
Economy, global: see Global Economy
Education: 92, 95, 100-101, 110, 152
Employer Sanctions: 170-174
Energy: 26-27, 32-33, 36-39, 46, 50, 53-54, 73
Enforcement of Environmental Regulations: 51-52, 187
Entrepreneurial Immigrants: 91-92
Environment: 14-31, 32-42, 43-54, 73-75, 119, 134, 146, 176-182,185-193
Environment, psychological needs: see Psychological-Lifestyle Needs
Environmental Enforcement: see Enforcement of Environmental Regulations
Environmental Groups: 1, 5, 21-23, 32-33, 84, 125-126, 193

Ethics of Helping The Third World Wisely and Americans First: 41-42, 73, 75, 77-78, 116, 120-121, 123-124, 129-131, 136-159, 160-164, 191
Ethnic Networking: 91
Europe, comparisons: 18-19, 30-31, 134, 165-167, 169-175

Family Reunification: 89, 111-112, 171, 183, 191-192
Fertility: see Birth Rates
Fishing: see Outdoors Sports
Foreign Workers, need for: 94-101
Free-Market Solutions: 43, 49-51, 95, 101-102
Freedom: 30-31, 37-41, 59, 61-63, 114, 116, 121-124, 134, 141-143, 169-174, 176-183, 192

Gap Between Rich and Poor: see Economic Disparity
Global Economy: 76-77, 98,99, 101-102, 111
Globalism: 72-83, 154-155, 157-159
Government Interference: see Freedom
Growth Advocates: 4, 29, 34, 80, 125, 133-135, 136-138, 149-150, 155-156, 190-192
Growth, economic need for: see Economic Need for Growth
Growth Philosophy: 55-65

Haven, safe: see Refuge
Hispanics: see Latinos
History, conservation: 19-21, 36, 44-47, 51
History, immigration: see Tradition
History, population: 55-58
Hotel and Restaurant Workers: 95-97
Housing: 37-41, 62-64
Humanitarianism: see Ethics of Helping
Hunting: see Outdoors Sports

ID Cards: see Employer Sanctions
Illegal Immigration: 165-175
Immigrant Bashing: 131-132
Immigrants as Percentage of Population: 119-120
Immigration Made America Great: 113-124
Immigration as Source of Skills: see Skills
Indians: see Indigenous Americans
Indigenous Americans: 81-83
Irredentism: 79-83

Jewish Positions: 68-69, 154-157
Job Creation by Immigrants: see Entrepreneurial Immigrants

Labor Concerns: see Economic Disparity & Labor Shortage
Labor Shortage: 92-101, 111, 152-153
Land Use Restrictions: 37-40
Latinos: 83, 93, 105, 127-128, 157
Legislation: see Congress

Mass Transit: see Carpooling
Middle Class, threats to: see Economic Disparity
Migrant Work: 94-95

Name-Calling: 125-135
Nannies: see Childcare Workers
Nation of Immigrants: 115-116
National Security: 65, 79-81
Nativism: 131-132, 193

Oceans for Food: 29-30
Outdoors Sports: 30, 179-180

Parks: see Psychological-Lifestyle Needs
Peace: see Domestic Tranquility
Plenty of Room for Growth: 14-31
Polls: see Public Opinion
Pollution: 2-3, 14, 20, 47-49
Population Density: see Crowding

Population Distribution: see Distribution
Population Goals: 39, 54, 188-193
Population Projections: 1-2, 5-6, 8-13, 30-31, 84-85, 90, 105, 120, 189-190
Population, world: 72-74, 77, 136-140, 145-146, 162-164
Psychological-Lifestyle Needs For Natural Areas: 25, 30-31, 40, 50-51, 57-59, 179-181
Public Opinion: 1-2, 7, 126-128, 186
Privacy Threats: 169-174

Recreation: see Psychological-Lifestyle Needs
Racial Tensions: 104-105, 108, 110, 121
Racism: see Bigotry
Recycling: 36
Refuge: 116, 121-124, 141-143, 170-172, 191-192
Refugees: see Refuge
Regulation: see Freedom
Religion: 66-71, 79, 82, 114, 154-158
Remittances: 144-145
Resource Scarcity: 49-51, 60

Safe Haven: see Refuge
Safety Valve: 145-146
Scapegoating: 131-132
Skills, importing through immigration: 52-53, 99-101, 143-144, 191
Social Security: 88-90
Space for Growth: 14-31
Sprawl: see Crowding and Sprawl
Statue of Liberty: 121-124

Technology: 43-54
Third World: 35-36, 41, 72-74, 77-78, 136-148, 157, 160-164, 166-167, 179, 192
Tradition: 107-108, 113-124, 126-127, 129-131, 133-134, 152-153, 193
Traffic: 2-3, 37-39, 58

Urban Needs: 91-92, 118, 181-182

Waste: 32-42
Welfare: 89
West, The: 15-17
Worker Identification: see Employer Sanctions
World Population: see Population, World

Xenophobia: 132-135, 193

Zoning: see Land Use Restrictions

Recommended Reading

Colony of the World: The United States Today, Eugene McCarthy, 120pp (Hippocrene Books, Inc., 171 Madison Avenue, New York, N.Y. 10016).

The Disuniting of America, Arthur M. Schlesinger, Jr. (W. W. Norton & Company, 500 Fifth Avenue, New York, N.Y. 10110)

Elephants In The Volkswagon: Facing the Tough Questions About Our Overcrowded Country, Lindsey Grant, 272pp (W. H. Freeman and Company, 41 Madison Avenue, New York, N.Y. 10010).

How Many Americans? Population, Immigration and the Environment, Leon F. Bouvier and Lindsey Grant, 174pp (Sierra Club Books, 730 Polk Street, San Francisco, Calif. 94109).

The Immigration Invasion, Wayne Lutton and John Tanton, 190pp (The Social Contract Press, 316 1/2 E. Mitchell Street, Petoskey, Mich. 49770).

Living Within Limits: Ecology, Economics and Population Taboos, Garrett Hardin, 339pp (Oxford University Press, Inc., 200 Madison Avenue, New York, N.Y. 10016).

Mass Immigration and the National Interest, Vernon M. Briggs, Jr., 276pp (M. E. Sharpe, Inc., 80 Business Park Drive, Armonk, N.Y. 10504).

Peaceful Invasions, Leon Bouvier, 234pp (University Press of America, 4720 Boston Way, Lanham, Md. 20706).

Population Politics: The Choices that Shape Our Future, Virginia D. Abernethy, 350 pp (Plenum Press, 233 Spring Street, New York, N.Y. 10013).

Population vs. Liberty, Jack Parsons, 417pp (Pemberton Books, available from 316 1/2 E. Mitchell Street, Petoskey, Mich. 49770).

Acknowledgements

Many thanks are owed Robert Kyser — managing editor of *The Social Contract* and a Presbyterian (U.S.A.) minister — for his tireless day-to-day editorial attention throughout this project and his theological consultation on the moral and ethical issues handled herein. Gratitude also is due Sean O'Brien, and to Peggy Raddatz, Niki Calloway and Dorothy Koury of *The Social Contract* staff, who handled many of the other logistics in the production of the book.

John Tanton, editor and publisher of *The Social Contract*, provided valuable editing and suggestions. An honored conservationist who has been a national leader in the Sierra Club and other groups, Dr. Tanton has thought and written on the subjects of this book for 30 years. He laid a foundation for this book through his diligent efforts over those years to identify and stimulate the work of experts in myriad related fields. Together, they have given us a much clearer vision of Americans' needs in creating a sustainable, high quality of life in terms of our natural environment, our workplace and our communities. Many of those experts read early versions of this book and offered helpful critiques. The overall analysis in the book, of course, does not necessarily reflect that of *The Social Contract* or of the experts whose work is on display in the book.

The Social Contract is a quarterly journal. Each issue includes 60 to 90 pages of original research, analysis, book reviews and reportage, as well as reprints from other publications, about immigration-related issues, written from the U.S. and abroad. The analysis is non-partisan and runs the spectrum from liberal to conservative, but most of it has a point of view in support of environmental quality, improved conditions for the American laborer, opportunities for the economic underclass, or the nurturing of social cohesiveness that helps ensure domestic tranquility in our communities. With the wonders of modern communication, most of *The Social Contract* staff are able to live in northern Michigan, where the environmental resources remain relatively healthy and beautiful, in no small measure because of long-time local activism by persons associated with the journal.

Annual subscriptions to the journal are $25 for individuals, libraries and institutions; $10 for students; complimentary for the news media. Contact:

The Social Contract
316 1/2 E. Mitchell St.
Suite 4
Petoskey, MI 49770
(616)347-1171

About the Author

Roy Beck is a veteran newspaper reporter whose recent articles about immigration-related issues have been featured in *The Atlantic Monthly, National Review, New York Newsday, Los Angeles Times, San Diego Union, New York Times, Population-Environment* journal, the *SEJournal* (Society of Environmental Journalists) and many others. He has lectured on these issues at the Smithsonian Institution's annual convocation for college deans, to universities and public-issue forum groups, to congressional briefings and national environmental conferences.

A native of the Missouri Ozarks, he now lives in Arlington, VA. He is married to a pediatric physical therapist who has converted the first floor of their home into a clinic; they spent their honeymoon backpacking in the Smokies and Adirondacks in 1970. During the writing of this book, their first son left home to begin college and their other son began high school.

Mr. Beck graduated from the University of Missouri School of Journalism where he was honored for science writing. He was the first environmental reporter for the daily *Columbia Missourian* in 1969. His work as environmental reporter and columnist for the *Grand Rapids* (Mich.) *Press* garnered national recognition, especially for articles on areas of solid waste management, toxic contamination and the effects of suburban sprawl. He was Sunday business news editor for the *Cincinnati Enquirer*, and associate editor of the national *United Methodist Reporter* (Dallas), where he received international honors for coverage of religion and social issues in the U.S., Asia and Latin America. He focused on Congress as the Chief Washington Correspondent for the Booth chain of daily newspapers before becoming the Washington Editor of *The Social Contract*.

His other books are: *On Thin Ice: A Religion Reporter's Memoir* (1988) and *Prophets and Politics: Handbook on the Washington Offices of U.S. Churches* (1994).

For additional copies of

RE-CHARTING AMERICA'S FUTURE

at $9.95 plus $2.50 postage and handling

contact

THE SOCIAL CONTRACT PRESS
316½ E. Mitchell Street
Suite 4
Petoskey, Michigan 49770

Phone: (616) 347-1171
FAX: (616) 347-1185